# DB2 for
# Application
# Programmers

**Prentice Hall Mainframe Software Series**

Essential Resources, Inc. (ERI) with Jan Diamondstone, *Using VAX/VMS*

Gildersleeve, *The CICS Companion: A Reference Guide to COBOL Command Level Programming*

Hoffman/Hicks, *The CMS User's Guide*

Inmon, *Optimizing Performance in DB2*

Lee, *CICS/VS Command Level Programming with COBOL Examples*

Lee, *CICS/VS Online System Design and Implementation Techniques*

Lee, *IMS/VS DB/DC Online Programming Using MFS and DL/1*

Lee, *IMS/VS DL/1 Programming with COBOL Examples*

Lee, *VSAM Coding in COBOL and VSAM AMS*

Lim, *DB2 for Application Programmers*

Martin, *Fourth-Generation Languages: Principles*, Volume 1

Martin/ARBEN, *Fourth-Generation Languages: Representative 4 GLS*, Volume II

Martin/ARBEN, *Fourth-Generation Languages: 4 GLS from IBM*, Volume III

Martin/ARBEN, *SNA: IBM's Networking Solution*

Martin/ARBEN, *VSAM: Access Method Services and Programming Techniques*

Narayan, *Data Dictionary: Implementation, Use, and Maintenance*

Nussbacher, *The VM/CMS Primer*

Rindfleisch, *OS and VS Job Control Language and Utility Programs, second edition*

Roetzheim, *Structured Computer Project Management*

# DB2 for Application Programmers

**Pacifico Amarga Lim**

**Prentice Hall,** Englewood Cliffs, New Jersey 07632

Library of Congress Cataloging-in-Publication Data

LIM, PACIFICO A.
    DB2 for application programmers/Pacifico Amarga Lim.
       p. cm.
    Includes index.
    ISBN 0-13-199795-5
       1. Data base managment.  2. IBM Database 2 (Computer system)
I. Title
QA76.9. D3L55     1990
005.75'65 — dc20

89-3910
CIP

Editorial/production supervision and
    interior design: *Jean Lapidus*
Cover design: *Wanda Lubelska Design*
Manufacturing buyer: *Mary Ann Gloriande*

**Prentice Hall Mainframe Software Series**

 © 1990 by Prentice-Hall, Inc.
A Division of Simon & Schuster
Englewood Cliffs, New Jersey 07632

This book can be made available to businesses
and organizations at a special discount when
ordered in large quantities. For more information
contact:

Prentice-Hall, Inc.
Special Sales and Markets
College Division
Englewood Cliffs, N.J. 07632

Printed in the United States of America
10  9  8  7  6  5  4  3  2  1


ISBN   0-13-199795-5


PRENTICE-HALL INTERNATIONAL (UK) LIMITED, *London*
PRENTICE-HALL OF AUSTRALIA PTY. LIMITED, *Sydney*
PRENTICE-HALL CANADA INC., *Toronto*
PRENTICE-HALL HISPANOAMERICANA, S.A., *Mexico*
PRENTICE-HALL OF INDIA PRIVATE LIMITED, *New Delhi*
PRENTICE-HALL OF JAPAN, INC., *Tokyo*
SIMON & SCHUSTER ASIA PTE. LTD., *Singapore*
EDITORA PRENTICE-HALL DO BRASIL, LTDA., *Rio de Janeiro*

TAB BOOKS Inc. offers software for sale. For information and a catalog, please contact
TAB Software Department, Blue Ridge Summit, PA 17294-0850.

**In memory of our father, *Victor Cuarto Lim*.**

We will always miss him.

# Contents

**Preface**                                                                    **xix**

*PART I  INTRODUCTION TO DB2*                                                  *1*

**1  Introduction**                                                            **1**

    1    What is a Database?  1

    2    Three Models of Database Systems  1

        *2.1  The Hierarchical Model, 1*
        *2.2  The Network Model, 2*
        *2.3  The Relational Model, 3*

**2  Introduction to Relational Database**                                     **4**

    1    History  4

    2    The Relational Model  4

    3    What Constitutes the Relational Model?  5

4    Advantages of the Relational Model   7

5    Basic Data Extraction   7

     5.1   Selection, 7
     5.2   Projection, 8
     5.3   Join, 8


3    **Introduction to DB2**                                                          **11**

     1    What is DB2?   11
     2    The DB2 Environment   11
     3    DB2 Objects   12

          3.1   Creating DB2 Objects, 13

     4    Tables as "Real" Tables   14

          4.1   Tables, 14

     5    Views as Virtual Tables   15

          5.1   View as a Security Measure, 15
          5.2   View to Simplify User Access, 15
          5.3   View to Help Reduce Data Redundancy, 15
          5.4   Examples of a View, 15
          5.5   Creating a View, 16
          5.6   Update Restrictions on Views, 16

     6    The Significance of SQL   17

          6.1   Most Common SQL Statements, 17
          6.2   Advantages of SQL, 17
          6.3   SQL Without an Application Program, 18
          6.4   SQL in an Application Program, 19
          6.5   Table/View Naming Conventions, 19
          6.6   Column Naming Conventions, 19

     7    Data Security/Integrity Facilities   20

          7.1   Data Security, 20
          7.2   Data Integrity, 20

     8    The DB2 Catalog   21

          8.1   The Role of the Catalog, 21

**PART II     SQL IN SPUFI**                                                               **22**

**4     The SQL Statements in SPUFI**                                          **22**

    1     The Common SQL Verbs and Statements  22
    2     The SELECT Statement  22

        *2.1   Clauses in the SELECT Statement, 22*

    3     The INSERT, UPDATE, and DELETE Statements  23
    4     Executing SQL in SPUFI  24

        *4.1   Log On to TSO, 24*
        *4.2   Invoke DB2I, 24*
        *4.3   Invoke SPUFI in DB2I, 24*
        *4.4   Entering the SPUFI Main Panel, 25*
        *4.5   Changing Current SPUFI Defaults, 26*
        *4.6   Entering/Saving SQL Statements, 27*
        *4.7   Running the SQL Statements, 28*
        *4.8   Browsing the Output, 28*
        *4.9   Committing Any Insert/Update/Delete SQL*
              *Statement, 30*

**5     Selecting Columns**                                                             **31**

    1     The Employee Table  31
    2     Select All Columns from Source Table(s)/Views  31

        *2.1   Select All Columns: Example #1, 32*
        *2.2   Select All Columns: Example #2, 32*
        *2.3   Problems With "SELECT *" in Application*
              *Programs, 32*

    3     Select Specific Columns from Source Table(s)/Views  33

        *3.1   Columns With Identical Names, 33*

    4     SELECT "DISTINCT" Source Column  33
    5     Select Computed Source Column  34
    6     Select Using Built-in Functions  34

        *6.1   The SUM Built-in Function, 34*
        *6.2   The MIN Built-in Function, 35*
        *6.3   The MAX Built-in Function, 36*
        *6.4   The AVG Built-in Function, 36*
        *6.5   The COUNT Built-in Function (Version 1), 37*
        *6.6   The COUNT DISTINCT Built-in Function*
              *(Version 2) 37*
        *6.7   Multiple Columns Using Built-in Function, 38*

**6    Specifying Source Tables and Views**                                          **39**

1    Specifying a Single Source Table or View   39
2    Specifying Multiple Source Tables/Views   39

  *2.1   Example of Selecting from Multiple Tables, 40*

**7    Selecting the Rows**                                                                 **41**

1    The WHERE Operand   41

  *1.1   Operands of WHERE, 42*
  *1.2   The NOT Negation Operator, 42*
  *1.3   Hierarchy of Evaluation on Compound Conditions, 42*

2    The Comparison Operators   42
3    The Arithmetic Operators   43
4    The BETWEEN . . . AND . . . Operators   43
5    The IN Operator   43
6    The LIKE Operator   43
7    The IS NULL Operator   44
8    Comparison on Conditions   44
9    The Join Operation   44

  *9.1   Indexes Useful in Join Operations, 45*

**8    Optional Clauses and Built-in Functions**                                 **46**

1    Clauses used in Built-in Functions   46

  *1.1   Current Data: Input Table, 46*

2    The GROUP BY Clause   46
3    The HAVING Clause   47

  *3.1   HAVING CLAUSE: First Function, 47*
  *3.2   HAVING CLAUSE: Second Function, 48*

4    The ORDER BY Clause   49

  *4.1   Ordering Sequence, 49*
  *4.2   ORDER BY and GROUP BY, 49*
  *4.3   Order By Column Position for Built-in Function Column, 50*
  *4.4   The Other ORDER BY Clause Uses, 50*

**9    SPUFI on INSERT/UPDATE/DELETE Operations**                         **51**

1    INSERT Operation   51

  *1.1   SQLCODE on INSERT Using SPUFI, 51*
  *1.2   Placement of Inserted Data Row, 52*

*1.3  Managing Free Space/Free Page of Data Pages, 52*
*1.4  Placement of New Index Entries, 53*
*1.5  Insert One Row: Principle, 54*
*1.6  SQL Example: Insert One Row, 55*
*1.7  Insert Multiple Rows: Principle, 56*
*1.8  SQL Example: Insert Multiple Rows, 56*

2    Update Row(s) in a Table or View   57

*2.1  The Expression in the SET Clause, 57*
*2.2  SQLCODE on UPDATE Using SPUFI, 57*
*2.3  SQL Example: Update Rows, 57*

3    Delete Row(s) from a Table   58

*3.1  SQLCODE on DELETE Using SPUFI, 58*
*3.2  SQL Example: Delete Rows, 58*

4    Committing any INSERT/UPDATE/DELETE SQL Statement   59

**PART III   SQL IN COBOL PROGRAMS**                                          *60*

**10    Coding the Cobol Program**                                            **60**

1    The Cobol Program   60

*1.1  Commit/Rollback for Cobol Programs, 60*
*1.2  The Cobol SQL Statement Delimiter, 61*

2    Coding the Working-Storage Section   61

*2.1  The SQL Communication Area (SQLCA), 61*
*2.2  Define the Tables/Views to be Used, 65*
*2.3  Define Host Variables, 67*
*2.4  The Indicator Variables, 68*

3    Coding the Procedure Division   70

*3.1  COMMIT/ROLLBACK and the Unit of Recovery, 70*
*3.2  The Commit Process, 71*
*3.3  The ROLLBACK Statement, 73*
*3.4  CICS COMMIT/ROLLBACK, 73*

4    Basic Program Skeleton   73
5    Program Example (as Coded)   74

**11    The Program Preparation Process**                                     **76**

1    Steps in Program Preparation   76

*1.1  Significance of the BIND Process, 78*
*1.2  How Many Programs (DBRMs) per Plan? 78*
*1.3  DB2's Automatic Rebind of Invalidated Plan, 78*

2    Using DB2I to Prepare and Test Programs    79

    *2.1    Saving the Generated JCL Statements, 79*
    *2.2    Invoke DB2I in TSO, 80*
    *2.3    Invoke Function in DB2I, 80*
    *2.4    The Program Preparation Panel, 80*

3    The DB2I Default Panel    82
4    The Precompile Panel    84

    *4.1    Output of CICS Command Translation, 85*
    *4.2    Output of Precompile, 85*

5    The BIND Panel    85
6    The COMPILE/LINK/RUN Panel    87
7    Executing the Program Preparation Steps    87
8    Executing the Program Preparation Steps Using JCL    88

**12    Select Operations**    **89**

1    Processing One Row from Source Table(s)/View    89

    *1.1    SQLCODE for Select ("Read-only") Operations, 89*
    *1.2    DCLGEN Output for XLIM.EMPTABLE, 90*
    *1.3    Current Data on XLIM.EMPTABLE, 90*
    *1.4    Program Logic: One-row Selection, 90*
    *1.5    Program Listing: One-row Selection, 91*
    *1.6    Additional JCL Statements and In-line Card File, 95*
    *1.7    Output Listing: One-row Selection, 95*

2    Processing Multiple Rows (by using a Cursor)    96

    *2.1    Defining the Cursor, 96*
    *2.2    Opening the Cursor to Start Processing, 98*
    *2.3    FETCH Statement to Read One Row, 98*
    *2.4    Closing the Cursor at End of Processing, 98*
    *2.5    Basic Program Logic: Multiple Rows, 98*
    *2.6    Program Example: Multiple-row Selection, 99*

**13    UPDATE/DELETE Using the Current Cursor**    **104**

1    UPDATE Using the Current Cursor    104

    *1.1    The DECLARE Statement, 104*
    *1.2    The OPEN/FETCH/CLOSE Cursor-name Statements, 105*
    *1.3    UPDATE/DELETE Using the Current Cursor, 105*
    *1.4    SQLCODE For UPDATE/DELETE/INSERT Operations, 106*
    *1.5    Program Logic: Update the Current Row, 107*
    *1.6    Program Example: Update the Current Row, 108*
    *1.7    COMMIT Using Cursor Processing, 112*

2    DELETE Using the Current Cursor   117

    *2.1   DELETE Using Cursor and Temporary Cursor Table, 118*
    *2.2   Program Logic: Delete the Current Row, 118*
    *2.3   Program Example: Delete the Current Row, 119*

**14    UPDATE/DELETE/INSERT Without Using Current Cursor          123**

1    UPDATE/DELETE Without Using Current Cursor   123
2    Non-cursor Update of One or More Rows   123

    *2.1   Current XLIM.EMPTABLE: Noncursor Update, 124*
    *2.2   Program Listing: Noncursor Update, 124*
    *2.3   Additional JCL Statements to be Included, 126*
    *2.4   Output Table: Noncursor Update, 126*

3    Noncursor Delete   126

    *3.1   Program Listing: Noncursor Delete, 127*
    *3.2   Additional JCL Statements to be Included, 128*
    *3.3   Output Table: Noncursor Delete, 129*

4    INSERT   129

    *4.1   Insert: No Cursor Required, 129*
    *4.2   Program Listing: Insert One Row, 129*
    *4.3   Additional JCL Statements to be Included, 132*
    *4.4   Output Table: Insert One Row, 132*
    *4.5   Mass Insert from a Table, 132*

*Part IV*  **BASIC DESIGN PRINCIPLES**                                   *133*

**15    Basic Logical Design: Preliminary Phase                         133**

1    Logical and Physical Design   133

    *1.1   Logical Design, 133*
    *1.2   Physical Design, 133*

2    Phases in the Logical Design Process   134
3    The Preliminary Design Phase   134

    *3.1   Identify the Entities, 134*
    *3.2   Entity Relationships, 136*
    *3.3   Identify the Properties of Entities, 137*

**16    Basic Logical Design: Final Phase                                  140**

1    The Final Phase Approach   140

    *1.1   Output of the Final Phase, 140*

2       Normalization   140

    *2.1   The Ideal Table, 141*
    *2.2   Levels of Normal Forms, 141*
    *2.3   Normalize to What Degree? 141*
    *2.4   The First Normal Form, 141*
    *2.5   The Second Normal Form, 142*
    *2.6   The Third Normal Form, 144*
    *2.7   The Fourth Normal Form, 146*
    *2.8   The Fifth Normal Form, 148*

**17      Physcial Design**                                                                 **149**

1       Size of a Data Row   149

    *1.1   Size of a Data Row as Seen by the User, 149*
    *1.2   Size of a Data Row on Disk (Physical Record), 149*

2       Number of Data Rows in a Page   150

    *2.1   Overhead in Page, 150*
    *2.2   Maximum Number of Data Rows in Page, 150*
    *2.3   Record Size that Wastes Disk Space, 150*

3       Computation for Space Needed for a Table   150

    *3.1   Compute for Percentage of Initially Usable Space, 151*
    *3.2   Compute for Number of Data Rows Per Page, 151*
    *3.3   Compute for Number of Pages for Table, 151*
    *3.4   Compute for Final Total Pages for Table, 151*
    *3.5   Compute for Table Size in Kilobytes, 151*
    *3.6   Computation Example, 151*

4       The Physical Index   153

    *4.1   The Leaf Pages, 153*
    *4.2   Nonleaf Pages, 153*
    *4.3   Root Page, 153*

**PART V   ADVANCED TOPICS**                                                           **154**

**18      Subquery and Union**                                                             **154**

1       Subquery   154

    *1.1   Use of a Subquery, 154*
    *1.2   Example of Subquery Using IN, 155*
    *1.3   Rules of the Subquery, 155*
    *1.4   Other Subquery Examples, 156*
    *1.5   Subquery in UPDATE and DELETE, 158*

*1.6   The Correlated Subquery, 158*
*1.7   Subqueries Versus Joins, 159*

2     Union of Tables   160

*2.1   Union of Tables: Format, 160*
*2.2   Union of Tables: Example, 160*


**19    Effeciency Techniques**                                    **162**

1     Introduction   162
2     Efficiency in Coding SQL Statements   162

*2.1   Basic SQL Efficiency Techniques, 162*
*2.2   Advanced SQL Efficiency Techniques, 164*

3     Efficiency Techniques in DB2 Resource Management   168

*3.1   Optimize the Speed of the DB2 Subsystem, 168*
*3.2   Improve the Utilization of Disk Devices, 171*
*3.3   Improve Virtual Storage Utilization, 172*
*3.4   Optimize Concurrency, 172*
*3.5   Validate During the BIND/REBIND Process, 173*
*3.6   On Page Locking Use Cursor Stability, Not*
*        Repeatable Read, 173*


**20    Creating and Dropping DB2 Objects**                        **175**

1     The Role of the System Administrator and DBA   175
2     Creating a Storage Group   175

*2.1   Example of Creating a Storage Group, 176*

3     Creating a Database   176

*3.1   Example of Creating a Database, 176*

4     Creating a Table Space   177

*4.1   Simple Versus Partitioned Table Space, 177*
*4.2   Creating a Simple Table Space, 177*
*4.3   Creating a Partitioned Table Space, 179*
*4.4   Number of Tables in a Table Space, 180*

5     Creating Tables   181

*5.1   The Table Owner, 182*
*5.2   Significance of NULL/NOT NULL WITH DEFAULT, 182*
*5.3   Table Exit Routines, 184*

6     Create a View   184

7     Create an Index   185

    *7.1   When Are Index Entries Created?   185*
    *7.2   Format of CREATE INDEX for Table in Simple*
    *Table Space, 185*
    *7.3   Format of CREATE INDEX for Partitioned*
    *Table Space, 186*

8     Creating a Synonym   188

    *8.1   Dropping a Synonym, 188*

9     Dropping DB2 Objects   188

    *9.1   Dropping a Table Space, 188*
    *9.2   Dropping a Table or View, 188*

10    Altering Table Spaces and Tables   189

    *10.1   Altering a Table, 189*

**21    Other Avanced Topics**                                                               **190**

1     The Locking Mechanism   190

    *1.1   Purposes of Locking, 190*
    *1.2   The Lock Owner, 191*
    *1.3   Object and Size of Locked Resource, 191*
    *1.4   Duration of Locks, 192*
    *1.5   Mode of Locking for Page Locks, 194*
    *1.6   The LOCK TABLE Statement, 195*

2     Granting Authorization   196

    *2.1   No Authorization Needed for Non-DB2 Activities, 196*
    *2.2   Authorization for DB2 Activities, 196*

3     Revoking Authorization   198
4     DB2 and CICS   198

    *4.1   How CICS and Batch Programs are Similar, 199*
    *4.2   How CICS and Batch Programs are Different, 199*

5     Referential Integrity   200

    *5.1   Referential Integrity with Subordinate and*
    *Association Tables, 200*
    *5.2   Referential Integrity with Primary/Foreign*
    *Tables, 200*
    *5.3   Data Inconsistency on DELETE, 200*
    *5.4   Data Inconsistency on INSERT, 202*
    *5.5   Data Inconsistency on UPDATE, 203*

**22    Important DB2 Utilities/Program Products                                204**

1    Introduction    204
2    The Data Extract Facility    204

    *2.1    Using DXT, 205*

3    Tuning the Database    205

    *3.1    The RUNSTAT Utility, 205*
    *3.2    The STOSPACE Utility, 207*

4    The Explain Statement    207

    *4.1    Format of the EXPLAIN Statement, 208*
    *4.2    Creating the PLAN_TABLE, 208*
    *4.3    Meaning of Fields in the PLAN_TABLE, 209*
    *4.4    Using the EXPLAIN Statement, 211*

5    Data Recovery    212

    *5.1    Data Recovery and the DB2 Locking Feature, 212*
    *5.2    The Image Copies of Table Space, 212*

6    QMF    213
    **Index                                                                                    215**

# *Preface*

For many years now, organizations have seen the advantages in placing their data in one centralized location, instead of in a multitude of separate files. Among the many advantages, one of the most important is the elimination of data inconsistency that is inherent when the same piece of data has to appear in different files.

Years ago when I worked for a department store, my address in the Accounts Receivable file (I had discount privileges) was inconsistent with my address in the Payroll file. My address in the former was always up to date since statements for any merchandise I bought were mailed to me. However, the latter carried the address I had when I first joined the company, and I never thought of informing the company on any change of address since both my payroll checks and W-2 forms were hand delivered to me. I only realized the problem when I left the company and my W-2 form was mailed to the wrong address.

This problem would have been avoided if we had a database system, where information is centralized. In database systems, the user only has to insert or update a piece of data once and that will be in effect for all applications. In some cases, a certain amount of redundancy is tolerated for the sake of efficiency. However, a database system such as DB2 still avoids data inconsistency since duplicate data may be updated all at once with a single transaction.

However, a big problem has always remained. In current databases of the hierarchical and network models, users can extract data only by navigating through a maze of linkages and pointers. Like a driver who must know both the intricacies of the road or street system and where he or she is currently located to successfully go from point A to point B, the database user must also know both the intricacies of the hierarchy or network and where in that hierarchy or network the program is currently pointing to. For both driver and database user, the key work is "navigate." The more complex the hierarchy or network is and the less experienced the person is, the greater the chance for error.

Several computer professionals (principally E. F. Codd) were the first to decry this problem. In the late 1960s, they postulated a new model of database, which they called relational. In it, data are contained in tables and are accessed via simple procedures such as Selection, Projection, and so on, where the user merely specifies what he or she wants, without any need to know the linkages between the data.

With relational database, it is similar to the driver going from point A to point B merely by saying, "I want to get from point A to point B" and the car automatically does the navigation for the driver. The driver does not have to know the street or road system.

The relational model is therefore easier to use than either the hierarchical or network model. DB2 is IBM's version of it and is written to work under the MVS/XA and MVS/SP operating systems. (A basically identical version called SQL/DS runs in VSE and VM systems.) This book explains to the application programmer and other user personnel how to manipulate data in DB2.

This book is divided into five parts. The first three chapters provide an introduction to DB2, followed by six chapters on how to access data in general (with or without Cobol programs). The next five chapters discuss how to access data specifically in Cobol programs. Three chapters follow on design techniques, and the final five chapters discuss advanced topics.

The examples in this book are straightforward and are very easy to follow. The SPUFI examples and the eight Cobol programs were fully tested under an MVS/XA system.

*Pacifico Amarga Lim*

# 1

# *Introduction*

## 1 WHAT IS A DATABASE?

A database is a centralized collection of data that serves the whole organization. Because of this centralized control, an organization is able to implement a better security and integrity procedure for data, as well as keep data redundancy to a minimum.

## 2 THREE MODELS OF DATABASE SYSTEMS

There are three models of database. The hierarchical and network models are the earlier ones used and the relational model is the latest one.

### 2.1 The Hierarchical Model

Figure 1.1 shows the hierarchical model.
The following rules apply:

1. Each node at any level may have only one parent node, the node at the next higher level it belongs to. Naturally, the highest-level node, which is called the root node, has no parent.

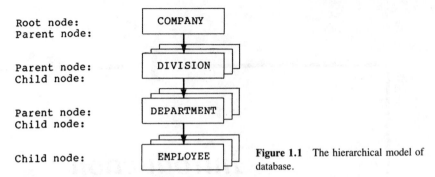

```
Root node:                 COMPANY
Parent node:

Parent node:              DIVISION
Child node:

Parent node:             DEPARTMENT
Child node:

Child node:               EMPLOYEE
```

**Figure 1.1**   The hierarchical model of database.

2. Each node at any level may have one or more children, the node(s) at the next lower level that belong(s) to it.

3. Each node except the root node can be accessed only via its parent node. Thus, to get the records of employees belonging to a department, the programmer has first to find the division that department belongs to.

**2.1.1. Disadvantages of the hierarchical model.**   While this model of database is currently in use (IMS/DLI is an example) and relatively easy to understand, it has several major problems. They are:

1. The biggest problem is that to access the data, the programmer must navigate through the hierarchy via a series of statements such as GET UNIQUE, GET NEXT, GET UNIQUE WITHIN PARENT, and so on. Thus, processing can become quite complicated and involved. In contrast, in the relational model, the programmer extracts data without having to navigate through the database.

2. Deletion of a parent node results in the deletion of the children. When a department record is deleted, all employees in that department are deleted. The user must therefore be very careful when doing deletes.

3. If a child has more than one parent, implementation is awkward with the child node becoming redundant since it has to appear for each parent. An example is a medical record which belongs to both patient and doctor.

## 2.2 The Network Model

Figure 1.2 shows the network model.

Each child node belongs to more than one parent node. A medical record belongs to one patient, but also to one (or more) doctors.

**2.2.1. Disadvantages of the network model.**   While the network model is natural to many situations (a medical record belongs to both patient and doctor, a grade belongs to both student and course offering, and so on), as with the hierarchical model, the programmer must also navigate through the network by specifying how to get to the desired data. Consequently, processing can also become quite complicated.

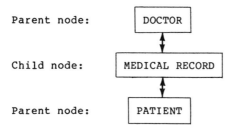

Figure 1.2   The network model of database.

## 2.3 The Relational Model

This is the simplest model to use, since the programmer gets the desired data simply by specifying exactly what is wanted, while the DBMS (such as DB2) takes care of navigating through the database.

# 2

# *Introduction to Relational Database*

## 1 HISTORY

The person credited with developing the formal concept of the relational model is E. F. Codd. He and a few other computer professionals noted the growing complexity in the structures of both the hierarchical and network models. They particularly decried the abundance of linkages between parent and child nodes and especially the fact that such linkages tended to multiply as new applications were added, resulting in more tangled webs for the programmer to navigate.

What was needed was a model that offered the user an easier means of manipulating data. The first papers on the subject were published in the late 1960s.

## 2 THE RELATIONAL MODEL

Figure 2.1 shows the relational model.
The following apply:

1. All data are contained in one or more tables that resemble traditional sequential files.

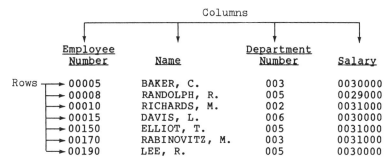

Figure 2.1   A table of data in the relational model.

2. Each row (record) in a table contains several columns (fields). In Figure 2.1, the rows are employee records; the columns are employee number, employee name, department number, and annual salary.

3. In relational database theory, the rows are not in any logical or physical sequence (therefore unordered). *However, as implemented in DB2, the user may choose to place the rows in physical sequence by key (ordering of rows is automatically done during the initial mass load of rows or at table reorganization) by specifying a clustered index for the key (see page 186).* A clustered index may promote greater overall efficiency for a table with a large degree of sequential read-only access where the rows are accessed in their physical order. However, note that it is DB2 that decides for each access request whether any existing index will be used, meaning it promotes greater efficiency. See page 168 for the discussion on when to define an index.

4. Although in relational database theory, all tables have a primary key (employee number for the Employee table, department number for the Department table, and so on), DB2 does not require any key at all. Access to data is based on the value of one or more columns of a table (i.e., Select all rows where salary is greater than $30,000). In DB2, a primary key, if one exists, is defined with an index, usually further defined as UNIQUE (thus, no duplicates) and CLUSTER (rows in physical sequence). In addition, no one is granted UPDATE permission on any of the column(s) that comprise the index.

5. Each table is independent of another and the programmer may use any of them singly or in combination to get the data needed.

6. There is no parent/child linkage among the tables as in the hierarchical and network models.

## 3  WHAT CONSTITUTES THE RELATIONAL MODEL?

The following apply:

1. The data are contained in tables.
2. A table has only two dimensions, the rows and columns. This is shown in

| Item No. | Units | Price |
|----------|-------|-------|

| Item No. | Units | Price |
|----------|-------|-------|

| Order Number | Item No. | Units | Price | Other fields |
|--------------|----------|-------|-------|--------------|

(a)

**Figure 2.2A**   An invalid DB2 table.

| Order Number | (Items Ordered) | | | Other fields |
|--------------|---------|-------|--------|--------------|
|              | Item No. | Units | Price |              |
| 000007 | 0083005 | 50 | 006075 | |
|        | 0007548 | 10 | 004600 | |
|        | 0643222 | 25 | 015000 | Etc. |
| 000450 | 0007548 | 15 | 004600 | |
|        | 1038876 | 10 | 016400 | Etc. |

(b)

**Figure 2.2B**   Example of an invalid DB2 table.

Figure 2.1. If a table is first designed with a third dimension, it is simplified via normalization (see Chapter 16).

Figure 2.2A shows an invalid table that has to be normalized (to the first normal form) before it can be used. There is a third dimension, the number of items in the order. Figure 2.2B is an example of an invalid table. Order number 000007 has three items, order number 000450 two items.

3. Each row in a table represents an entity, such as one employee or one inventory item, and each column represents a property of that entity, such as name or address. In Figure 2.1, we have the Employee table, which represents the "employee" entity containing the properties employee number, employee name, department number, and annual salary.

4. In relational database theory, each row in a table is identified by a primary key (one or more columns). *However, as implemented in DB2, a key is not required.* If a table has a primary key, it is defined with the CREATE UNIQUE INDEX statement, and often further defined as CLUSTER, so it is also physically sequenced by the primary key. In addition, the key is further protected from being changed by not allowing any UPDATE authorization on any of the column(s) that comprise the index.

5. The tables can be manipulated to form new tables that the programmer wants (see Basic Data Extraction in Section 5).

## 4 ADVANTAGES OF THE RELATIONAL MODEL

The relational model provides several advantages over the hierarchical and network models. They are:

1. *Data manipulation is much simpler and more straightforward.* From the table(s) that the user is allowed to access, the programmer extracts the required data with simple "cut and paste" operations. The data are "cut" (by specifying the rows and columns) from one or more tables and "pasted" (displayed) immediately at the terminal or brought one row at a time to be processed in the program.

2. *The user does not navigate through pointers to manipulate the data.* It is the DBMS (for instance, DB2), not the application programmer, that navigates through the database. The programmer is therefore free of the problem that had always existed in the hierarchical and network models.

3. *Among the three models of database, this offers the highest degree of data independence.* Pointers to data (implemented via indexes) are not needed for data manipulation and are totally independent of the data. As long as the manipulation statement is correct, the data will be manipulated correctly. However, the judicious use of indexes will allow the DBMS to manipulate such data faster in certain situations. Indexes are therefore defined for efficiency but are never specified by the user in data manipulation statements.

## 5 BASIC DATA EXTRACTION

There are three most basic operations for extracting data from a relational database. They are all "cut and paste" methods, based on relational algebra, which take one or more input tables as the operand(s) and generate an output table. The rows comprising the output table may be immediately displayed on a terminal (if using the interactively facility of the DBMS) or brought one row at a time to the application program.

Both Selection and Projection operations are implemented in DB2 with the same SELECT statement; therefore, while different in theory, they are basically identical to the practicing programmer.

### 5.1 Selection

Selection gives the programmer a new table which consists of a "horizontal" subset of the rows in the old table; which rows are selected depends on the selection criteria (the WHERE clause in DB2). *Selection is row extraction* (as opposed to Projection, which is column extraction).

| Employee Number | Name | Department Number | Salary |
|---|---|---|---|
| 00008 | RANDOLPH, R. | 005 | 0029000 |
| 00150 | ELLIOT, T. | 005 | 0031000 |
| 00190 | LEE, R. | 005 | 0030000 |

**Figure 2.3**   Selection output from Fig. 2.1.

In theory, all original columns are extracted. However, as implemented in DB2 (with the verb SELECT, with the WHERE clause specifying how rows are selected), the user may also specify the columns.

Using Figure 2.1 as the input table, we can generate Figure 2.3 as shown in the following Selection operation (in pseudocode):

```
Select from the table in Fig. 2.1
    where the department number is '005'.
```

The user may now process this output table. Note that only those rows in Figure 2.1 with department number equal to '005' (the selection criteria) are generated in the output table.

## 5.2 Projection

Projection gives the programmer a new table which consists of a "vertical" subset of the columns in the old table; the programmer specifies the column(s) in the new table. *Projection is column extraction* (as opposed to Selection, which is row extraction).

It is also implemented in DB2 with the SELECT verb, but without the WHERE clause. The columns selected are specified following the verb.

Using Figure 2.1 as the input, we can generate Figure 2.4 in the following Projection operation (in pseudocode):

```
Select employee number, name, salary
    from the table in Fig. 2.1.
```

Here the programmer is interested only in the employee number, name, and salary for all rows in Figure 2.1. The department number is left out.

## 5.3 Join

Join gives the programmer a new table which is the result of the concatenation of rows from two or more tables. Concatenation (not merging, which is accomplished with the UNION operation) is done with the selected columns from Table 1 appearing on the left, the selected columns from Table 2 concatenated on the right, and so

| Employee Number | Name | Salary |
|---|---|---|
| 00005 | BAKER, C. | 0030000 |
| 00008 | RANDOLPH, R. | 0029000 |
| 00010 | RICHARDS, M. | 0031000 |
| 00015 | DAVIS, L. | 0030000 |
| 00150 | ELLIOT, T. | 0031000 |
| 00170 | RABINOVITZ, M. | 0031000 |
| 00190 | LEE, R. | 0030000 |

**Figure 2.4**   Projection output from Fig. 2.1.

on. Join is also implemented in DB2 with the SELECT verb, with the FROM clause specifying the "source" tables.

**5.3.1 Natural join (equijoin).**    Natural Join is a join based on the same data value of certain columns (department number, item number, and so on). The WHERE clause specifies the column(s) to be matched.

Given Figure 2.5 as another table (a Department table):

```
Department Number        Department Name

        002              Accounts Payable
        003              Data Processing
        005              Administration
        006              Finance              Figure 2.5  The department table.
```

Using Figures 2.1 and 2.5, we can generate Figure 2.6 in the following natural join operation (in pseudocode):

```
Select employee number, name, department number,
                    department name
     from the tables in Fig. 2.1 and Fig. 2.5.
     where the department numbers in both tables are equal
```

Here the programmer wants the employee number, name, department number, and department name from both the Employee and Department tables where the department numbers in the Employee table match those in the Department table.

```
Employee                      Dept.      Dept.
Number        Name            Number     Name

00005        BAKER, C.        003        Data Processing
00008        RANDOLPH, R.     005        Administration
00010        RICHARDS, M.     002        Accounts Payable
00015        DAVIS, L.        006        Finance
00150        ELLIOT, T.       005        Administration
00170        RABINOVITZ, M.   003        Data Processing
00190        LEE, R.          005        Administration
```

**Figure 2.6**  Join output from Fig. 2.1 and Fig. 2.5.

**5.3.2 Other joins.**    In the natural join (or equijoin) operation, we match two or more tables and join rows where values are identical. Actually, rows are joined (not necessarily natural join) as long as the join criteria (in DB2, specified in the WHERE clause) is TRUE. For instance, given Figure 2.7:

```
Employee                 Department
Number        Name       Number      Salary

00005        BAKER, C.     003       0030000
00008        RANDOLPH, R.  005       0029000   Figure 2.7  A table of data.
```

We will generate Figure 2.8 if we execute the following (nonequijoin) join operation:

```
Select employee number, name, department name
     from the tables in Fig. 2.7 and Fig. 2.5
     where the department numbers in both tables are not equal
```

```
Employee
Number        Name            Dept.
                              Name

00005       BAKER, C.        Accounts Payable
00005       BAKER, C.        Administration
00005       BAKER, C.        Finance
00008       RANDOLPH, R.     Accounts Payable
00008       RANDOLPH, R.     Data Processing
00008       RANDOLPH, R.     Finance
```

**Figure 2.8** Nonequijoin output from Fig. 2.7 and Fig. 2.5.

This result, which is actually meaningless, is explained in the next section. But as per the join criteria (the department numbers in both tables are not equal), each row in Figure 2.7 (the first table) is joined with all rows in Figure 2.5 (the second table) where the department numbers are indeed not equal.

Thus, the improper use of the join operation can result in quite meaningless output.

**5.3.3 Output rows generated in join operations.** For a join operation using two tables, each row in Table 1 will generate as many output rows as that row and all rows in Table 2 satisfy as TRUE the condition for join, or else no output is generated for that row in Table 1. Thus, each row in Table 1 is matched against all rows in Table 2. If there are three tables, any matched Table 1–Table 2 pair (using the technique just mentioned) will generate as many output rows as the pair and all rows in Table 3 satisfy the condition for join, or else no output is generated by that matched pair.

Thus, on a join operation using two tables, if there are two rows in Table 1 that satisfy the condition with three rows in Table 2, then six output rows will be generated. This is in fact what happened in Section 5.3.2.

# 3

# *Introduction to DB2*

## 1 WHAT IS DB2?

DB2 is IBM's relational database management system for large IBM mainframes. It runs as a subsystem in MVS/XA and MVS/SP environments. It supports an easy-to-use database language with which the user can define tables, access tables, and specify authorization for access. In addition, there are separate user-friendly, menu-driven program products that may be used to access the database and print meaning-ful reports from it.

A version called SQL/DS runs in VSE and VM systems.

## 2 THE DB2 ENVIRONMENT

Figure 3.1 shows the DB2 operating environment.

DB2 allows access to DB2 resources (rows and columns from tables, indexes, table spaces, and so on) in the following ways:

1. *Via a batch application program* written in a language such as Cobol, PL/I, and so on. The job runs under TSO background, since TSO is used for data

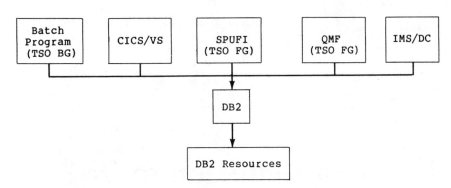

**Figure 3.1**   The DB2 operation environment.

communications. *The regular, batch processing of information is best done this way.*

2. *Via CICS/VS* as the front end for application programs written in command-level. *The regular, online processing of information is best done this way.*

3. *Via SPUFI* (SQL Processing Using File Input), a function under the built-in DB2 Interactive (DB2I) facility that is accessed via TSO foreground. It allows the execution of SQL statements without the need for an application program (but is expensive to use) and *is mostly used by the system administrator and the DBA to perform such housekeeping functions as create tables, grant authorization, and so on. However, application programmers learning DB2 may conveniently use it to learn how SQL statements work.*

4. *Via QMF* (Query Management Facility), a separate piece of software that goes beyond what SPUFI can provide. An interactive, user-friendly product, it runs under TSO foreground and allows the user to print well-formatted reports (including subtotals, range checking, and so on). In addition, the user may conveniently access data using the menu-driven query-by-example (QBE) feature, instead of coding SQL statements. *It is mostly used by nontechnical user personnel to print one-time reports on an as-needed basis.*

5. *IMS/DC.* IMS/DC (not IMS batch) can access DB2 resources.

## 3 DB2 OBJECTS

Chapter 20 gives a more complete discussion of DB2 objects. Briefly, they are resources that can be created or manipulated by the user. These are:

1. *Database.* A collection of one or more tables and their associated indexes. Each database generally contains all data for an application or a group of related applications. There is a Personnel database, a Purchase Order database, an Accounts Receivable database, and so on.

2. *Storage group.* A set of DASD volumes of the same type predefined by the system administrator and contains the data in tables and indexes.

3. *Table space*. A VSAM ESDS (entry-sequenced data set) that can contain up to 64 gigabytes. It is implemented in either of two ways.

    a. *Simple table space*. This contains one or more tables implemented in one storage group.

    b. Or, *partitioned table space*. A single table partitioned (physically implemented) in several storage groups. This is most useful for large tables.

4. *Table*. The DB2 object that contains the data in the form of rows and columns. It is not a data set (the table space is) but is only a logical component of a table space. It is implemented as one or more VSAM control intervals. Examples of tables are the Employee table, the Department table, the Purchase Order table, and the Inventory table. A table can be up to 64 gigabytes long (meaning, only one table in that table space). *Generally, a table with 250 pages or more is best placed in a table space of its own (see Chapter 17 for the computation of number of pages)*. Most tables would actually fit this category. Some tables, such as the Department table is often less than 250 pages long.

5. *Index*. A pointer to one or more rows in a table, based on the value of a column or group of columns. It is optionally defined by the user. A table may have several indexes and like a table space, it is also implemented as a VSAM ESDS. Note that an index cannot be defined for a view, only for a table.

6. *View*. An alternative way of representing data, the user's window to the data. For security reasons, to provide a simplied picture of the data or to help reduce data redundancy, it is the one that many users are allowed to access. Each view is derived from the selected rows and columns of one or more tables. There is no limit to what a view is. It may result from a Join, Union, or grouping of rows of one or more tables.

Figure 3.2 is an example of one installation's DB2 objects.
The following apply:

1. We have a database called "REGISTER", which is on student registration. This database has two table spaces.

2. A large table called "STUDENT" is implemented in a partitioned table space. It has two partitions, one implemented in storage group STGP1, the other in storage group STGP2.

    a. For each partition, we have an index. The indexes are implemented in the same storage group as their corresponding partitions. Thus, partition 1 and index PARTX1 are implemented in storage group STGP1.

3. Two smaller tables implemented in a simple table space called "REGOTHER". This is implemented in storage group 2.

## 3.1 Creating DB2 Objects

The creation of DB2 objects is shown in Chapter 20. This function is done by the system administrator and database administrator (DBA), not the application pro-

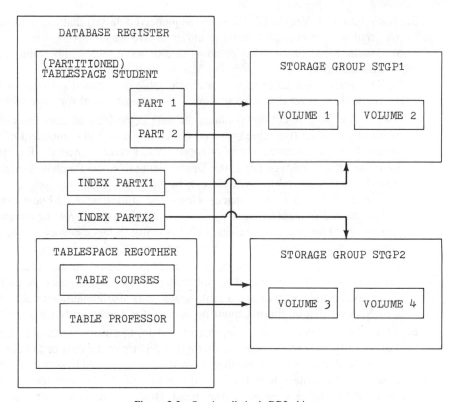

**Figure 3.2**  One installation's DB2 objects.

grammers. Certain objects such as tables, indexes, and views are decided on by the systems designer and user management, but also created by the DBA.

After creation, permission to insert, update, delete, and select database data (rows and columns in tables and views) is then provided by the DBA to individual users. For views, certain updates are not allowed (see section 5.6).

## 4 TABLES AS "REAL" TABLES

When users access data, they access either "real" tables and/or facsimiles of tables. Which ones are accessed depends on management and the systems designer.

### 4.1 Tables

The tables that logically result from the design process are "real" tables. They contain the rows and columns of data that comprise the database information. Examples are the Employee table, the Department table, and so on.

As implemented in DB2, each table is only a logical subdivision of a physical data set, the table space, the latter being a VSAM ESDS. A similar concept is a partitioned data set where a member is only a logical subdivision of the PDS.

# 5 VIEWS AS VIRTUAL TABLES

In many cases, users do not see the table(s) as is. Instead, they are provided (by the DBA) with a view, a specific picture of the database, which is only what management wants them to see.

Each user may have one or more views. Each is actually just a definition maintained in the DB2 catalog (see Section 8) and has no corresponding internal representation in physical devices. It is therefore known as a "virtual" table, formed from the selected columns of one or more real tables.

However, the user cannot tell a "virtual" table from a real table and since views are generally used for read-only data, may operate on the view as if it were a real table. There are, however, several limitations if the view is used to update the corresponding tables. See Section 5.6.

## 5.1 View as a Security Measure

One reason for a view is security. For instance, certain personnel should not be allowed to see all the information in a table. The manager of a department may be given a view that allows access to rows (for employees) that belong to his or her department only and not to other departments. Clerical personnel may be allowed access to certain columns in the Personnel database, but not the salary column.

## 5.2 View to Simplify User Access

Another reason for a view is to provide a user a more simplified picture of the data. In one example, a view may contain only the three columns a user needs, not the 30 columns in the original table. In another example, a user may get a view that is already a join between two or more tables.

## 5.3 View to Help Reduce Data Redundancy

If a user requires data that may be generated from existing tables (that is, they are currently not in the form that the user can immediately use), then a view avoids the need to maintain such data somewhere else, and thus help reduce data redundancy. For instance, a division manager may get a view from the existing Employee table, where each row in the view contains the computed total salary or average salary of the departments within the division. There is therefore no need to create a separate table containing such divisional information.

## 5.4 Examples of a View

Figure 3.3A shows a real table. Figures 3.3B and 3.3C are two views from that table.

One view from Figure 3.3A is Figure 3.3B. From the original four columns, we have two columns in the view.

Another view from Figure 3.3A is Figure 3.3C. From the original four columns, we have three columns in the view.

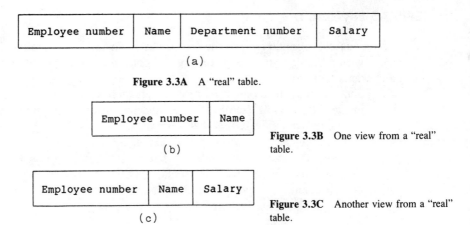

(a)

**Figure 3.3A**   A "real" table.

**Figure 3.3B**   One view from a "real" table.

**Figure 3.3C**   Another view from a "real" table.

## 5.5 Creating a View

Chapter 20 shows how the CREATE VIEW view-name statement is used to create a view. As mentioned before, selected rows from one or more tables generate one view.

For instance, in Figure 3.4, View1 gets selected rows and columns from Table1 and Table2 (join or union), View2 gets selected rows and columns from Table1, Table2 and Table3 (join or union), while View3 gets selected rows and columns from Table4 only (selection, projection).

## 5.6 Update Restrictions on Views

While a view is mostly used for read-only access, update functions are allowed, except for the following restrictions:

1. An INSERT, UPDATE, or DELETE is not allowed if a view is generated from more than one table (say, from a join).
2. An INSERT, UPDATE, or DELETE is not allowed if a view is generated from a built-in function or the GROUP BY or DISTINCT clauses.
3. An INSERT is not allowed if a view does not contain a column in the original table which was defined as NOT NULLS.

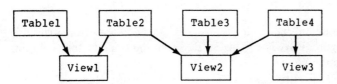

**Figure 3.4**   Views from tables.

**4.** If a column of a view is computed (such as SALARY * 1.1).
   a. An INSERT is not allowed (obviously, there is no way to update the original column in the table).
   b. An UPDATE is not allowed on the column.

Note that when we update via a view, we are in fact updating the original table.

# 6 THE SIGNIFICANCE OF SQL

SQL (Structured Query Language) is the database language of DB2. Except when using the query-by-example (QBE) facility of QMF, it is the language used to access DB2 objects. Thus, it is to DB2 what DL/I is to IMS/DLI.

Specifically, it is used by application programs to request database service within Cobol, PL/I, and so on, by user personnel to access data interactively, without any application program (SPUFI and QMF); by database administrators, the system administrator, and others, to create tables, grant or revoke authorization for data access, and so on.

It is very easy to use, even for occasional users, and has become the de facto language for relational databases.

## 6.1 Most Common SQL Statements

SQL is most commonly used to:

1. Create and drop tables/views (CREATE/DROP).
2. "Read" selected rows and columns (SELECT).
3. Insert new rows into a table (INSERT).
4. Delete existing rows from a table (DELETE).
5. Update certain rows and columns (UPDATE).
6. Add columns to a table or view (ALTER).
7. Grant or revoke specific access privileges to nonowners (GRANT/REVOKE).

## 6.2 Advantages of SQL

SQL offers several advantages.

1. *Easy to use*.
   a. It requires only a short initial learning period.
   b. It is a nonprocedural language. Users specify what they want, rather than how to do it. For example:

```
SELECT EMPNO, EMPNAME
   FROM XLIM.EMPTABLE
   WHERE EMPDEPT = '005'
```

which selects the employee number and the corresponding name for those employees belonging to department number '005'.

  c. It is totally data independent. The user does not specify any access path via indexes or physical sequence. Any indexes or physical sequencing may be used by DB2 if it will provide a faster access to the data.

  d. There is high-level programming support so that application programmers may write Cobol, PL/I, Assembler and Fortran programs to process the data. Such application programs are used for planned, regularly-used applications.

2. *Useful aid facilities for the User.*

  a. DB2 allows large tables, up to 64 gigabytes in size.

  b. In a pinch, or for one-time use, the user may use SPUFI or QMF, which allow database without an application program.

  c. The database administrator also uses SPUFI to define and modify tables on line without interrupting DB2 operations.

  d. The DB2 Interactive facility (DB2I), of which SPUFI is only one of the functions, runs under TSO. It allows the programmer to interactively prepare application programs, use DB2 utilities, and so on.

  e. DB2 provides enhancement for improved performance:

    1) Extended access path selection to provide more efficient access to data.

    2) More concurrency, allowing more transactions to run simultaneously.

3. Faster data access for programs that process the database in physical record sequence.

4. Utility enhancements which reduce I/O operations and elapsed time.

5. Temporary data sets may be placed on multiple volumes, eliminating contention for the temporary files used by the DB2 sort operation.

### 6.3 SQL Without an Application Program

SPUFI and QMF allow the user to code SQL statements to access (including insert, update, and delete records) DB2 resources independent of any application program. The former is a function under the built-in DB2 Interactive facility, while the latter, a much more powerful facility, is a separate piece of software.

Some typical functions are:

1. List all or parts of a table on either the terminal or a printer (QMF only).

2. Insert, update, and delete data.

3. Sort or sequence the data.

4. Format the output to include more descriptive column headings.

For example, assuming that the table in Figure 2.1 has been cataloged in DB2 as XLIM.EMPTABLE, with the corresponding columns cataloged as EMPNO, EMPNAME, EMPDEPT, and EMPSALARY. If we code in SPUFI:

| <u>EMPNO</u> | <u>EMPNAME</u> | <u>EMPSALARY</u> |
|-------|----------------|----------|
| 00005 | BAKER, C.      | 0030000  |
| 00008 | RANDOLPH, R.   | 0029000  |
| 00010 | RICHARDS, M.   | 0031000  |
| 00015 | DAVIS, L.      | 0030000  |
| 00150 | ELLIOT, T.     | 0031000  |
| 00170 | RABINOVITZ, M. | 0031000  |
| 00190 | LEE, R.        | 0030000  |

**Figure 3.5**   Terminal display output of SPUFI.

```
SELECT EMPNO, EMPNAME, EMPSALARY
      FROM XLIM.EMPTABLE;
```

The output table as displayed in a terminal is Figure 3.5.

Note that this is a straightforward display; however, the user may modify the column headings to make them more descriptive.

## 6.4 SQL in an Application Program

For repetitive, planned access to the database, application programs are used. Programmers use the very same SQL statements used in SPUFI and QMF, plus additional ones. For instance, the output table generated from a Selection, Projection, or Join operation is not brought "as is" to the program; instead, the programmer defines a cursor and fetches this output table, one row at a time.

SQL in Cobol programs will be discussed in Chapters 10 to 14.

## 6.5 Table/View Naming Conventions

Table/view names consist of two parts, separated by a period. The first part is the userid of the table/view owner, which is the same one explicitly specified when the table/view is created (by the DBA); otherwise it is the TSO userid of the creator (the DBA). The second part may be up to 18 characters long, and specifies a descriptive name for the table/view.

As an example, the table name for an Employee table may be XLIM. EMPTABLE, that of the Department table, XLIM.DEPTABLE.

### 6.5.1 The userid in statements.
When using the table name in SQL statements, the owner does not have to specify his or her userid since DB2 will append it if missing; all other users (assuming of course that they are granted authorization to access the table) must specify the owner's userid in statements.

## 6.6 Column Naming Conventions

The user is also allowed 18 characters for column names. The names have to be unique for a table, but may have duplicates across tables. However, when columns with identical names (naturally, from different tables) are specified in a single SQL statement (say, in a join operation), the columns are differentiated by prefixing the

corresponding table names. Thus, XLIM.EMPTABLE.DEPTNO and XLIM.
DEPTABLE.DEPTNO.

## 7 DATA SECURITY/INTEGRITY FACILITIES

DB2 offers comprehensive facilities for data security and integrity.

### 7.1 Data Security

DB2 users have four methods to ensure that only authorized personnel may be allowed to perform certain functions.

**7.1.1 View as security measure.**    We have previously discussed that the creation of views provides a certain measure of data security since by doing so, only selected information may be accessed by certain users.

**7.1.2 The resource access control facility (RACF).**    IBM's RACF may be used to control access. Specifically:

1. *DB2 Connection Control*. Prevents unauthorized users to access DB2.
2. *Data Set Protection*. Protects the VSAM data sets that contain the data from unauthorized access or deletion.
3. *DASD Volume Protection*. Prevents unauthorized access to a DASD volume.

Note that RACF cannot be used to protect DB2-defined resources such as tables and views. They are protected instead by the DB2 authorization control (see Section 7.1.4).

**7.1.3 VSAM data set passwords.**    In RACF is not available, the user may use VSAM's built-in password-protection facilities to protect the VSAM data sets that contain DB2 data.

**7.1.4 DB2 authorization control.**    DB2 authorization control is discussed in more detail in Chapter 20. Briefly, it controls access by allowing a function (create a table, update a column in a row, and so on) only if the particular user attempting to perform that function is authorized to do so.

This is done via a rigid set of rules that allow the user to define to DB2 userids which have implicit or explicit authorization for certain functions.

### 7.2 Data Integrity

Data integrity is managed in two ways, mostly under the direct control of DB2, although it is influenced to some degree by the user.

**7.2.1 DB2 locking.**    The DB2 locking feature makes sure that data changed by a user (that is, logically changed in the buffer) but not yet committed (that is, not yet physically written by DB2 to the physical device) cannot be accessed by other users until the changes are indeed committed as final or rolled back wherein the changes are disregarded. Locking is explained in more detail in Chapter 21.

**7.2.2 DB2 recovery feature.**    DB2 also offers a comprehensive and integrated recovery facility that includes data recovery on a program or system failure or any physical data corruption. Recovery from program or system failure uses DB2 logging of "before" and "after" images of rows updated and is either done automatically (on a program failure) or as part of the emergency restart procedure (on a system crash, for instance).

Recovery from physical data corruption uses the "after" images of updated rows, in conjunction with the built-in DB2 utilities that are used to periodically copy (COPY utility) table spaces and the utility that recovers (RECOVER utility) the table space using these copies. Data recovery is explained in more detail in Chapter 22.

# 8 THE DB2 CATALOG

The DB2 catalog is the DB2 data dictionary and contains information on every object that DB2 manages, such as data, storage, programs, and authorization. It is itself a DB2 database consisting of tables and indexes, and is contained in VSAM data sets.

This catalog is updated every time a new DB2 object is defined or an old one changed. It contains such information as table names, view names, the owners, indexes, authorization for access, the columns, the name of the database containing the objects, the name of the table space containing the objects, and so on.

In addition, certain DB2 utilities such as RUNSTAT and STOSPACE also update this catalog with statistical information.

## 8.1 The Role of the Catalog

This catalog is used by DB2 during the BIND process to determine the validity of SQL statements as well as select the most efficient way to implement the statement.

Authorized users may access this catalog through SQL statements (in effect treating it as data) to get information about the objects, as well as statistical information generated by utilities such as RUNSTAT, STOSPACE, and so on.

# 4

# *The SQL Statements in SPUFI*

## 1 THE COMMON SQL VERBS AND STATEMENTS

In SPUFI, users access DB2 tables and views with four SQL verbs, all self-defining. They are SELECT, INSERT, UPDATE, and DELETE. In application programs, the same four verbs are used, in addition to OPEN, CLOSE, and FETCH, the latter of which brings the output table into the program, one row at a time.

Complete discussions on the use of SQL statements start in the next chapter.

## 2 THE SELECT STATEMENT

The SELECT statement extracts rows and columns from one or more tables or a view and produces an output table.

### 2.1 Clauses in the SELECT Statement

The user specifies clauses to further define the selection process. Only the FROM clause is mandatory, although others may become mandatory depending on other clauses.

*Clauses must be specified in the following exact order.*

**2.1.1 The SELECT columns clause.**    In the next chapter, we will learn that by default the programmer can select all the columns in the source table(s) or view. Or optionally, he or she selects specific columns; for instance, employee number and employee name only. Or, only summary data from groups of rows; for instance, the total salary for the employees belonging to each department.

Selecting columns is explained in the next chapter.

**2.1.2 The FROM source table(s) or view clause.**    The user must code the FROM operand to specify the table(s) and/or view used.

Selecting table(s) and views is explained in Chapter 6.

**2.1.3 The WHERE row selection clause.**    If the user wants all rows to be included (that is, process all rows in the input table), then this option is not needed; otherwise, the user specifies the criteria with the WHERE clause (for instance, WHERE department number = '003').

Note that the WHERE clause works with a column name compared to either a data-name or literal. In application programs, a data-name is generally used.

Selecting rows is explained in Chapter 7.

**2.1.4 The GROUP BY clause.**    If the user generates summaries only (DB2 built-in function SUM, AVG, and so on), this clause specifies the column(s) determining the "control break" upon which columns are added together, averaged, and so forth.

For instance, if SUM(annual salary) is specified with the GROUP BY department-number clause, then all rows belonging to a specific department number will have a single output row that is the sum of annual salaries for that department.

The GROUP BY clause is explained in Chapter 8.

**2.1.5 The HAVING clause.**    This specifies a further delimiter for groups selected via the GROUP BY clause. For instance, groups with only one row may be bypassed during selection.

The HAVING clause is explained in Chapter 8.

**2.1.6 The ORDER BY clause.**    This specifies the sequence in which the output will be presented to the user. If the specified sequence also has an index defined for it, DB2 will decide if using that index is more efficient than sorting the output; if so, it is used. Note that the GROUP BY clause does not sequence the output.

The ORDER BY clause is explained in Chapter 8.

# 3 THE INSERT, UPDATE, AND DELETE STATEMENTS

These statements are explained in Chapter 9.

## 4 EXECUTING SQL IN SPUFI

There are several steps needed to execute SQL statements in SPUFI.

### 4.1 Log On to TSO

SPUFI is a function of the DB2 Interactive (DB2I) facility, which runs under TSO. Therefore, the operator must first sign on to TSO, then invoke DB2I.

After logging on to TSO, the programmer may go directly to any panel he or she wants, by concatenating panel numbers. For instance, in one system the author has used, "ISPF s.5.1" immediately got the panel in Figure 4.3. In another system, "2.1.1" got the same Figure 4.3.

### 4.2 Invoke DB2I

To illustrate the steps properly, let us now go through the panels one by one. After TSO logon, the operator selects DB2I which may or may not be via the ISPF Primary Option Menu. One display might be Figure 4.1:

```
------------------- ISPF PRIMARY OPTION MENU ---------------
  SELECT OPTION ===>

  0   ISPF PARMS     - SPECIFY TERMINAL AND ISPF PARAMETERS
  1   BROWSE         - DISPLAY SOURCE DATA/COMPUTER LISTING
  2   EDIT           - CREATE OR CHANGE SOURCE DATA
  3   UTILITIES      - PERFORM ISPF UTILITY FUNCTIONS
  4   .....
  5   DB2I           - DATABASE2 INTERACTIVE
  6   .....
  7   .....
  8   .....
  9   .....
```

**Figure 4.1**  The ISPF primary option menu.

The operator selects option 5.

### 4.3 Invoke SPUFI in DB2I

Once in DB2I, the operator selects SPUFI in the DB2I Primary Option Menu. A typical display is Figure 4.2:

The operator selects option 1, which as we mentioned before, is only one of many functions of DB2 Interactive (DB2I).

```
                        DB2I PRIMARY OPTION MENU
===>

Select one of the following and press ENTER

   1   SPUFI              (Process SQL statements)
   2   DCLGEN             (Generate SQL and source language declarations)
   3   PROGRAM PREPARATION (Prepare a DB2 application program to run)
   4   PRECOMPILE         (Invoke DB2 precompiler)
   5   BIND/REBIND        (BIND/REBIND/FREE application plans)
   6   RUN                (RUN an SQL program)
   7   DB2 COMMANDS       (Issue DB2 commands)
   8   UTILITIES          (Invoke DB2 utilities)
   9   EXIT               (Leave DB2I)



PRESS:   ENTER to process      END to exit      HELP for more information
```

**Figure 4.2**   The DB2 primary option menu.

## 4.4 Entering the SPUFI Main Panel

The SPUFI main panel specifies the input and output of the SQL statements. A typical panel is shown in Figure 4.3.

The following apply:

1. The input data set will contain the SQL statements to be executed. This must have been previously allocated. If the user wants to use an existing partitioned data set, he or she simply specifies a new member name (or an old one to be reused).

2. The sequential output data set need not be allocated. This will hold the output generated by the SQL statement(s). "OUT1", "OUT2", or any other self-defining names may be conveniently utilized.

3. The processing options:
   a. "Y" for CHANGE DEFAULTS allows the user to change SPUFI default values. A panel is then displayed from which the operator may change such things as maximum number of rows generated by the SELECT statement, the output table specifications (such as block size and record format) and so on.
   b. "Y" for EDIT INPUT allows the operator to enter SQL statements.
   c. "Y" for EXECUTE will execute the SQL statements.
   d. "Y" for AUTOCOMMIT will make DB2 commit (write into the physical table) all changes to DB2 data if the SQL run is successful.
   e. "Y" for BROWSE automatically displays the output at the terminal, where it can be browsed using standard ISPF browse PF keys.

```
                        SPUFI
===>

Enter the input data set name:    (Can be sequential or partitioned)
 1 DATA SET NAME ... ===> 'DB2.TEST.SPUFI(QUERY1)'
 2 VOLUME SERIAL ... ===>         (Enter if not cataloged)
 3 DATA SET PASSWORD ===>         (Enter if password protected)

Enter the output data set name:   (Must be sequential)
 4 DATA SET NAME ... ===> OUT1

Specify processing options:
 5 CHANGE DEFAULTS   ===> Y       (Y/N - Display SPUFI defaults panel?)
 6 EDIT INPUT ...... ===> Y       (Y/N - Enter SQL statements?)
 7 EXECUTE ......... ===> Y       (Y/N - Execute SQL statements?)
 8 AUTOCOMMIT ...... ===> Y       (Y/N - Commit after successful run?)
 9 BROWSE .......... ===> Y       (Y/N - Browse output data set?)


PRESS:   ENTER to process      END to exit      HELP for more information
```

**Figure 4.3**  The SPUFI main panel.

## 4.5 Changing Current SPUFI Defaults

If the CHANGE DEFAULTS processing option in Figure 4.3 is "Y", Figure 4.4 is
displayed for the operator. Then default values may be changed.
      The following apply:

```
                    CURRENT SPUFI DEFAULTS
===>

Enter the following to control the SPUFI session:
 1   ISOLATION LEVEL   ===> CS     (RR=repeatable read, CS=cursor stability)
 2   MAX SELECT LINES  ===> 300    (Maximum number of lines returned from
                                       a SELECT)

Enter the output data set characteristics:
 3   RECORD LENGTH ... ===> 200    (Logical record length)
 4   BLOCK SIZE ...... ===> 4000   (Size of one block)
 5   RECORD FORMAT ... ===> FB     (RECFM=F, FB, V, VB, FBA, VBA)
 6   DEVICE TYPE ..... ===> SYSDA  (Must be DASD unit name)

Enter the output format characteristics:
 7   MAX NUMERIC FIELD ===> 15     (Maximum width for numeric fields)
 8   MAX CHAR FIELD .. ===> 70     (Maximum width for character fields)
 9   COMMON HEADING .. ===> NAMES  (NAMES, LABELS, ANY or BOTH)


PRESS:   ENTER to process      END to exit      HELP for more information
```

**Figure 4.4**  The current SPUFI defaults panel.

1.  The ISOLATION LEVEL entry is either CS or RR. CS is more efficient (see Chapter 19).
2.  The output data set characteristics define the record length, block size, record format, and device type of the output.
3.  The output format characteristics define the maximum width for numeric and character fields, and the heading used in the output (generally NAMES, which means the original column names). Naturally, computed columns do not have original column names.

### 4.6 Entering/Saving SQL Statements

If the EDIT INPUT processing option in Figure 4.3 is "Y", Figure 4.5 is displayed for the operator. He or she may then add, change, and delete SQL statements in the output data set.

The programmer uses standard ISPF keys to enter the statements. Since to SPUFI, two dashes in columns 7 and 8 (first two positions for entering statements) indicate a note, it is best for the programmer to start coding the statements starting in column 10.

The following apply:

1.  The semicolon (;) at line 000300 is required if there is another SQL statement following, which is lines 000600 to 000800. If there is only one SQL statement, the semicolon is optional.
2.  Lines 000400 to 000500 are taken as a comment because of the two dashes at the beginning. They become executable SQL statements if these two dashes are removed.

```
Edit --- userid.DB2.TEST.SPUFI(QUERY1)
COMMAND INPUT ===>
****** *****************  TOP OF DATA *********************
000100    SELECT EMPNO, EMPNAME, EMPSALARY
000200        FROM XLIM.EMPTABLE
000300        WHERE EMPDEPT = '003';
000400 -- DELETE FROM XLIM.EMPTABLE
000500 --     WHERE EMPNO = '000010';
000600    SELECT EMPNO, EMPNAME, EMPSALRY
000700        FROM XLIM.EMPTABLE
000800        WHERE EMPDEPT = '125';
****** **************** BOTTOM OF DATA ********************
```

**Figure 4.5**  The SPUFI SQL statement panel.

3. The operator saves the statements either with the SAVE command or the END PF key (PF3/PF15).

## 4.7 Running the SQL Statements

If PF3/PF15 is used and the EXECUTE option of Figure 4.3 is "Y", Figure 4.5 is automatically executed, unless it was not modified at all. In this case, Figure 4.3 reappears with a prompt for the operator to choose between continuing and abandoning the execution. To continue, the operator simply hits the ENTER key.

DB2 will execute all the statements and place the result in the output data set.

## 4.8 Browsing the Output

If the BROWSE option is "Y", the output data set is automatically displayed at the terminal where it may be browsed using standard browse PF keys. Besides looking at the output, the operator may also check the SQLCODE.

An example of an output is Figure 4.6. Note that if a computed column is in the display, it will have no column names. Also, any NULLs value in the output will generate dashes in the display.

Note the following:

1. The first SQL statement is redisplayed for reference.
2. The rows selected by the statement are displayed, showing the column names and corresponding data. Note that if a computed column is in the display, it

```
BROWSE --- userid.OUT1 --------------------- LINE 000008 COL   001 080
COMMAND ===>                                          SCROLL ===> PAGE
*************************** TOP OF DATA ***************************
---------+---------+---------+---------+---------+---------+---------+
      SELECT EMPNO, EMPNAME, EMPSALARY
         FROM XLIM.EMPTABLE
            WHERE EMPDEPT = '005';
---------+---------+---------+---------+---------+---------+---------+
EMPNO  EMPNAME                    EMPSALARY
00008  RANDOLPH, R.               029000
00150  ELLIOT, T.                 031000
00190  LEE, R.                    030000
DSNE610I NUMBER OF ROWS DISPLAYED IS 3
DSNE616I STATEMENT EXECUTION WAS SUCCESSFUL, SQLCODE IS 100
---------+---------+---------+---------+---------+---------+---------+
---------+---------+---------+---------+---------+---------+---------+
DSNE617I COMMIT PERFORMED, SQLCODE IS 0
DSNE616I STATEMENT EXECUTION WAS SUCCESSFUL, SQLCODE IS 0
---------+---------+---------+---------+---------+---------+---------+
DSNE601I SQL STATEMENTS ASSUMED TO BE BETWEEN COLUMNS 1 AND 72
DSNE620I NUMBER OF SQL STATEMENTS PROCESSED IS 1
*************************** BOTTOM OF DATA ***************************
```

**Figure 4.6**   The SPUFI output.

will have no column names. Also, any NULLS value in the output will generate dashes in the display.

    a. Columns are separated by 2 spaces.

    b. A column containing nulls is displayed with dashes (----).

**3.** Statistics on number of rows displayed are shown. In this example, it is 3. In addition, the SQLCODE is displayed, which for a SELECT statement is always 100.

**4.** The fact that we did an autocommit (or not) is displayed.

**5.** If there are additional SQL statements, numbers 1 to 4 are repeated for each additional statement.

**6.** The number of SQL statements is displayed.

**7.** If there is overflow to another page, or the result has more columns than can fit on the display, the programmer may use standard ISPF browse functions to see all the output.

**4.8.1 The SQL return code (SQLCODE) in SPUFI.**   The SQLCODE (whether in SPUFI or when running an application program) is the return code generated by DB2 on the execution of an SQL statement. When executing an application program, DB2 returns more than SQLCODE. (See page 61.) General guidelines for SQLCODE values in SPUFI are:

**1.** For a SELECT statement, SQLCODE is always equal to 100 (unless the statement did not execute, in which case it is negative), with the number of rows selected indicated. In our example, there are three rows.

**2.** For other statements:

    a. SQLCODE should be 0 to indicate an error-free execution.

    b. SQLCODE is 100 for UPDATE and DELETE if there were no rows updated or deleted.

    c. If SQLCODE is negative, there is a major error for which the statement was unsuccessful. For instance, $-803$ means on an insert (INSERT) operation, an identical value already exists for a column defined in the table as UNIQUE. Another example is $-407$, which means that on an insert operation, a column defined as NOT NULL did not have a value.

**4.8.2 Explaining the return code from the help function.**   SPUFI provides the operator with several help aids while at screen displays that state at the bottom, "HELP for  more information". This is the case for most SPUFI displays as can be seen in Figures 4.2, 4.3, and others.

The traditional key used is PF1. This generates Figure 4.7.

*4.8.2.1 The SQLCODE help function.*   In Figure 4.7, the function selected is "C". This will display another panel where the operator enters the SQLCODE to be explained.

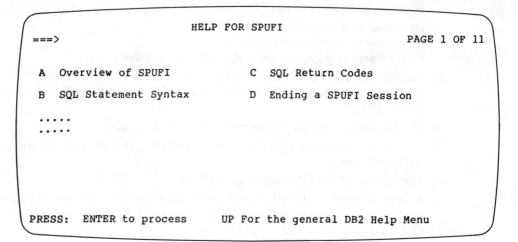

```
                          HELP FOR SPUFI
===>                                                      PAGE 1 OF 11


   A   Overview of SPUFI           C   SQL Return Codes

   B   SQL Statement Syntax        D   Ending a SPUFI Session

   . . . . .
   . . . . .




PRESS:   ENTER to process       UP For the general DB2 Help Menu
```

**Figure 4.7**   The HELP FOR SPUFI display.

## 4.9 Committing Any Insert/Update/Delete SQL Statement

The AUTOCOMMIT option (processing option 8 on the SPUFI panel) must be either
"Y" or "N". If "Y", DB2 will commit changes to the database if all SQL statements
in that run do not have any error; if there is any error, all changes are backed out. If
"N", after the execution, DB2 will display a panel to force the user to commit
(COMMIT) the changes, back out (ROLL BACK) the changes, or DEFER the decision, say, until after the execution of another set of SQL statements. In the latter case,
the user will tie up resources, especially the pages containing the updated rows.

# 5

# *Selecting Columns*

[Author's note: The SPUFI SQL statements shown in this chapter are also used in Cobol programs. However, there is a difference in how values are specified. In SPUFI, they are entered by the operator as literals; in Cobol, they are contained in data-names. See Chapters 10 to 14.]

## 1 THE EMPLOYEE TABLE

We will use Figure 5.1 in our SQL examples.

## 2 SELECT ALL COLUMNS FROM SOURCE TABLE(S)/VIEWS

The format is: SELECT *.

The "*" selects all columns in the source table(s) and/or view(s) and they appear in their original order in the table(s). If we are using multiple tables (for instance, in a join operation), columns for Table 1 will appear first, followed by those of Table 2, and so on.

| Employee Number (EMPNO) | Name (EMPNAME) | Department Number (EMPDEPT) | Salary (EMPSALARY) |
|---|---|---|---|
| 00005 | BAKER, C. | 003 | 0030000 |
| 00008 | RANDOLPH, R. | 005 | 0029000 |
| 00010 | RICHARDS, M. | 002 | 0031000 |
| 00015 | DAVIS, L. | 006 | 0030000 |
| 00150 | ELLIOT, T. | 005 | 0031000 |
| 00170 | RABINOVITZ, M. | 003 | 0031000 |
| 00190 | LEE, R. | 005 | 0030000 |

**Figure 5.1** The XLIM. EMPTABLE employee table.

### 2.1 Select All Columns: Example #1

Given the SQL statement:

```
SELECT *
    FROM XLIM.EMPTABLE;
```

Using Figure 5.1 as input, this selects all columns from the Employee table. In addition, all rows are also selected because the WHERE clause is missing. The result is exactly Figure 5.1. We are in fact selecting all data in the original table.

### 2.2 Select All Columns: Example #2

Given the SQL statement:

```
SELECT *
    FROM XLIM.EMPTABLE
    WHERE EMPDEPT = '005';
```

Using Figure 5.1 as input, this selects all columns from those rows in the Employee table where the department number is '005'. The result is Figure 5.2.

### 2.3 Problems With "SELECT *" in Application Programs

Using the "*" character is generally not good when used in application programs, even if all columns are selected. One problem is that the user loses data independence. If a row is later added to the table, the program becomes inconsistent. It is therefore far better in application programs to specify individual columns as shown in Section 3.

In addition, if all columns are not needed in the first place, there is inefficiency. This is especially the case when there is sorting.

| Employee Number (EMPNO) | Name (EMPNAME) | Department Number (EMPDEPT) | Salary (EMPSALARY) |
|---|---|---|---|
| 00008 | RANDOLPH, R. | 005 | 0029000 |
| 00150 | ELLIOT, T. | 005 | 0031000 |
| 00190 | LEE, R. | 005 | 0030000 |

**Figure 5.2** "All-columns" selection output on XLIM. EMPTABLE employee table.

## 3 SELECT SPECIFIC COLUMNS FROM SOURCE TABLE(S)/VIEWS

The format is: SELECT column-name1, column-name2, . . .

The columns to be selected are separated by commas and are in the order specified. The following is an example:

```
SELECT EMPNO, EMPNAME, EMPSALARY
     FROM XLIM.EMPTABLE;
```

Using Figure 5.1 as input, this selects the employee number, employee name, and salary, for all rows in the Employee table. The result is Figure 5.3.

| Employee Number (EMPNO) | Name (EMPNAME) | Salary (EMPSALARY) |
|---|---|---|
| 00005 | BAKER, C. | 0030000 |
| 00008 | RANDOLPH, R. | 0029000 |
| 00010 | RICHARDS, M. | 0031000 |
| 00015 | DAVIS, L. | 0030000 |
| 00150 | ELLIOT, T. | 0031000 |
| 00170 | RABINOVITZ, M. | 0031000 |
| 00190 | LEE, R. | 0030000 |

**Figure 5.3** "Selected-columns" selection output on XLIM.EMPTABLE employee table.

### 3.1 Columns With Identical Names

A column-name is unique within a table, but may have duplicates across tables. If such column-names are specified together in the same SQL statement, the programmer must differentiate them to DB2. This is done by prefixing the table names to the column-name.

Thus, XLIM.EMPTABLE.DEPTNO and XLIM.DEPTABLE.DEPTNO differentiate the two columns.

## 4 SELECT "DISTINCT" SOURCE COLUMN

The format is: SELECT DISTINCT column-name.

The output, in the ascending sequence of column-name (unless an ORDER BY clause is coded specifying DESC), will show one row per distinct value of column-name, including one for Nulls (if present). If there is an index defined for the column, DB2 will decide on whether to use it or do a sort. As an example.

```
SELECT DISTINCT EMPDEPT
     FROM XLIM. EMPTABLE;
```

Using Figure 5.1 as input, this generates an output table where the department number is not duplicated in any row. The result is Figure 5.4.

Note that the duplicates for department numbers 003 and 005 as seen in the original table (Fig. 5.1) are eliminated.

```
Department
Number
(EMPDEPT)

  002          Figure 5.4  "Select
  003          DISTINCT" output on XLIM.
  005          EMPTABLE employee table.
  006
```

## 5 SELECT COMPUTED SOURCE COLUMN

One or more columns in the table are calculated from the source columns(s). The following rules apply:

1. Only columns containing numeric data may be used.
2. The +, −, *, and / expressions are used.
3. Parentheses may be used for clarity. As an example:

```
SELECT EMPNO, (EMPSALARY/4)
        FROM XLIM.EMPTABLE;
```

This selects the employee number and quarterly salary (assume that EMPSALARY is the annual salary) of all rows in the Employee table. Using Figure 5.1 as input, the result is Figure 5.5.

```
Employee
Number        Salary / 4
(EMPNO)

 00005        0007500
 00008        0007250
 00010        0007750
 00015        0007500          Figure 5.5  "Select computed column"
 00150        0007750          output on XLIM.
 00170        0007750          EMPTABLE employee table.
 00190        0007500
```

## 6 SELECT USING BUILT-IN FUNCTIONS

One or more columns in the output table are a summary value computed from the values of columns belonging to one or more rows. Thus, the SUM, MIN, AVG, and other such functions may be used together in a single statement.

If the WHERE clause is specified, only those rows so selected are used in the calculation. For instance, "WHERE EMPDEPT = '003'" will use as input only those rows where the department number is '003'.

### 6.1 The SUM Built-in Function

The format is: SUM(column-name).
The following rules apply:

1. The subtotals (if the optional GROUP BY clause is specified) or a single overall total of the specified numeric source column is generated in the output table.

2. The optional GROUP BY clause specifies the group of input rows which will be summed together to generate a row in the output table (for instance, GROUP BY department number); otherwise, there is only one overall sum for all selected input rows.

3. Except for the column specified in the GROUP BY clause, which is used in grouping, any other column specified must also use a built-in function. For instance,

```
SELECT EMPDEPT, SUM(EMPSALARY)
    FROM XLIM.EMPTABLE
        GROUP BY EMPDEPT;
```

Using Figure 5.1 as input, this selects the total annual salary of each department using all rows in the Employee table. The result is Figure 5.6.

Note that the GROUP BY clause did not generate the output in department number sequence. If the user so desires, then the optional ORDER BY clause is specified.

| Department Number (EMPDEPT) | Salary |
| --- | --- |
| 003 | 0061000 |
| 005 | 0090000 |
| 002 | 0031000 |
| 006 | 0030000 |

**Figure 5.6** "Select SUM" output on XLIM.EMPTABLE employee table.

## 6.2 The MIN Built-in Function

The format is: MIN(column-name).

The following rules apply:

1. The minimum value of the specified numeric source column is brought to the output table.

2. The optional GROUP BY clause specifies the group of input rows which will be considered together to determine the minimum in the group (for instance, GROUP BY department number); otherwise, all selected input rows are considered together to generate a single minimum value.

3. Except for the column specified in the GROUP BY clause, which is used in grouping, any other column specified must also use a built-in function, as in the following example:

```
SELECT EMPDEPT, MIN(EMPSALARY)
    FROM XLIM.EMPTABLE
        GROUP BY EMPDEPT;
```

| Department Number (EMPDEPT) | Salary |
|---|---|
| 003 | 0030000 |
| 005 | 0029000 |
| 002 | 0031000 |
| 006 | 0030000 |

**Figure 5.7** "Select MIN" output on XLIM.EMPTABLE employee table.

Using Figure 5.1 as input, this selects the lowest annual salary of each department for all rows in the Employee table. The result is Figure 5.7.

### 6.3 The MAX Built-in Function

The format is: MAX(column-name).
The following rules apply:

1. The maximum value of the specified numeric source column is brought to the output table.
2. The optional GROUP BY clause specifies the group of input rows which will be considered together to determine the maximum in the group (for instance, GROUP BY department number); otherwise, all selected input rows are considered together to generate a single maximum value.
3. Except for the column specified in the GROUP BY clause, which is used in grouping, any other column specified must be also use a built-in function. To illustrate:

```
SELECT EMPDEPT, MAX(EMPSALARY)
        FROM XLIM.EMPTABLE
            GROUP BY EMPDEPT;
```

Using Figure 5.1 as input, this selects the highest annual salary of each department for all rows in the Employee table. The result is Figure 5.8.

### 6.4 The AVG Built-in Function

The format is: AVG(column-name).
The following rules apply:

1. The average value of the specified numeric source column is generated in the output table.

| Department Number (EMPDEPT) | Salary |
|---|---|
| 003 | 0031000 |
| 005 | 0031000 |
| 002 | 0031000 |
| 006 | 0030000 |

**Figure 5.8** "Select MAX" output on XLIM.EMPTABLE employee table.

**2.** The optional GROUP BY clause specifies the group of input rows which will be considered together to determine the average in the group (for instance, GROUP BY department number); otherwise, all selected input rows are considered together to generate a single average value.

**3.** Except for the column specified in the GROUP BY clause, which is used in grouping, any other column specified must also use a built-in function. For example,

```
SELECT EMPDEPT, AVG(EMPSALARY)
      FROM XLIM.EMPTABLE
         GROUP BY EMPDEPT;
```

Using Figure 5.1 as input, this selects the average annual salary of each department using all rows in the Employee table. The result is Figure 5.9.

### 6.5 The COUNT Built-in Function (Version 1)

The format is: COUNT(*).

The number of rows that satisfy the search condition are counted. For example:

```
SELECT COUNT(*)
      FROM XLIM.EMPTABLE
         WHERE EMPDEPT = '003';
```

This generates a count of the number of employees belonging to department '003'. The result is 3.

### 6.6 The COUNT DISTINCT Built-in Function (Version 2)

The format is: COUNT
(DISTINCT column-name).

The number of distinct rows that satisfy the search condition are counted. For example:

```
SELECT COUNT (DISTINCT EMPDEPT)
      FROM XLIM.EMPTABLE;
```

This generates a count of the number of distinct department numbers contained in the Employee table. The resulting count is 4 (department numbers, 002, 003, 005, and 006).

| Department Number (EMPDEPT) | Salary | |
|---|---|---|
| 003 | 0030500 | |
| 005 | 0030000 | **Figure 5.9** "Select AVG" |
| 002 | 0031000 | output on XLIM.EMPTABLE employee |
| 006 | 0030000 | |

## 6.7 Multiple Columns Using Built-in Function

We mentioned before that we can combine SUM, AVG, MIN, and so on in a single statement. For instance:

```
SELECT EMPDEPT, MIN(EMPSALARY), AVG(EMPSALARY)
       FROM XLIM.EMPTABLE
       GROUP BY EMPDEPT;
```

# 6

# *Specifying Source Tables and Views*

[Author's note: The SPUFI SQL statements shown in this chapter are also used in Cobol programs. There is, however, a difference in how values are specified. In SPUFI, they are entered by the operator as literals; in Cobol, they are contained in data-names. See Chapters 10 to 14.]

## 1 SPECIFYING A SINGLE SOURCE TABLE OR VIEW

The format is: FROM table-name (or view-name).
    Examples are shown in Chapter 5.

## 2 SPECIFYING MULTIPLE SOURCE TABLES/VIEWS

The format is: FROM table-name1/view-name1,
                    table-name2/view-name2, . . .

The following rules apply:

1. An example of one use is in the equijoin operation, where two or more tables generate a single output table.
2. In this case, the WHERE clause specifies the column(s) in each table/view which must match to identify a pair of rows to be joined.

## 2.1 Example of Selecting from Multiple Tables

Given Figure 6.1 as the input table:

| Employee Number (EMPNO) | Name (EMPNAME) | Department Number (EMPDEPT) | Salary (EMPSALARY) |
|---|---|---|---|
| 00005 | BAKER, C. | 003 | 0030000 |
| 00008 | RANDOLPH, R. | 005 | 0029000 |
| 00010 | RICHARDS, M. | 002 | 0031000 |
| 00015 | DAVIS, L. | 006 | 0030000 |
| 00150 | ELLIOT, T. | 005 | 0031000 |
| 00170 | RABINOVITZ, M. | 003 | 0031000 |
| 00190 | LEE, R. | 005 | 0030000 |

**Figure 6.1** The XLIM.EMPTABLE employee table.

Also, given Figure 6.2:

| Department Number (EMPDEPT) | Department Name (DEPTNAME) |
|---|---|
| 002 | Accounts Payable |
| 003 | Data Processing |
| 005 | Administration |
| 006 | Finance |

**Figure 6.2** The XLIM.DEPTABLE department table.

An example of using two source tables is the following equijoin operation:

```
SELECT EMPNO, EMPNAME, XLIM.EMPTABLE.EMPDEPT, DEPTNAME
    FROM XLIM.EMPTABLE, XLIM.DEPTABLE
    WHERE XLIM.EMPTABLE.EMPTDEPT = XLIM.DEPTABLE.EMPDEPT;
```

This extracts the employee number, name, department number, and department name from both the Employee and Department tables and join them where the department numbers in the Employee table match those in the Department table. Note the use of table name prefix to identify which table the specific EMPDEPT column belongs to. The result is Figure 6.3.

| Employee Number (EMPNO) | Name (EMPNAME) | Dept. Number (EMPDEPT) | Dept. Name (DEPTNAME) |
|---|---|---|---|
| 00005 | BAKER, C. | 003 | Data Processing |
| 00008 | RANDOLPH, R. | 005 | Administration |
| 00010 | RICHARDS, M. | 002 | Accounts Payable |
| 00015 | DAVIS, L. | 006 | Finance |
| 00150 | ELLIOT, T. | 005 | Administration |
| 00170 | RABINOVITZ, M. | 003 | Data Processing |
| 00190 | LEE, R. | 005 | Administration |

**Figure 6.3** Output of join using two tables.

# 7

# *Selecting the Rows*

[Author's note: The SPUFI SQL statements shown in this chapter are also used in Cobol programs. There is, however, a difference in how values are specified. In SPUFI, they are entered by the operator as literals; in Cobol, they are contained in data-names. See Chapters 10 to 14.]

## 1 THE WHERE OPERAND

This specifies the criteria for selecting the rows in the source table(s) or view. If the condition (which may be a compound condition with ANDs and ORs) is true for that row, it will be selected.

If the SELECT statement specifies a DB2 built-in function (SUM, MAX, and so on), the selected row is used in the computation but will not appear in the output table, since only summary rows are generated. If there is no such DB2 built-in function, the selected row will appear in the output.

*Note that if the WHERE operand is missing, all rows will be selected.* This is then equivalent to a sequential read of the rows.

### 1.1 Operands of WHERE

The WHERE clause is followed by an optional NOT negation operator, a column-name, an operator (comparison, arithmetic, and so on), and finally a data-name or a literal.

The format is: WHERE [NOT] column-name operator [data-name | literal] . . . . .
Examples are:

```
#1:  WHERE EMPDEPT > '003'
#2:  WHERE NOT EMPDEPT = '006'
```

### 1.2 The NOT Negation Operator

Note that the NOT negation operator is coded after the WHERE but before the specific condition it negates. In compound conditions (ANDs and ORs), it only negates one condition, unless parentheses are used. Thus:

```
#1: WHERE NOT EMPDEPT = '010' AND EMPSALARY > 25000
    Only the condition "EMPDEPT = '010'" is negated.
#2: WHERE NOT (EMPDEPT = '010' AND EMPSALARY > 25000)
    The whole compound condition is negated.
```

### 1.3 Hierarchy of Evaluation on Compound Conditions

The WHERE clause allows compound conditions (ANDs and ORs, and also NOTs) as previously illustrated. Unless parentheses are used to change the order, within the same level DB2 evaluates the NOT clause first, then the AND clause, and finally the OR clause.

## 2 THE COMPARISON OPERATORS

They are:

|    |    |
|----|----|
| =  | Equal to. |
| ¬= | Not equal to. |
| <  | Less than. |
| >  | Greater than. |
| <= | Less than or equal to. |
| >= | Greater than or equal to. |

An example is:

```
WHERE EMPDEPT = '007' AND EMPSALARY > 10000
```

Note that the fifth and sixth comparison operators are respectively $<=$ (not $=<$) and $>=$ (not $=>$); otherwise, there is an operator error, with SQLCODE of $-104$.

## 3 THE ARITHMETIC OPERATORS

They are:

| | |
|---|---|
| $+$ | Add. |
| $-$ | Subtract. |
| $*$ | Multiply. |
| $/$ | Divide. |

An example is:

```
WHERE (EMPSALARY / 4) > 8000
AND EMPDEPT = '015'
```

' This selects those rows whose department number is '015' and where the quarterly salary is greater than \$8,000 (assume EMPSALARY is the annual salary).

## 4 THE BETWEEN...AND...OPERATORS

An example is:

```
WHERE column-name BETWEEN 3 AND 7.
```

This is more efficient and produces the same result as:

```
WHERE column-name >= 3 AND column-name <= 7.
```

## 5 THE IN OPERATOR

The format is: IN (string1, string2, . . . , stringn). An example is:

```
WHERE EMPDEPT IN ('003', '005')
```

This selects all rows where the department number has the value '003' or '005'.

## 6 THE LIKE OPERATOR

The format is: LIKE string.

This is used to search for a column value that has the pattern specified in the supplied value. The following rules apply:

**1.** Each underscore ("_") character stands for any character.

**2.** A single "%" character stands for a string of 0 or more characters. Example:

WHERE column-name LIKE '%3_'.

If the length of the column is six digits, this will select rows where the value of column-name is something like 123730, 000031, 106732, and so on. Note that the first four digits can be anything, followed by a 3 (the fifth digit), followed by any digit.

## 7 THE IS NULL OPERATOR

This is used if the user wants rows where the value of the column specified is null. A null value is generated for a column on the INSERT statement if it was defined as NULL when the table was created (CREATE TABLE table-name) and the row inserted had no value for that column. Such a column may also have a NULL value if it originally contained a value but was changed to NULL in an UPDATE statement. An example is WHERE EMPDEPT IS NULL.

## 8 COMPARISON ON CONDITIONS

Values are compared when:

**1.** There are comparison operators.
**2.** MAX, MIN, or DISTINCT are used.
**3.** GROUP BY or ORDER BY are used.

The rules on comparison are:

**1.** Only equal data formats are compared.
 a. Character strings versus character strings.
 b. Graphic strings versus graphic strings.
 c. Numeric strings versus numeric strings.
**2.** DB2 performs conversion where needed.
 a. On numeric strings, there is conversion if say, one is binary, the other decimal.
 b. On character strings, if one is longer, a temporary copy of the shorter string is made, padded with spaces on the right.
 c. Note that compared fields may be designed or coded as similar in format to avoid the inefficiency resulting from conversion.

## 9 THE JOIN OPERATION

The Join operation is explained on pages 8 to 10. An example using SQL in SPUFI is shown on page 40 (selecting from multiple tables).

## 9.1 Indexes Useful in Join Operations

Note that because of the mechanism of the join operation (especially equijoin), where DB2 uses the values of column for control, improved efficiency may ensue if such columns used in the WHERE clause are defined with indexes, especially if the tables are large. If so, DB2 will decide whether the index can shorten the process to search for the true conditions (where a join of rows is made); otherwise DB2 will presort the table(s). (See Chapter 20 for the creation of indexes.)

# 8

# *Optional Clauses and Built-in Functions*

[Author's note: The SPUFI SQL statements shown in this chapter are also used in Cobol programs. There is, however, a difference in how values are specified. In SPUFI, they are entered by the operator as literals; in Cobol, they are contained in data-names. See Chapters 10 to 14.]

## 1 CLAUSES USED IN BUILT-IN FUNCTIONS

There are three clauses used to control the built-in functions.

### 1.1 Current Data: Input Table

For the examples in this chapter, Figure 8.1 is the input data.

## 2 THE GROUP BY CLAUSE

The format is: GROUP BY (column-name1, . . . column-namen)
    The following rules apply:

| Employee Number (EMPNO) | Name (EMPNAME) | Department Number (EMPDEPT) | Salary (EMPSALARY) |
|---|---|---|---|
| 00005 | BAKER, C. | 003 | 0030000 |
| 00008 | RANDOLPH, R. | 005 | 0029000 |
| 00010 | RICHARDS, M. | 002 | 0031000 |
| 00015 | DAVIS, L. | 006 | 0030000 |
| 00150 | ELLIOT, T. | 005 | 0031000 |
| 00170 | RABINOVITZ, M. | 003 | 0031000 |
| 00190 | LEE, R. | 005 | 0030000 |

**Figure 8.1**   The XLIM.EMPTABLE employee table.

1. The column(s) specified in the clause must be columns also specified in the SELECT statement. For instance, for "GROUP BY EMPDEPT", the select statement must be in the format "SELECT column-name1, . . . , EMPDEPT, built-in function . . .

2. This clause groups multiple source rows into one output row, based on each distinct value of the column-name(s), with column-name1 as major and column-namen as minor. If missing, there is only one output row generated for all selected source rows. Nulls is considered a distinct value.

3. This clause does not generate the groups in any specific sequence; the ORDER BY clause does that. An example is:

```
SELECT EMPDEPT, SUM(EMPSALARY)
     FROM XLIM.EMPTABLE
        GROUP BY EMPDEPT;
```

Using Figure 8.1 as input, this extracts the total annual salary in each department using all rows in the Employee table. The result is Figure 8.2.

| Department Number (EMPDEPT) | Salary |
|---|---|
| 003 | 0061000 |
| 005 | 0090000 |
| 002 | 0031000 |
| 006 | 0030000 |

**Figure 8.2**   Output of the GROUP BY clause of select.

Note that the GROUP BY clause did not generate the table in department number sequence. If the user so desires, the optional ORDER BY clause is specified.

## 3 THE HAVING CLAUSE

This clause has two functions.

### 3.1 HAVING CLAUSE: First Function

The first function of the HAVING clause is to determine for a built-in function whether the corresponding group is generated after all. For instance, we sum the salaries of input rows and group the output by department numbers. The HAVING clause can specify that we generate in the final output only those departments (assume the clause GROUP BY EMPDEPT) where the sum of salaries is less than say, $85,000.

*Thus, in the same manner that the WHERE clause determines if an input row is selected, one function of the HAVING clause is to determine if the computed group is generated in the output table after all.*

An example of this first function of the clause is:

```
SELECT EMPDEPT, SUM(EMPSALARY)
    FROM XLIM.EMPTABLE
        GROUP BY EMPDEPT
        HAVING SUM(EMPSALARY) < 85000;
```

This selects only those departments where the sum of the salary is less than $85,000. Using Figure 8.1 as input, the result is Figure 8.3.

| Department Number (EMPDEPT) | Salary |
|---|---|
| 003 | 0061000 |
| 002 | 0031000 |
| 006 | 0030000 |

**Figure 8.3** Output of the HAVING clause: function number 1.

Compare this to Figure 8.2. Note that department number '005' in Figure 8.2 is not included because the total salary of $90,000 is indeed greater than $85,000.

## 3.2 HAVING CLAUSE: Second Function

The second function of the HAVING clause is to determine for a built-in function whether a potential group is be generated because it consists of a certain number of rows. For instance, we sum the salaries of input rows and group the output by department numbers. The HAVING clause can specify that we generate in the final output only those departments (assume the clause GROUP BY EMPDEPT) with more than one input row.

An example of this second function of the clause is:

```
SELECT EMPDEPT, SUM(EMPSALARY)
    FROM XLIM.EMPTABLE
        GROUP BY EMPDEPT
        HAVING COUNT( * ) > 1;
```

This selects only those departments with more than one input row (employee row). Using Figure 8.1, the result is Figure 8.4.

| Department Number (EMPDEPT) | Salary |
|---|---|
| 003 | 0061000 |
| 005 | 0090000 |

**Figure 8.4** Output of the HAVING clause: function number 2.

Compare this to Figure 8.2. Note that department numbers '002' and '006' in Figure 8.2 are not included because they have only one employee.

## 4 THE ORDER BY CLAUSE

This clause puts the output rows in the sequence of the specified column(s), from major to minor. If there is an index defined for the same column(s), DB2 will decide whether using that index is more efficient than sorting the output.

The format is:

```
ORDER BY ([column-name1|column-position] [ASC|DESC],
         . . . column-namen|column-positionn] [ASC|DESC])
```

The programmer may specify the original column name or the position of the column (starting with 1) as stated in the SELECT statement. Specifying the position is the only way to sequence the output via a computed built-in function, since it does not have a column name of its own. See Section 4.2 for ordering by column position.

In case of multiple columns and/or column positions, column-name1/column-position1 is the major, column-name2/column-position2 . . . are minors.

Ascending sequence (ASC) is the default.

### 4.1 Ordering Sequence

Ordering is by EBCDIC collating sequence, with blanks as the lowest value and Nulls as the highest.

### 4.2 ORDER BY and GROUP BY

This clause is often used to put groups specified in the GROUP BY clause into a specific sequence. Usually the operands of both clauses are identical, or if the ORDER BY clause specifies multiple columns, the major column is the same as that specified by GROUP BY. Example:

```
SELECT EMPDEPT, SUM(EMPSALARY)
   FROM XLIM.EMPTABLE
      GROUP BY EMPDEPT
      ORDER BY EMPDEPT;
```

Using Figure 8.1 as input, this puts the generated output table in department number sequence. The result is Figure 8.5.

| Department
Number
(EMPDEPT) | Salary | |
|---|---|---|
| 002 | 0031000 | |
| 003 | 0061000 | |
| 005 | 0090000 | **Figure 8.5**  Output of the GROUP BY |
| 006 | 0030000 | clause. |

### 4.3 Order By Column Position for Built-in Function Column

Optionally, the user may specify integers instead of column-names as the objects of the ORDER BY clause. These are the column position(s) of the columns in the SELECT statement and is the only way to request sequencing via one of the built-in functions (which has no column-name).

For instance, if we code:

```
SELECT EMPDEPT, SUM(EMPSALARY)
    FROM XLIM.EMPTABLE
        GROUP BY EMPDEPT
        ORDER BY 2;
```

The use of the numeric literal 2 requests the output to be sequenced according to the sum of salaries, in ascending sequence (the default).

Note that we may use column positions even if a column-name is available. ORDER BY 1 sequences the output by employee department number.

### 4.4 The Other ORDER BY Clause Uses

The ORDER BY clause may be used outside a built-in function. It is in fact used whenever the user wants an output to be in a specific sequence. Suppose we want the output to be in sequence by salary, we code the ORDER BY clause as follows:

```
SELECT EMPNO, EMPSALARY
    FROM XLIM.EMPTABLE
    ORDER BY [EMPSALARY|2];
```

We can specify either EMPSALARY or the numeric literal 2.

# 9

# *SPUFI on INSERT/UPDATE/ DELETE Operations*

[Author's note: The SPUFI SQL statements shown in this chapter are also used in Cobol programs. There is, however, a difference in how values are specified. In SPUFI, they are entered by the operator as literals; in Cobol, they are contained in data-names. See Chapters 10 to 14.]

## 1 INSERT OPERATION

The user may either insert one row at a time (by entering the data for that row) or extract rows from existing tables and do a mass insert to another table.

### 1.1 SQLCODE on INSERT Using SPUFI

When doing an insert in SPUFI, if any SQL statement in that input data set has an error (negative value of SQLCODE), no insert operation is done and any row previously inserted by any previous statement in that run—remember that SPUFI can execute multiple SQL statements (see Fig. 4.5)—is backed out.

## 1.2 Placement of Inserted Data Row

Rows are physically located in pages, each one equivalent to a VSAM control interval (either 4K or 32K long). The row to be inserted is placed on a given page depending on whether the current page has space on it or not.

**1.2.1 Row insertion with space on current page.**   Figure 9.1 shows an insertion where there is space for two more rows in the current page. DB2 will simply insert the new row after the last row (row 3) in that page, the new row now becoming row 4. This is the case even if the table is defined with a clustered index (where on the initial mass insert or reorganization, the rows are in physical sequence), since DB2 will not resequence the rows in the page, but simply insert the new row at the first available slot on the page.

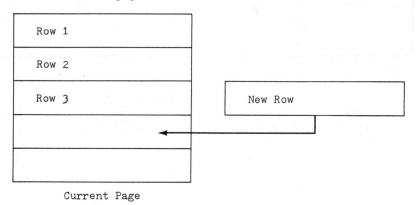

Current Page

**Figure 9.1**   Row insertion with space on current page.

Having space on the current page therefore promotes efficiency if there is a large number of insertions. Otherwise, DB2 will have to perform additional I/O to look for space in other pages.

**1.2.2 Row insertion without space on current page.**   Figure 9.2 shows an insertion where the current page (page A) does not have space for the row. DB2 will look for a page that has space (row B, which could be many pages beyond page A) and insert the row there. This is inefficient, especially with a large number of insertions since DB2 will have to read additional pages to do a single insert. In addition, if we have a clustered index, rows will be far out of sequence, and the sequential read later on will become more inefficient.

## 1.3 Managing Free Space/Free Page of Data Pages

The proper user management of data free space and free pages is a factor in the efficiency of insert operations.

**1.3.1 Defining original free space and free page.**   When creating or altering a table space (CREATE TABLESPACE, ALTER TABLESPACE), PCTFREE

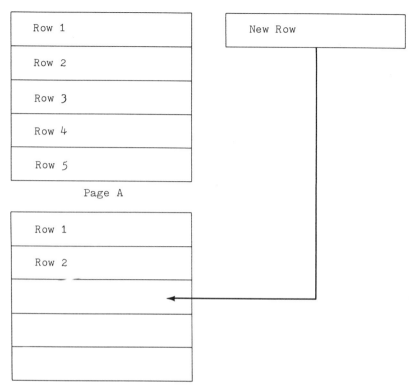

Page B

**Figure 9.2**   Row insertion without space on current page.

specifies the percentage on a page that is left free (for future insertions) on the initial mass load of rows or at reorganization. For tables with a large number of insertions, a number greater than the default of 5 percent should be used.

FREEPAGE meantime specifies the number of pages after which a completely free page is generated (also for future insertions). In general though, this is best left at the default of 0, while free space for insertions is defined purely by PCTFREE.

PCTFREE and FREEPAGE are discussed in more detail in Chapter 20, in the section on creating table space.

**1.3.2 Reclaiming used free space.**   Note that a large number of insertions will eventually use up all free spaces originally defined, making further insertions inefficient. At this point, a reorganization (DB2 REORG utility) run is done to reclaim the free space.

The RUNSTAT utility is effectively used to generate statistics to aid the user.

## 1.4 Placement of New Index Entries

Figure 9.3A shows the index entries before data insertion. Each index entry contains the key (the columns defined with the index) and a four-byte pointer column for each row that entry is pointing to. In our example, our indexes are nonunique (otherwise, there would be only one pointer per entry) and key A and key B currently point to one row while key D points to three rows.

We now insert three rows (data rows), with the first two having the key value of A, and the third having the key value of C. The result is Figure 9.3B.

Key A expands because it now points to two additional rows. A new entry for key C is inserted between the original key B and key D entries.

*Note that unlike those for data, where the rows are not placed in sequence during insertion, index entries are always placed in sequence by the key.*

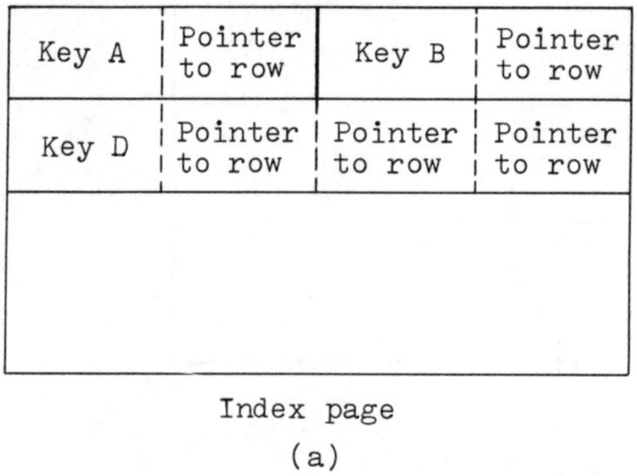

| Key A | Pointer to row | Key B | Pointer to row |
|-------|----------------|-------|----------------|
| Key D | Pointer to row | Pointer to row | Pointer to row |
|       |                |       |                |

Index page

(a)

**Figure 9.3A**  Index page before data insertion.

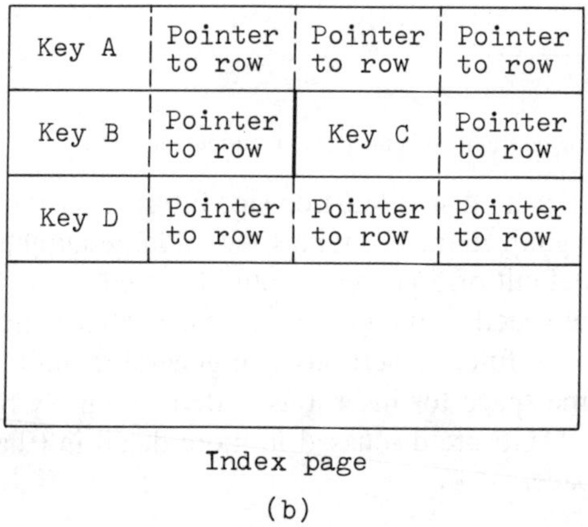

| Key A | Pointer to row | Pointer to row | Pointer to row |
|-------|----------------|----------------|----------------|
| Key B | Pointer to row | Key C | Pointer to row |
| Key D | Pointer to row | Pointer to row | Pointer to row |
|       |                |       |                |

Index page

(b)

**Figure 9.3B**  Index page after data insertion.

## 1.5 Insert One Row: Principle

The format is:

```
INSERT INTO [table-name|view-name]
     [(column-name1, column-name2, . . . ,)]
     VALUES (value1, value2, . . . . ,);
```

The following apply:

1. The column list (column names) is optional. If it is not specified, the sequence of values correspond to the sequence of the columns of the table or view as originally defined. If it is specified, the column-names and values have a one-to-one correspondence and do not have to match the sequence of the columns in the original table or view.

2. Inserting a row into a table.
   a. If a column is missing in the column list and it was defined as "NOT NULL WITH DEFAULT" when the table was created, DB2 will generate the default value (zeros for numeric columns, spaces for nonnumeric columns).
   b. If a column is missing and it was defined as "NOT NULL", there is an error and the insert operation is not done.
   c. If an index is defined as UNIQUE, no insert is done if that value in the column(s) already exists.

3. Inserting a row into a view.
   a. If the insert is successful, the row is actually inserted into the corresponding table since a view has no data of its own, it being only a definition in the DB2 catalog.
   b. If the view is a join of two or more tables, the insert operation is not allowed.
   c. If the view consists of summary rows (DB2 built-in functions such as SUM, AVG, MIN, and so on), the insert operation is likewise not allowed.
   d. If a table column not part of a view is defined as NOT NULL, the insert is not allowed, otherwise null values are generated (NULL defined) or default values (NOT NULL WITH DEFAULT).

Note that as in any SQL statement, the user must be authorized to do an insert operation.

## 1.6 SQL Example: Insert One Row

We will use Figure 9.4 as the input for examples in this chapter.

| Employee Number (EMPNO) | Name (EMPNAME) | Department Number (EMPDEPT) | Salary (EMPSALARY) |
|---|---|---|---|
| 00005 | BAKER, C. | 003 | 0030000 |
| 00008 | RANDOLPH, R. | 005 | 0029000 |
| 00010 | RICHARDS, M. | 002 | 0031000 |
| 00015 | DAVIS, L. | 006 | 0030000 |
| 00150 | ELLIOT, T. | 005 | 0031000 |
| 00170 | RABINOVITZ, M. | 003 | 0031000 |
| 00190 | LEE, R. | 005 | 0030000 |

**Figure 9.4**  The XLIM.EMPTABLE employee table.

An example of inserting one row is:

```
INSERT INTO XLIM.EMPTABLE
        (EMPNO, EMPNAME, EMPDEPT, EMPSALARY)
        VALUES ('00200', 'MILLER, S.', '010', 25000);
```

Using Figure 9.4 as input, the output is Figure 9.5.

| Employee Number (EMPNO) | Name (EMPNAME) | Department Number (EMPDEPT) | Salary (EMPSALARY) |
|---|---|---|---|
| 00005 | BAKER, C. | 003 | 0030000 |
| 00008 | RANDOLPH, R. | 005 | 0029000 |
| 00010 | RICHARDS, M. | 002 | 0031000 |
| 00015 | DAVIS, L. | 006 | 0030000 |
| 00150 | ELLIOT, T. | 005 | 0031000 |
| 00170 | RABINOVITZ, M. | 003 | 0031000 |
| 00190 | LEE, R. | 005 | 0030000 |
| 00200 | MILLER, S. | 010 | 0025000 |

**Figure 9.5**  Ouput of INSERT of one row.

### 1.7 Insert Multiple Rows: Principle

The format is:

```
INSERT INTO [table-name|view-name]
        [(column-name1, column-name2, . . . . . ,)]
        SELECT [*|column1, column2, . . . . .]
        FROM clause
        [WHERE clause];
```

We use the SELECT statement to extract the rows from another table. The functions of the column names, the FROM clause, and the WHERE clause are as in any SELECT statement.

### 1.8 SQL Example: Insert Multiple Rows

An example of inserting multiple rows is:

```
INSERT INTO TEMP.EMPDEPT
        SELECT EMPNO, EMPNAME, EMPDEPT, EMPSALARY
        FROM XLIM.EMPTABLE
        WHERE EMPDEPT IN ('003', '005');
```

Assuming TEMP.EMPDEPT is originally empty and using Figure 9.4 as the source of rows, the result is Figure 9.6.

| Employee Number (EMPNO) | Name (EMPNAME) | Department Number (EMPDEPT) | Salary (EMPSALARY) |
|---|---|---|---|
| 00005 | BAKER, C. | 003 | 0030000 |
| 00008 | RANDOLPH, R. | 005 | 0029000 |
| 00150 | ELLIOT, T. | 005 | 0031000 |
| 00170 | RABINOVITZ, M. | 003 | 0031000 |
| 00190 | LEE, R. | 005 | 0030000 |

**Figure 9.6**  Output of INSERT of multiple rows.

Because of the WHERE clause, only records with department numbers '003' and '005' are inserted.

## 2 UPDATE ROW(S) IN A TABLE OR VIEW

The format is:

```
UPDATE [table-name|view-name]
    SET column-name1 = expression1,
        column-name2 = expression2, . . . .
    [WHERE clause];
```

The SET operand specifies the column(s) and the corresponding value(s) for the update; the WHERE clause specifies the criteria for selecting the rows to be updated and is very important because *all rows will be updated if the WHERE clause is missing*.

### 2.1 The Expression in the SET Clause

In the "SET column-name = expression clause", the expression may be:

1. A literal. Replace the column's current value with this literal. This is generally the style used in SPUFI.
2. A host variable. Replace the column's current value with the value of this host variable. This is generally the style used in application programs.
3. A column name. Replace the column's current value with the value of this column in that same row.
4. NULL. Replace the column's current value with nulls. Note that this is not allowed if the row is defined with NOT NULL.
5. USER. Replace the column's current value with the userid of the person executing the program.

### 2.2 SQLCODE on UPDATE Using SPUFI

When doing an update in SPUFI, if any SQL statement in that input data set has an error (negative value of SQLCODE), no update operation is done and any row previously "updated"—remember that SPUFI can execute multiple SQL statements (see Fig. 4.5)—by any previous statement in that run is backed out.

### 2.3 SQL Example: Update Rows

An example for updating row is:

```
UPDATE XLIM.EMPTABLE
    SET EMPDEPT = '020'
    WHERE EMPDEPT = '005';
```

Using Figure 9.4 as the input, the result is Figure 9.7.
All department numbers '005' are replaced with '020'.

| Employee Number (EMPNO) | Name (EMPNAME) | Department Number (EMPDEPT) | Salary (EMPSALARY) |
|---|---|---|---|
| 00005 | BAKER, C. | 003 | 0030000 |
| 00008 | RANDOLPH, R. | 020 | 0029000 |
| 00010 | RICHARDS, M. | 002 | 0031000 |
| 00015 | DAVIS, L. | 006 | 0030000 |
| 00150 | ELLIOT, T. | 020 | 0031000 |
| 00170 | RABINOVITZ, M. | 003 | 0031000 |
| 00190 | LEE, R. | 020 | 0030000 |

**Figure 9.7**   Output of UPDATE of rows.

## 3 DELETE ROW(S) FROM A TABLE

The format is:

```
DELETE FROM table-name
    [WHERE clause]
```

The WHERE clause specifies the criteria for selecting the rows to be deleted. Just like that of UPDATE, this clause is very important because *all rows will be deleted if the WHERE clause is missing*.

### 3.1 SQLCODE on DELETE Using SPUFI

When doing a delete in SPUFI, if any SQL statement in that input data set has an error (negative value of SQLCODE), no delete operation is done and any row previously "deleted"—remember that SPUFI can execute multiple SQL statements (see Fig. 4.5)—by any previous statement in that run is backed out.

### 3.2 SQL Example: Delete Rows

An example is:

```
DELETE FROM XLIM.EMPTABLE
    WHERE EMPNO = '00010';
```

Using Figure 9.4 as the input, the output is Figure 9.8.
Employee number 00010 is deleted.

| Employee Number (EMPNO) | Name (EMPNAME) | Department Number (EMPDEPT) | Salary (EMPSALARY) |
|---|---|---|---|
| 00005 | BAKER, C. | 003 | 0030000 |
| 00008 | RANDOLPH, R. | 005 | 0029000 |
| 00015 | DAVIS, L. | 006 | 0030000 |
| 00150 | ELLIOT, T. | 005 | 0031000 |
| 00170 | RABINOVITZ, M. | 003 | 0031000 |
| 00190 | LEE, R. | 005 | 0030000 |

**Figure 9.8**   Output of DELETE of rows.

## 4 COMMITTING ANY INSERT/UPDATE/DELETE SQL STATEMENT

The AUTOCOMMIT option (processing option 8 on the SPUFI panel) must be either "Y" or "N". If "Y", DB2 will commit changes to the database if all SQL statements in that run do not have any error; if there is any error in any statement, all changes are backed out. If "N", after the execution, DB2 will display a panel to force the user to commit (COMMIT) the changes, back out (ROLL BACK) the changes, or DEFER the decision, say, until after the execution of another set of SQL statements. In the latter case, the user may tie up resources since there is a lock on pages containing updated rows.

# 10

# *Coding the Cobol Program*

[Author's note: We will deal only with batch Cobol programs.]

## 1 THE COBOL PROGRAM

The Cobol programs are written in the usual way, except that access to DB2 resources are done via SQL statements, not READ file-name, WRITE record-name, and so on (batch Cobol) or READ DATASET, WRITE DATASET, and so on (Cobol running under CICS/VS). The programmer therefore uses the same SELECT, INSERT, UPDATE, and DELETE statements we have previously discussed. In addition, the FETCH, OPEN, and CLOSE statements are also used.

### 1.1 Commit/Rollback for Cobol Programs

The program generally executes the COMMIT or ROLLBACK statement to commit or roll back information issued to update rows (INSERT, UPDATE, DELETE). Otherwise, all uncommitted updates are committed only at normal end of job (batch program) or normal task termination (CICS application programs).

See Section 3.1 for a complete discussion on commit/rollback.

## 1.2 The Cobol SQL Statement Delimiter

One minor difference between SQL statements in Cobol and those used in SPUFI is that the former are delimited by the "EXEC SQL" and "END-EXEC" statements. The semicolon (;) delimiter is not used. Thus:

```
EXEC SQL
      SELECT EMPDEPT, SUM(EMPSALARY)
             . . . . .
      END-EXEC
```

Instead of:

```
SELECT EMPDEPT, SUM(EMPSALARY) . . . . . ;
```

# 2 CODING THE WORKING-STORAGE SECTION

In addition to the usual data areas defined in the WORKING-STORAGE section, the programmer includes specific data areas (see Section 2.1 and others following). The SQL statements to execute the logic (INSERT, UPDATE, FETCH, and so on) are naturally coded in the Procedure Division.

## 2.1 The SQL Communication Area (SQLCA)

The SQLCA is a data area that must be present in the WORKING-STORAGE section. On each execution of an SQL statement, DB2 returns certain information to the program concerning the success or failure of the statement. The program has the option of using or disregarding any information returned.

There are three fields that are very important. They are:

1. *SQLCODE*. The return code. The values are:
   a. Zeroes. The SQL statement executed without any error, or with a minor error such as truncation (see SQLWARN0 as follows).
   b. A positive value. The statement executed but with an exceptional condition. An example is +100 for the various "no rows found" conditions such as "end of table" when processing multiple rows via the FETCH statement, "no rows found" on an UPDATE or DELETE operation, and so on.
   c. A negative value. The statement was unsuccessful. An example is −407 for an INSERT operation where a column defined as NOT NULL has no data at all.

2. *SQLERRD (3)*. The number of rows updated, inserted, or deleted by DB2.

3. *SQLWARN0*. If equal to "W", then at least one of the warning flag fields (SQLWARN1 to SQLWARNA) is set to a value. This field may contain a "W" even if SQLCODE is zeroes. See Section 2.1.3.3.

**2.1.1 Define SQLCA.**    There are two ways to do this. The easiest way is to allow the precompiler to generate this area with the following statement in the WORKING-STORAGE section:

```
EXEC SQL
        INCLUDE SQLCA
END-EXEC.
```

Optionally, the user may use the Cobol COPY statement to copy the area from a source statement library.

**2.1.2 The precompiler-generated SQLCA.**    Figure 10.1 shows the typical SQLCA as generated by the precompiler.

```
01  SQLCA.
        05  SQLCAID             PIC X(8).
        05  SQLCABC             PIC S9(9) COMP.
        05  SQLCODE             PIC S9(9) COMP.
        05  SQLERRM.
                49   SQLERRML   PIC S9(4) COMP.
                49   SQLERRMC   PIC X(70).
        05  SQLERRP             PIC X(8).
        05  SQLERRD             OCCURS 6 TIMES
                                PIC S9(9) COMP.
        05  SQLWARN.
                10   SQLWARN0   PIC X(1).
                10   SQLWARN1   PIC X(1).
                10   SQLWARN2   PIC X(1).
                10   SQLWARN3   PIC X(1).
                10   SQLWARN4   PIC X(1).
                10   SQLWARN5   PIC X(1).
                10   SQLWARN6   PIC X(1).
                10   SQLWARN7   PIC X(1).
                10   SQLWARN8   PIC X(1).
                10   SQLWARN9   PIC X(1).
                10   SQLWARNA   PIC X(1).
        05  SQLEXT              PIC X(5).
```

**Figure 10.1**  The SQLCA as generated by the precompiler.

**2.1.3 Using the SQLCA.**    After the execution of each SQL statement, the programmer may investigate any field in the SQLCA. The most important fields are discussed in the following sections.

*2.1.3.1 Using the SQLCODE field.*    There are two common uses of the SQLCODE field. First, it is used to determine if any error occurred on the execution of an SQL statement; checking is therefore usually done right after the execution of the SQL statement. For instance:

```
EXEC SQL
        SELECT . . . . .
END-EXEC
IF SQLCODE EQUAL TO ZEROES
        OK, continue
else execute error routine
```

A second use is when processing the output table row by row via a cursor (FETCH statement: see the next chapter). A value of 100 signifies the "no record found" condition, which for the FETCH statement, means "end of rows".

***2.1.3.2 The WHENEVER exceptional condition.***    The method of using SQLCODE as previously explained is the only way to process exceptional conditions if we prefer to treat each condition differently from the others. For most programs, this is the safest and best method, not subject to errors when a program is modified. In addition, the programmer may take any action (say, doing a CALL, which is not allowed in the following alternate method).

However, if we prefer to treat each condition the same way anywhere in the program, the programmer may actually just use the SQLCODE indirectly by simply specifying the WHENEVER exceptional condition, which may be coded anywhere in the Procedure Division but must execute ahead of the SQL statement we want to control.

The format is:

```
EXEC SQL
     WHENEVER [NOT FOUND | SQLWARNING | SQLERROR]
          [GO TO label | CONTINUE]
END-EXEC.
```

The following apply:

1. The only actions allowed are GO TO label or CONTINUE (continue execution).
2. Each NOT FOUND, SQLWARNING, or SQLERROR condition is paired with either a GO TO label or CONTINUE. The programmer may specify all three conditions in a single statement.
   a. NOT FOUND is true if SQLCODE is 100.
   b. SQLWARNING is true if SQLWARN0 = 'W' or SQLCODE is positive, but not 100.
   c. SQLERROR is true if SQLCODE is negative.
3. Multiple WHENEVER statements may be coded in the program. The latest one executed will then take effect.
4. After executing each SQL statement (except the WHENEVER statement), DB2 checks whether any WHENEVER statement is active; if so, the action (GO TO label or CONTINUE) is done if the condition is true.

An example is:

```
EXEC SQL
     WHENEVER NOT FOUND
          GO TO Error-routine
END-EXEC
. . . . .
. . . . .
EXEC SQL
     SELECT . . . . .
END-EXEC
```

If the "NOT FOUND" condition is true for the SELECT statement (SQL-CODE = 100), the program then automatically executes "Error-routine".

### 2.1.3.3 The meaning of SQL fields.

1. *SQLCAID:* Set to 'SQLCA' to identify the field in a dump.
2. *SQLCABC:* Length of SQLCA, set by DB2 when your program first uses the structure.
3. *SQLCODE:* The SQL return code.
   a. A zero value denotes successful execution.
   b. A positive value denotes normal conditions but with a warning. This is mostly the "no record found" condition (SQLCODE value of 100).
   c. A negative value denotes an abnormal condition such that the statement was unsuccessful. For example, a value of $-803$ means that on an insert operation, the value of a column already exists for a column that was defined with an index defined as UNIQUE.
4. *SQLERRC:* Error message that usually goes with the SQLCODE.
5. *SQLERRP:* If the SQLCODE is negative (abnormal condition), this contains the name of the DB2 routine that discovered the error. This field is used with SQLERRD in debugging.
6. *SQLERRD:* This describes the current internal state of DB2. SQLERRD #3 is significant for it specifies the number of rows processed on an INSERT, UPDATE, and DELETE operation.
7. *SQLWARN:* Characters that warn of various conditions encountered during the processing on your statement. Alternately, specific warnings may be indicated by positive value in the SQLCODE field.
8. *SQLWARN0:* Has the value 'W' if one of the following warning characters is set to 'W' and thus serves as a quick test for the existence of any warning. It has a value of 'S' (severe) if SQLWARN6 is let to 'S'.
9. *SQLWARN1:* Has the value of 'W' if at least one column's value was truncated in the host variable. This always happens when truncating character data items but may or may not happen for numeric items.
10. *SQLWARN2:* Has the value of 'W' if null values were ignored in the computation of a built-in function (AVG, SUM, and so on). This value is set only during preprocessing, never at run time.
11. *SQLWARN3:* Has the value of 'W' if the number of items in the SELECT list is not equal to the number of target variables in the INTO caluse.
12. *SQLWARN4:* Has the value of 'W' if an UPDATE or DELETE statement has been used without a WHERE clause. You should verify that the update or delete was intended unconditionally on the entire table. This value is set only during preprocessing, never at run time.
13. *SQLWARN5:* Has the value of 'W' if a WHERE clause associated with a SELECT statement has exceeded a DB2 internal limitation.

14. *SQLWARN6:* Has the value of 'W' if the last SQL statement executed caused DB2 to terminate a logical unit of work. This is set to 'S' when DB2 issues an SQLCODE that is severe (−805, −806, and so on).

15. *SQLWARN7:* Reserved for DB2 use.

16. *SQLWARN8:* Has the value of 'W' if a statement has been disqualified for blocking for reasons other than storage.

17. *SQLWARN9:* Has the value of 'W' if blocking was cancelled for a cursor because of insufficient storage in the user partition.

18. *SQLWARNA:* Has the value of 'W' if blocking was cancelled for a cursor because a blocking factor of at least two rows could not be maintained.

19. *SQLTEXT:* Reserved for DB2 use.

## 2.2 Define the Tables/Views to be Used

Although optional, the programmer should define the table(s) or views to be used. It both serves as a documentation, as well as provides an extra measure of control since during the precompile step (see Section 4), DB2 will verify it against the names used in SQL statements.

There are two options in defining tables.

### 2.2.1 Define the tables/views via DCLGEN.
The DCLGEN function is option 2 of the DB2 Interactive (DB2I) Primary Option Menu (see Fig. 4.2). It may also be invoked directly in TSO via the TSO command "DSN" with the subcommand "DCLGEN". Lastly, it may be run in batch.

The two advantages of using DCLGEN over the DECLARE TABLE statement (see Section 2.2.2) is that it uses the table definition in the DB2 catalog and there are therefore no possible coding errors. In addition, the corresponding Cobol record description (see host variable, Section 2.3) is also generated.

The typical DCLGEN panel is shown in Figure 10.2.

Note the following:

1. The SOURCE TABLE NAME entry is the table or view from which we generate the DECLARE statement and Cobol data-names.

2. DATA SET NAME contains the output of DCLGEN. The library name is used in the Precompile panel (Fig. 11.6) and Compile/Link/Run panel (Fig. 11.8) of Chapter 11. The member name is the one specified in the EXEC SQL INCLUDE statement Section 2.2.2) that brings the declaration and Cobol data-names into the Working-storage section.

3. The DATA SET PASSWORD entry is used if the output of DCLGEN is password protected.

4. ACTION is ignored for sequential data sets. For partitioned data sets, REPLACE will replace an old version or create a new one; ADD creates a new version.

```
                              DCLGEN
===>

Enter table name for which declarations are required:
  1    SOURCE TABLE NAME ===> 'XLIM.EMPTABLE'

Enter destination data set:          (Can be sequential or partitioned)
  2    DATA SET NAME ... ===> 'XLIM.DB2.COBOL(EMPTABDL)'
  3    DATA SET PASSWORD ===>          (If password protected)

Enter options as desired:
  4    ACTION ......... ===> ADD     (ADD new or REPLACE old declaration)
  5    COLUMN LABEL .... ===> NO      (Enter YES for column label)
  6    STRUCTURE NAME .. ===>                 (Optional)
  7    FIELD NAME PREFIX ===>                 (Optional)




PRESS:   ENTER to process    END to exit    HELP for more information
```

**Figure 10.2**   The DCLGEN panel.

**5.** COLUMN LABEL is normally NO.

**6.** STRUCTURE NAME (up to 31 characters) specifies the generated data structure name (01-level group item); if missing, DB2 will generate the table or view name prefixed with "DCL". In this case, our output would become "01 DECLEMPTABLE."

**7.** FIELD NAME PREFIX (up to 28 characters) specifies the prefix for the fields in the generated output (which correspond to table or view columns). The fields will then be generated as prefix001, prefix002, and so on. The prefix is usually not specified so the field names will be instead identical to the column names in the table or view.

**2.2.2 DECLARE TABLE statement generated by DCLGEN.**   Hit ENTER at Figure 10.2 to get the message "EXECUTION COMPLETE, MEMBER EMPTABDL REPLACED". Figure 10.3 is then the DECLARE TABLE output portion of EMPTABDL. Note that EMPTABDL also contains the record description for the table row (Fig. 10.4).

**2.2.3 Including the DCLGEN output.**   To bring the DECLARE TABLE output into the application program, the programmer codes in the working-storage section:

```
EXEC SQL
    INCLUDE EMPTABDL
END-EXEC
```

```
****************************************************************
* DCLGEN TABLE(XLIM.EMPTABLE)                                  *
*        LIBRARY(XLIM.DB2.COBOL(EMPTABDL)                      *
*        ACTION(REPLACE)                                       *
*        APOST                                                 *
* ... IS THE DCLGEN COMMAND THAT MADE THE FOLLOWING STATEMENTS *
****************************************************************
      EXEC SQL DECLARE XLIM.EMPTABLE TABLE
      ( EMPNO              CHAR(5) NOT NULL,
        EMPNAME            CHAR(30) NOT NULL WITH DEFAULT,
        EMPDEPT            CHAR(3) NOT NULL WITH DEFAULT,
        EMPSALARY          DECIMAL(7,0) NULL
      ) END-EXEC.
```

**Figure 10.3**    DECLARE TABLE statement generated by DCLGEN.

**2.2.4 Coding the DECLARE TABLE statement.**    As we have seen, the DECLARE statement is one of the outputs of the DCLGEN procedure (the other is the Cobol record description). If DCLGEN is not used, the DECLARE statement may be coded by the programmer and the format is similar to one for creating the tables or views. The format is:

```
EXEC SQL DECLARE table-name TABLE
    (column-name1    data-type,
     column-name2    data-type, . . .)
END-EXEC
```

Note that the literal "TABLE" is always used, whether we are defining a table or view. Unlike using DCLGEN, this method does not generate the record definition of the host variables.

## 2.3 Define Host Variables

Host variables are those that are used in the application program. Naturally, they are defined according to the rules of the programming language (Cobol, for instance). Those for the tables or views are either automatically generated in DCLGEN or specifically defined by the programmer.

**2.3.1 Table row description generated by DCLGEN.**    When DCLGEN is not used, the programmer must code the host variables for the tables and views, a process that is error prone. Using DCLGEN is thus better since the DB2 catalog is used. An example of the table row generated by DCLGEN is Figure 10.4.

**2.3.2 Using host variables in SQL statements.**    *When used in SQL statements, Cobol data-names must be prefixed with a colon (:). It goes without saying*

```
*********************************************************************
* COBOL DECLARATION FOR TABLE XLIM.EMPTABLE                        *
*********************************************************************
 01  DCLEMPTABLE.
     10  EMPNO                    PIC X(5).
     10  EMPNAME                  PIC X(30).
     10  EMPDEPT                  PIC XXX.
     10  EMPSALARY                PIC S9(7) COMP-3.
*********************************************************************
* THE NUMBER OF COLUMNS DESCRIBED BY THIS DECLARATION IS 4         *
*********************************************************************
```

**Figure 10.4**   Table row description generated by DCLGEN.

that they do not have the colon prefix when used in regular Cobol statements (meaning non-SQL statements).

Examples (as used in SQL clauses) are:

```
1) WHERE EMPNO = :EMPNO.
2) SET EMPSALARY = :EMPSALARY.
3) VALUES (:EMPNO, :EMPNAME).
```

Note that in the three previous examples, the ones with the colon prefix are the Cobol data-names generated by DCLGEN and those without prefixes are the original table column names. The names will always be identical if we use DCLGEN and we ignore the "FIELD NAME PREFIX" entry of Figure 10.2.

### 2.4 The Indicator Variables

An indicator variable is defined in working storage for a column that can have a NULL value. On a SELECT or FETCH statement, DB2 will place a negative value in the variable if the column has a NULL value. The corresponding Cobol data-name is not changed and therefore retains whatever value it received from a previous SELECT or FETCH statement. On an UPDATE or INSERT statement, the programmer places a negative value in the variable to indicate to DB2 that a NULL value is to be used for the column. In this case, the column cannot be defined in the table as NOT NULL.

*Unless an indicator variable is used for a field, on an input operation (SELECT, FETCH) there is an SQL error if the field does contain NULLs; on an output operation (INSERT, UPDATE), DB2 will not be able to insert or update NULLs into the field.*

#### 2.4.1 Defining the indicator variable.   Each indicator variable is a half-word integer (PIC S9(4) COMP). If defined as an array (OCCURS clause), then it

may be used for a list of columns with the first occurrence of the indicator variable corresponding to the first column in that list. (For an example, see Section 2.4.2, item 2.)

Examples of indicator variables follow:

```
01 INDICATOR-VARIABLES.
   05 EMPSALARY-IND                          PIC S9(4) COMP.
   05 EMPTABLE-IND                           PIC S9(4) COMP OCCURS 3.
```

**2.4.2 Using indicator variables on "read" (SELECT, FETCH).**   An example of using a nonarray indicator variable is:

```
EXEC SQL
    SELECT EMPNAME, EMPSALARY
          INTO :EMPNAME, :EMPSALARY:EMPSALARY-IND
          FROM XLIM.EMPTABLE
          WHERE EMPNO = :EMPNO
END-EXEC
```

Note the following:

1. The indicator variable (EMPSALARY-IND) is immediately placed (prefixed with a colon) after the corresponding variable (here the Cobol data-name EMP-SALARY) that corresponds to the column.
   a. EMPSALARY-IND will have a negative value if the column EMP-SALARY has a NULL value. The programmer may or may not use this fact (depending on the contents of other fields) to process the row.
2. Other fields may or may not also have indicator variables. An example of using an array indicator variable is:

```
EXEC SQL
    SELECT EMPNO, EMPNAME, EMPDEPT, EMPSALARY
          INTO :DCLEMPTABLE:EMPTABLE-IND
          FROM XLIM.EMPTABLE
          WHERE EMPNO = :SEARCH-DEPT
END-EXEC
```

Note that a negative value in EMPTABLE-IND(1) means a NULL value in the first data-name under DCLEMPTABLE (which is EMPNO in Fig. 10.4); a negative value in EMPTABLE-IND(2) means a NULL value in the second data-name under DCLEMPTABLE (which is EMPNAME in Fig. 10.4), and so on.

**2.4.3 Using indicator variables on UPDATE and INSERT.**   On an UP-DATE or INSERT statement, it is the programmer who indicates (by placing a negative value in the appropriate indicator variable) that we will use nulls for a column used in the UPDATE or INSERT statement. Naturally, such a column must not be defined with the NOT NULL attribute.

An example of using an indicator variable in an insert operation is:

```
***** set EMPNO, EMPNAME, EMPSALARY to the correct values.
      IF condition-1
         MOVE 0 TO EMPSALARY-IND
      ELSE
         MOVE - 1 TO EMPSALARY-IND.
      EXEC SQL
         INSERT INTO XLIM.EMPTABLE
            (EMPNO, EMPNAME, EMPSALARY)
               VALUES (:EMPNO, :EMPNAME, EMPSALARY:EMPSALARY-IND)
      END-EXEC.
```

If condition-1 is true, we set EMPSALARY-IND to 0 and the value in the EMPSALARY data-name (which the programmer should previously set to the correct numeric value) will be used. If condition-1 is false, we set EMPSALARY-IND to −1 and DB2 will insert nulls for EMPSALARY. Note that in the latter case, if EMPSALARY is defined with NOT NULL WITH DEFAULT, the salary value as finally inserted in the row is zeroes.

## 3 CODING THE PROCEDURE DIVISION

The same SELECT, UPDATE, INSERT, and DELETE statements we have seen before are coded where needed right in the Procedure Division, and interspersed with regular Cobol statements. In addition, we will learn the use of the FETCH statement when processing rows in an application program.

### 3.1 COMMIT/ROLLBACK and the Unit of Recovery

A unit of recovery is that portion of processing where the program tells DB2 that all updates (successful INSERT, UPDATE, and DELETE statements) in that unit should be either committed (to be written to the physical device) or rolled back (disregarded). Because DB2 takes log records for a unit of recovery, a user's decision to commit or roll back will be done, even if the action is not completed because of an abnormal termination of processing (say, the DB2 subsystem crashes or your program abends). In this case, it is eventually done either by DB2 (if only the program bombs) or during emergency restart of DB2 or the system.

A unit of recovery has both a start and an end. At end, DB2 will do a physical write of updated rows if the end is triggered with the SQL COMMIT statement or normal end of job (for a batch program) or CICS SYNCPOINT command or normal task termination (for a CICS application program).

**3.1.1 Choosing the unit of recovery.**   In some cases, choosing the unit of recovery is a user judgment call. For instance, one may choose to wait for every 10 rows updated before they are committed as final if the user judges it to offer the best tradeoff between efficiency and allowing greater concurrency. *More commits incur a greater overhead processing, but allow more users to share the data.*

However, certain processing requires that a series of updates be within a unit of recovery. For instance, in an order entry application, a single customer order will insert one row in the Purchase order table, insert as many line-item rows as there are in the order, then update the same number of rows (the inventory items) in the Inventory table.

The update of these 3 tables must be synchronized as one unit of recovery since if one is not completed (say, due to a program bomb or power failure), we want all inserts and updates to be rolled back (not committed).

### 3.1.2 Start of unit of recovery.    The unit of recovery starts on the following:

1. At program start (batch program) or task start (CICS application program).
2. On the SQL COMMIT statement or CICS SYNCPOINT command. This starts another unit of recovery while also ending the current one.
3. On the SQL ROLLBACK statement or CICS SYNCPOINT ROLLBACK command. This starts another unit of recovery while also ending the current one.

### 3.1.3 End of unit of recovery.    The unit of recovery ends on the following:

1. On the SQL COMMIT statement or CICS SYNCPOINT command. This requests DB2 to physically write all changes to data done since the start of this unit of recovery. This also starts a new unit of recovery.
2. On the SQL ROLLBACK statement or CICS SYNCPOINT ROLLBACK command. This requests DB2 to roll back (therefore do not physically write, that is, ignore) all changes to data done since the start of this unit of recovery. This also starts a new unit of recovery.
3. When the program normally terminates (batch program) or task normally terminates (CICS application program). All uncommitted changes within this unit of recovery are also committed (not rolled back).

### 3.1.4 Incomplete unit of recovery.    By definition, an incomplete unit of recovery (that is, with no end) is not really a unit of recovery. Thus, if the program bombs, all uncommitted updates are lost (automatically rolled back).

## 3.2 The Commit Process

We have learned that under SPUFI, the SPUFI main panel will allow the user to select an automatic commit or roll back or defer that decision to a later time (at which point he or she may commit or roll back the changes).

For application programs, if the program does not so specify, DB2 will not commit any update, unless the batch application program normally ends or the CICS task normally terminates.

Note that only successful INSERT, UPDATE, and DELETE statements (SQL-CODE zeroes) will have the corresponding rows included in the unit of recovery.

### 3.2.1 The format of the COMMIT statement. The format of the statement is:

```
EXEC SQL
             COMMIT
END-EXEC
```

### 3.2.2 When to commit. Efficiency, the reduction of deadlocks, and data integrity are three reasons for the timing of the commit process.

*3.2.2.1 Commit for greater efficiency.* Since DB2 implicitly secures a lock on uncommitted updates (thus preventing other programs from accessing data in those pages), prolonging the commit process results in other programs having to wait longer to access DB2 data. For a heavily-used table, this promotes lower concurrency (lower degree of sharing among many users), hence less overall efficiency.

It is therefore important that the programmer does the commit or roll back as soon as feasible, especially for heavily-used tables, to allow a larger level of concurrency. DB2's data "blocks" are called pages and when updating single tables (especially if very large), we may issue the commit for each row if we are processing randomly; we may wait for several rows if we are processing in sequence. The physical rewrite of pages (which results from the commit) incurs some overhead and doing a single rewrite for multiple rows that are updated gains some efficiency.

If we are updating more than one table, and they must be synchronized, we may do the commit when we have reached a consistent unit of recovery. For instance, in an Order Entry application, once we have updated both the Order table and ordered-item table (to enter the order) and the Inventory table (to reduce inventory by the items being ordered), we may issue the SQL COMMIT statement.

*3.2.2.2 Commit to reduce deadlocks.* The problem of deadlocks is discussed in more detail on page 106. For now, let it suffice to say that the more pages users hold on to, the greater the chance that two or more users cannot continue processing because they need data on pages held by somebody else. The timely commit of updates therefore reduces this problem.

*3.2.2.3 Commit for data integrity.* If the system goes down or the program bombs, any uncommitted update is lost. Doing a commit therefore makes sure that updated rows are made final on the physical device.

### 3.2.3 DB2 action on commit. Any user request for commit only requests DB2 to commit all changes within that unit of recovery. DB2 writes log records to

guarantee that even if the system crashes or the program bombs before any physical write is done, the updates are eventually written out to the physical device.

DB2 does not immediately do a physical write since pages of updated data in the buffers are written out only at checkpoint intervals, which are specified at installation time. An exception is if the buffer pool is full and a user needs additional data to be brought to the buffer, DB2 will use the least frequently used page, writing it out first if it contains uncommitted updates. This actually allows more pages to be already in the buffer when users request data.

### 3.3 The ROLLBACK Statement

The SQL ROLLBACK statement rolls back all changes to rows, instead of committing them. In the same manner as the SQL COMMIT statement, it tells DB2 that the program is finished with the uncommitted rows and that changes in the current unit of recovery should be ignored. As far as improving concurrency, it has the same effect as the COMMIT statement.

**3.3.1 The format of the ROLLBACK statement.**   The format of the statement is:

```
EXEC SQL
      ROLLBACK
END-EXEC
```

### 3.4 CICS COMMIT/ROLLBACK

The SQL COMMIT and ROLLBACK statements are not valid in CICS. The programmer instead uses the CICS SYNCPOINT and SYNCPOINT ROLLBACK commands.

## 4 BASIC PROGRAM SKELETON

Actual program examples are shown in Chapters 12, 13, and 14. For the moment, we will just show how they will look like in Figures 10.5 and 10.6.

The basic program skeleton is:

The items, in the following order, are:

1. The INCLUDE for the DCLGEN output.
2. All needed indicator variables.
3. The INCLUDE for the SQLCA data block.

```
      WORKING-STORAGE SECTION.
      .....
         EXEC SQL
             INCLUDE member-name (output of DCLGEN)
         END-EXEC.
**** Code indicator variables (if any).
         EXEC SQL
             INCLUDE SQLCA
         END-EXEC.
      .....
      PROCEDURE DIVISION.
      .....
****   Here set the EMPNO dataname to the correct value.
****   For instance, the value may come from a file.

         EXEC SQL
             SELECT EMPNAME, EMPSALARY
               INTO :EMPNAME, :EMPSALARY
                  FROM XLIM.EMPTABLE
                     WHERE  EMPNO = :EMPNO
         END-EXEC.
         IF SQLCODE  EQUAL TO  ZEROS
               MOVE EMPNAME  TO  ...
         ELSE error routine.
```

**Figure 10.5**   Basic program skeleton.

4. The setting of the EMPNO data-name to the correct value.

5. The SELECT statement to select a specific row and bring it to the Cobol data-names EMPNAME and EMPSALARY.

6. The processing of the data if SQLCODE is zeroes.

## 5  PROGRAM EXAMPLE (AS CODED)

Figure 10.6 is an example of a coded program (with the DCLGEN output printed out and with certain Cobol program headers omitted). Here we display the employee number and name of employees in the Employee table based on employee numbers keyed in an "in-line" card file (//CARDIN DD * JCL entry).

The items, in the following order, are:

1. The SELECT statement for the CARDIN file.

2. The DCLGEN output, both the DECLARE TABLE statement and the table row descriptions.

3. The initial housekeeping routines such as the opening of the card file and the code for the main loop.

4. The SELECT statement to bring the data of one row (assuming EMPNO is defined with a unique index) into the EMPNAME data-name.

5. The processing of the data if SQLCODE is zeroes.

```
     .....
     SELECT EMPLOYEE-CARDIN ASSIGN TO CARDIN.
     .....
  WORKING-STORAGE SECTION.
  ********************************************************************
  * DCLGEN TABLE(XLIM.EMPTABLE)                                      *
  *        LIBRARY(XLIM.DB2.COBOL(EMPTABDL)                          *
  *        ACTION(REPLACE)                                           *
  *        APOST                                                     *
  * ... IS THE DCLGEN COMMAND THAT MADE THE FOLLOWING STATEMENTS     *
  ********************************************************************
     EXEC SQL DECLARE XLIM.EMPTABLE TABLE
     ( EMPNO                  CHAR(5) NOT NULL,
       EMPNAME                CHAR(30) NOT NULL WITH DEFAULT,
       EMPDEPT                CHAR(3) NOT NULL WITH DEFAULT,
       EMPSALARY              DECIMAL(7,0) NULL
     ) END-EXEC.
  ********************************************************************
  * COBOL DECLARATION FOR TABLE XLIM.EMPTABLE                        *
  ********************************************************************
  01  DCLEMPTABLE.
      10   EMPNO              PIC X(5).
      10   EMPNAME            PIC X(30).
      10   EMPDEPT            PIC XXX.
      10   EMPSALARY          PIC S9(7) COMP-3.
  ********************************************************************
  * THE NUMBER OF COLUMNS DESCRIBED BY THIS DECLARATION IS 4         *
  ********************************************************************
      01   W005-EMPLOYEE-NUMBER     PIC X(5).
      01   W005-END-OF-FILE-SW      PIC X.
           88  W005-CARDIN-HAS-ENDED      VALUE 'Y'.
      EXEC SQL
           INCLUDE SQLCA
      END-EXEC.

  PROCEDURE DIVISION.
      OPEN INPUT EMPLOYEE-CARDIN.
      MOVE 'N'  TO  W005-END-OF-FILE-SW.
      PERFORM C060-READ-EMPLOYEE-CARDIN.
      PERFORM C040-PROCESS-ONE-EMPLOYEE
                  UNTIL W005-CARDIN-HAS-ENDED.
      CLOSE EMPLOYEE-CARDIN.
      GOBACK.

  C040-PROCESS-ONE-EMPLOYEE.
      EXEC SQL
          SELECT EMPNAME
               INTO :EMPNAME
            FROM XLIM.EMPTABLE
            WHERE  EMPNO = :W005-EMPLOYEE-NUMBER
      END-EXEC.
      IF SQLCODE  EQUAL TO  ZEROS
         DISPLAY W005-EMPLOYEE-NUMBER ' ' EMPNAME
      ELSE DISPLAY W005-EMPLOYEE-NUMBER ' MAJOR ERROR'.
      PERFORM C060-READ-EMPLOYEE-CARDIN.

  C060-READ-EMPLOYEE-CARDIN.
      READ EMPLOYEE-CARDIN INTO W005-EMPLOYEE-NUMBER
           AT END, MOVE 'Y' TO W005-END-OF-FILE-SW.
```

**Figure 10.6**  Program example (as coded).

# 11

---

# *The Program Preparation Process*

---

## 1 STEPS IN PROGRAM PREPARATION

Figure 11.1 shows the five steps in preparing an application program.
The five steps accomplish the following:

1. The CICS translation step is the only optional step. It is only done for command-level CICS application programs and it generates two outputs.
   a. The translation listing in userid.temp.cxlist.
   b. The translated source program in userid.temp.cicsin.
2. The PRECOMPILE step checks that the SQL statements are free of syntax errors. In addition, if there is a DECLARE TABLE statement (automatically generated by DCLGEN), the table names and column names in the statement are verified. PRECOMPILE generates three outputs.
   a. The precompile listing in userid.temp.pclist.
   b. The database request module (DBRM), which contains a parse tree version of the SQL statements in a program. This will be the input to the BIND process in Step 3.

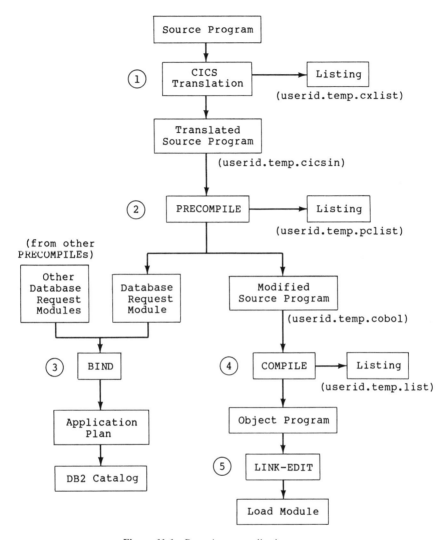

**Figure 11.1**   Preparing an application program.

   c. The modified source program in userid.temp.cobol, but with each SQL statement replaced mostly by a series of Call statements. Userid.temp.cobol is the input to the compile in Step 4.

**3.** The BIND process is DB2's version of a link-edit. It reads one or more database request modules (see Section 1.2) and "binds" them together into one application plan. This process accesses the DB2 catalog to verify table information, access authorization, and so on. Specifically, it does the following:
   a. It checks the SQL statements for valid table, view, and column names.

b. Unless this is postponed until program execution (VALIDATE(RUN) option), it checks if the person doing the bind is authorized to use the resources (tables, and so on) named in the SQL statements.

c. It determines via the Optimizer module how the data will be accessed, including whether to use any existing index or not.

d. It converts the DBRMs into one application plan. These are control structures used by DB2 during program execution. The application plan is stored
in the DB2 catalog. *In DB2, it is the plan, not the corresponding pro-
gram(s) that a user is authorized to execute.*

4. The compile process, which generates the usual output, including the listing in
userid.temp.list.

5. The link-edit process.

## 1.1 Significance of the BIND Process

The BIND process is done before the execution of the corresponding application.
Since data access is resolved during BIND, not at program execution, this results in
greater efficiency. Note that in SPUFI, data access is resolved during the execution
of SQL statements, thus making it inherently less efficient than the corresponding
application program.

In addition, checking for authorization during the BIND process, as opposed to
postponing it until program execution, enhances efficiency because this overhead is
not done during the program run.

## 1.2 How Many Programs (DBRMs) per Plan?

At PRECOMPILE, each program generates a single database request module
(DBRM). In turn, at BIND (as we said, DB2's version of link-edit), one or more
DBRMs generate a single plan.

*Unless otherwise required, (such as when a main program and several subpro-
grams — if the latter have SQL statements — form one run unit), the user should use
only one program per plan.* This allows for maximum flexibility. Unnecessarily putting multiple programs (DBRMs) in a single plan makes that plan more prone to being
invalidated, since a modification to a single program (change to tables, hence to
DCLGEN output, deletion of indexes, and so on) may invalidate the corresponding
DBRM. This in turn invalidates the whole plan. When this happens, all programs
within that plan cannot be executed, including those that were not modified in the first
place. However, as explained later, DB2 tries to help the user with this problem.

## 1.3 DB2's Automatic Rebind of Invalidated Plan

The user may do the rebind of any previous plan, including an invalidated plan. If
not, DB2 will attempt an automatic rebind of an invalidated plan without any user
intervention, at the time the plan is next run. However, if the attempt fails (for in-

stance, a program accesses a column that since the last bind has been deleted from the table), DB2 will inform the user and change the plan status from invalidated to deactivated. The plan cannot then be executed until the user makes corrections to programs, tables, and so on.

## 2 USING DB2I TO PREPARE AND TEST PROGRAMS

Once the programmer has coded the program (using TSO/ISPF), he or she may then execute the steps in Figure 11.1. There are two ways to do this:

1. One way is to directly submit JCL statements in TSO background. These state-ments reside in a data set previously saved by the programmer. See Section 8 later in this chapter.

2. Another way is to use the DB2 Interactive (DB2I) facility, which later auto-matically executes the program in TSO foreground or generates the JCL state-ments that are submitted to run in TSO background. Figure 11.2 shows that PROGRAM PREPARATION is one of the DB2I functions.

*Note that the interactive panels (for PRECOMPILE, BIND, RUN, and others) we will learn to use do not implement Figure 11.1 interactively. They merely gener-ate control information that implements Figure 11.1 when later run in TSO back-ground or foreground.*

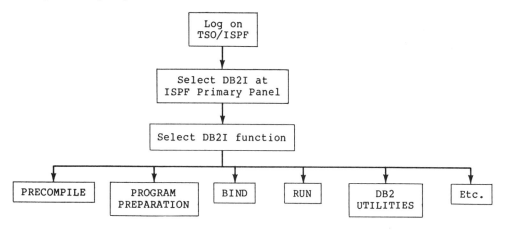

**Figure 11.2** The various DB2I functions.

### 2.1 Saving the Generated JCL Statements

If the programmer chooses "BACKGROUND" or "EDITJCL" in entry 3 of Figure 11.5, DB2 generates JCL statements in userid.temp.cntl, which will remain until TSO logoff. For option "EDITJCL", the programmer may include additional JCL

statements before submitting it for execution (needed if the program has batch files).
DB2 automatically saves userid.temp.cntl when the programmer leaves the panel.

An even better option is to copy userid.temp.cntl into a separate data set, since
the former is lost at TSO logoff. This is shown in Section 8 later in this chapter. This
saves time and effort since there is now no need to use the DB2I program preparation steps. The programmer simply recalls the saved JCL, generally changes a few
JCL statements (such as program name), then resubmits it to run in TSO batch.

Note however that each combination of functions selected (precompile only,
bind only, precompile-bind-run, etc.) generates a different procedure. Each one has
to be saved separately.

## 2.2 Invoke DB2I in TSO

Once in TSO, the programmer selects DB2I, possibly via the ISPF Primary Option
Menu. A typical display is Figure 11.3.

The programmer selects option 5.

```
------------------- ISPF PRIMARY OPTION MENU --------------
SELECT OPTION ===>

0   ISPF PARMS      - SPECIFY TERMINAL AND ISPF PARAMETERS
1   BROWSE          - DISPLAY SOURCE DATA/COMPUTER LISTING
2   EDIT            - CREATE OR CHANGE SOURCE DATA
3   UTILITIES       - PERFORM ISPF UTILITY FUNCTIONS
4   .....
5   DB2I            - DATABASE2 INTERACTIVE
6   .....
7   .....
8   .....
9   .....
```

Figure 11.3   The ISPF primary option menu.

## 2.3 Invoke Function in DB2I

Figure 11.4 is the DB2I Primary Option Menu.

## 2.4 The Program Preparation Panel

The programmer selects option 3, which will then generate the program preparation
panel in Figure 11.5.

```
                        DB2I PRIMARY OPTION MENU
===>

Select one of the following and press ENTER

    1   SPUFI               (Process SQL statements)
    2   DCLGEN              (Generate SQL and source language declarations)
    3   PROGRAM PREPARATION (Prepare a DB2 application program to run)
    4   PRECOMPILE          (Invoke DB2 precompiler)
    5   BIND/REBIND         (BIND/REBIND/FREE application plans)
    6   RUN                 (RUN an SQL program)
    7   DB2 COMMANDS        (Issue DB2 commands)
    8   UTILITIES           (Invoke DB2 utilities)
    9   EXIT                (Leave DB2I)



PRESS:   ENTER to process      END to exit      HELP for more information
```

**Figure 11.4**    The DB2I primary option menu.

```
                        DB2 PROGRAM PREPARATION
===>

Enter the following:
    1   INPUT DATA SET NAME .... ===> 'userid.DB2.COBOL(COBOL1)'
    2   DATA SET NAME QUALIFIER  ===> TEMP      (For building data set names)
    3   PREPARATION ENVIRONMENT  ===> EDITJCL   (FOREGROUND, BACKGROUND, EDITJCL)
    4   RUN TIME ENVIRONMENT ... ===> TSO       (TSO, CICS, IMS)
    5   STOP IF RETURN CODE >=   ===> 8         (Lowest terminating return code)
    6   OTHER OPTIONS .......... ===>

Select functions:         Display panel?          Perform function?
    7   CHANGE DEFAULTS ........ ===> Y (Y/N)       ............
    8   PL/I MACRO PHASE ....... ===> N (Y/N)       ===> N (Y/N)
    9   PRECOMPILE ............. ===> Y (Y/N)       ===> Y (Y/N)
   10   CICS COMMAND TRANSLATION ............       ===> N (Y/N)
   11   BIND ................... ===> Y (Y/N)       ===> Y (Y/N)
   12   COMPILE OR ASSEMBLE .... ===> Y (Y/N)       ===> Y (Y/N)
   13   LINK ................... ===> N (Y/N)       ===> Y (Y/N)
   14   RUN .................... ===> N (Y/N)       ===> Y (Y/N)

PRESS:   ENTER to process      END to exit      HELP for more information
```

**Figure 11.5**    The program preparation panel.

Note the following:

1. The INPUT DATA SET NAME is that of the program.
2. The DATA SET NAME QUALIFER is TEMP. This is used in the BIND process.

3. The PREPARATION ENVIRONMENT is usually EDITJCL for batch programs, which allows the generated JCL statements in userid.temp.cntl to be edited. This is needed to add the JCL statements for batch files (say, the printer). The programmer can then later SUBMIT userid.temp.cntl to run in TSO batch. If FOREGROUND, the steps is Figure 11.1 are executed in foreground, one step at a time, which gives the programmer an instantaneous feedback on the execution of each step.

4. The RUN TIME ENVIRONMENT is TSO, unless we access the DB2 resources via CICS or IMS.

5. The STOP IF RETURN CODE value is 8.

6. The OTHER OPTIONS entry is a list of parameters you want included in this program preparation process; for instance, options to the CICS/VS command language translator.

7. The CHANGE DEFAULT entry is usually Y the very first time so the programmer can see what the defaults are. In addition, the programmer usually codes the JCL Job statement that will be used instead of the default when the job is later submitted.

8. The PL/I macro phase is naturally only used in PL/I programs.

9. The PRECOMPILE options are both Y. Before it is executed, the corresponding panel is displayed.

10. The CICS COMMAND TRANSLATION entry is for CICS programs.

11. Like those of PRECOMPILE, the BIND options are both Y.

12. In like manner, the COMPILE OR ASSEMBLE options are both Y. Note that COMPILE, LINK (Item 13), and RUN (Item 14) use the same panel.

13. The LINK option has N for display since we will enter the necessary information along with the previous COMPILE OR ASSEMBLE step.

14. The RUN option has N for display since we will enter the necessary information along with the previous COMPILE OR ASSEMBLE step.


## 3 THE DB2I DEFAULT PANEL

Figure 11.6 is the DB2 Default panel.
Note the following:

1. This panel appears if we choose "Y" for the Display panel column of the CHANGE DEFAULTS entry of Figure 11.5.

2. The programmer may change the system defaults as shown on the display.

3. Entry 9 is the Job statement coded by the programmer and will be used in place of the defaults. This will appear in the generated JCL that is submitted to run (Fig. 11.10).

```
                          DB2I DEFAULTS

===>

Change defaults as desired:

1  DB2 NAME ...........  ===> DSN      (Subsystem identifier)
2  DB2 CONNECTION RETRIES  ===> 0      (How many retries for DB2 connection)
3  APPLICATION LANGUAGE  ===> COBOL    (COBOL, COB2, ASM, FORT, PLI)
4  LINES/PAGE OF LISTING  ===> 60      (A number from 5 TO 999)
5  MESSAGE LEVEL .......  ===> I        (Information, Warning, Error, Severe)
6  COBOL STRING DELIMITER  ===> '       (DEFAULT, ' OR ")
7  SQL STRING DELIMITER  ===> '         (DEFAULT, ' OR ")
8  DECIMAL POINT .......  ===> .        (. OR ,)

9  DB2I JOB STATEMENT:      (Optional if site has a SUBMIT exit)
   ===> //jobname JOB ....
   ===>
   ===>
   ===>


PRESS:   ENTER to process        END to exit      HELP for more information
```

**Figure 11.6**  The DB2I defaults panel.

## 4 THE PRECOMPILE PANEL

Figure 11.7 is the Precompile panel.

```
                          PRECOMPILE
===>

Enter precompiler data sets:

  1   INPUT DATA SET .... ===> 'userid.DB2.COBOL(COBOL1)'
  2   INCLUDE LIBRARY ... ===> 'userid.DB2.COBOL'

  3   DSNAME QUALIFIER .. ===> TEMP         (For building data set names)
  4   DBRM DATA SET ..... ===>

Enter processing options as desired:
  5   WHERE TO PRECOMPILE ===> EDITJCL      (FOREGROUND, BACKGROUND, or EDITCJL)
  6   OTHER OPTIONS ..... ===>




 PRESS:  ENTER to process        END to exit        HELP for more information
```

**Figure 11.7**   The PRECOMPILE panel.

Note the following:

1. This panel appears if we choose "Y" for the Display panel column of the PRE-COMPILE entry of Figure 11.5.
2. If this panel is accessed via the Program Preparation panel (Fig. 11.5), the INPUT DATA SET NAME contains the value specified in that panel.
3. The INCLUDE LIBRARY entry specifies the library containing members to be included by the precompiler, for instance, the library containing the output of the DCLGEN operation.
4. If this panel is accessed via the Program Preparation panel (Fig. 11.5), the DSNAME QUALIFIER entry contains the value specified in that panel.
5. The DBRM DATA SET entry is the DBRM library for the precompiler output (which becomes input to BIND). If this panel is accessed via the Program Preparation panel (Fig. 11.5), it is initially blanks. When you press ENTER, the value of DATA SET NAME QUALIFIER (here equal to "TEMP") is concatenated with ".DBRM" and becomes the DBRM DATA SET.
6. If this panel is accessed via the Program Preparation panel, the WHERE TO COMPILE entry is the same as the PREPARATION ENVIRONMENT of that panel.

**7.** The OTHER OPTIONS entry are precompiler options that will override the installation standards. Many of these are identical to the options for compile. Examples are APOST to specify the single quotes as the literal delimiter, FLAG(x,y) to specify the level of diagnostic messages, and so on.

### 4.1 Output of CICS Command Translation

**1.** If there is a command language translation step (CICS application program only), the translated program is in userid.temp.cicsin.

**2.** The output listing is in userid.temp.cxlist.

### 4.2 Output of Precompile

**1.** The modified source module is in userid.temp.cobol.

**2.** The precompile listing is in userid.temp.pclist.

## 5 THE BIND PANEL

Figure 11.8 is the BIND panel.

**Figure 11.8**   The BIND panel.

```
                          BIND
 ===>

   Enter DBRM data set name(s):
   1   LIBRARY(S) ............... ===> TEMP.DBRM
   2   MEMBER(S) ................ ===> COBOL1
   3   PASSWORD(S) .............. ===>

   4   MORE DBRMS? .............. ===> N              (Y to list more DBRMs)

   Enter options as desired:
   5   PLAN NAME ................ ===> COBOL1         (Required to create a plan)
   6   ACTION ON PLAN ........... ===> REPLACE        (REPLACE or ADD)
   7   RETAIN EXECUTION AUTHORITY ===> Y              (Y to retain user list)
   8   ISOLATION LEVEL .......... ===> CS             (RR or CS)
   9   PLAN VALIDATION TIME ..... ===> BIND           (RUN or BIND)
  10   RESOURCE ACQUISITION TIME. ===> USE            (USE or ALLOCATE)
  11   RESOURCE RELEASE TIME .... ===> COMMIT         (COMMIT or DEALLOCATE)
  12   EXPLAIN PATH SELECTION ... ===> N              (Y or N)


 PRESS:   ENTER to process        END to exit        HELP for more information
```

Note the following:

1. This panel appears if we choose "Y" for the Display panel column of the BIND entry of Figure 11.5.

2. If this panel is accessed via the program preparation steps, the LIBRARY entry contains the value specified in the DBRM DATA SET entry of the Precompile step.

3. The MEMBER entry is the DBRM itself. For a partitioned data set, its default value is the member name of the INPUT DATA SET NAME entry of the Program Preparation panel. For a sequential data set, it is the second qualifier of the data set.

4. The PASSWORD entry is used for a password.

5. The MORE DBRMS entry allows the programmer to enter more DBRMs via another panel.

6. The PLAN NAME entry is the name of the application plan created during BIND. The default value for a partitioned data set is the member name of the INPUT DATA SET NAME of the Program Preparation panel. For a sequential file, it is the second qualifier.

7. The ACTION OF PLAN entry is REPLACE or ADD. REPLACE will also add a new plan.

8. The RETAIN EXECUTION AUTHORITY entry is valid only if we are modifying an old plan. If Y, those authorized to bind or execute the old plan are to retain the authority for the modified plan.

9. The ISOLATION LEVEL entries are explained in Chapter 20. CS promotes greater concurrency; RR allows "repeatable read" by a single program.

10. The PLAN VALIDATION TIME specifies when full validity checking is to be done. BIND means do it during the BIND process, which is the efficient way. RUN means do it during program execution, which has to be used if authorization is not granted by the time BIND is done.

11. The RESOURCE ACQUISITION TIME entry determines when you want the system to acquire resources for your program. USE means acquire it when first used in the program; ALLOCATE means acquire it when first used in the plan is allocated (the program starts). Specifying USE promotes greater concurrency.

12. The RESOURCE RELEASE TIME entry determines when you want the system to release resources taken by your program. COMMIT means release them when committed (SQL COMMIT or SQL ROLLBACK statements); DEALLOCATE means wait until the program terminates. COMMIT promotes greater concurrency.

13. The EXPLAIN PATH SELECTION entry allows the user to query DB2 about how it navigates through the table to access the data.

## 6 THE COMPILE/LINK/RUN PANEL

Figure 11.9 is the COMPILE/LINK/RUN panel.

```
                PROGRAM PREPARATION: COMPILE, LINK, AND RUN
 ===>

 Enter compiler or assembler options:
 1   INCLUDE LIBRARY ===>
 2   INCLUDE LIBRARY ===>
 3   OPTIONS ....... ===> ADV, OPTIMIZE

 Enter linkage editor options:
 4   INCLUDE LIBRARY ===>
 5   INCLUDE LIBRARY ===>
 6   INCLUDE LIBRARY ===>
 7   LOAD LIBRARY .. ===> RUNLIB.LOAD
 8   OPTIONS ....... ===>

 Enter run options:
 9   PARAMETERS .... ===>
 10  SYSIN DATA SET  ===> TERM
 11  SYSPRINT DS ... ===> TERM




 PRESS:  ENTER to process        END to exit        HELP for more information
```

**Figure 11.9**   The COMPILE/LINK/RUN panel.

Note the following:

1. This panel appears if we choose "Y" for the Display panel column of the COMPILE OR ASSEMBLE entry of Figure 11.5.
2. The programmer may include up to two libraries for the compile phase.
3. The OPTIONS entry are compiler options that will override the installation standards, for instance, ADV.
4. Entries 4 to 6 allow up to three libraries containing members to be included in the linkage editor run.
5. The LOAD LIBRARY entry has the default of RUNLIB.LOAD.
6. The PARAMETERS entry is a list of parameters you want passed to the runtime processor or the program.
7. By default, the SYSIN DATA SET and SYSPRINT DS entries are TERM.

## 7 EXECUTING THE PROGRAM PREPARATION STEPS

With typical batch programs, "EDITJCL" is entered in the PREPARATION ENVI-RONMENT entry of the DB2 program preparation panel (Fig. 11.5). Before the run is done, DB2 displays a panel that shows the JCL statements it generated, and if the programmer entered a Job statement in the DB2I DEFAULT panel (Fig. 11.6), it will be used in place of the standard Job statement. The programmer may then insert JCL statements for batch files (say, printers).

Figure 11.10 shows this DB2-generated JCL.

```
000001 //jobname JOB .....      ◄─from JOB statement of Fig. 11.6
000002 //GO EXEC PGM .....      ⎫
000003 //.....                  ⎬ DB2-generated statements
......                          ⎭
000009 //LSTOUT DD SYSOUT=A     ⎫
000010 //CARDIN DD *            ⎪
000011 00005                    ⎪
000012 00010                    ⎬ user-added statements
000013 00015                    ⎪
000014 /*                       ⎭
......
000020 //SYSTSIN DD *           ⎫
......                          ⎪
000030 INPUT('''userid.DB2.COBOL(PROG1202)''')
......                          ⎪
000036 PLAN(plan name)          ⎬ DB2-generated statements
......                          ⎪
000039 RUN (TSO)                ⎪
......                          ⎪
000045 /*                       ⎪
000046 //                       ⎭
```

**Figure 11.10**   The DB2-generated JCL.

Note the following:

1. The JOB statement is from entry 9 of Figure 11.6.
2. DB2 saves the JCL statements in userid.temp.cntl. This data set will be retained until TSO logoff. As suggested in Section 8 later in this chapter, this is best copied into a programmer-owned data set.
3. The programmer adds JCL statements for the batch files. The programmer may now submit the job with the SUB command.

## 8 EXECUTING THE PROGRAM PREPARATION STEPS USING JCL

The DB2-generated JCL statements (in userid.temp.cntl) are lost at TSO logoff. Therefore, it is generally best for the programmer to copy it into his or her own data set. As mentioned before, note that each combination of functions selected (precompile only, bind only, precompile-bind-run, etc.) generates a different procedure. Each must be saved separately. The programmer may conveniently just resubmit one of the saved versions of the JCL, after making minor changes.

One change is the JCL statements for batch files. Others are the "INPUT" entry for the program data set name (line 000030 of Fig. 11.10) and the "PLAN" entry for the plan name (line 000036).

# 12

# *Select Operations*

## 1 PROCESSING ONE ROW FROM SOURCE TABLE(S) | VIEW

The programmer may select one row from a source table(s) or view and bring it immediately into the application program. *This option is used only if there is at most only one row selected because the column(s) used in the selection criteria (WHERE clause) only contains unique values (the column was defined with UNIQUE INDEX).* An example is a selection based on employee number (which is unique).

If this processing style is used where the selection criteria uses a column that may contain nonunique values, an error will result if DB2 finds more than one row.

### 1.1 SQLCODE for Select (Read-Only) Operations

For SELECT operations, there are only two values of SQLCODE that are of interest to the user: a value of 0 (no error) or a value of 100 ("no record found") on either the SELECT statement itself or the FETCH statement (if processing multiple rows). On a negative value, the row is not read into the program.

The use of SQLCODE is shown in the discussion of program logic and the program examples.

## 1.2 DCLGEN Output for XLIM.EMPTABLE

Figure 12.1 is the DCLGEN output for the XLIM.EMPTABLE Employee table. We will use it in all our program examples. Note that we have both the DECLARE TABLE statement and the table row description.

```
**********************************************************************
* DCLGEN TABLE(XLIM.EMPTABLE)                                        *
*        LIBRARY(XLIM.DB2.COBOL(EMPTABDL)                            *
*        ACTION(REPLACE)                                             *
*        APOST                                                       *
* ... IS THE DCLGEN COMMAND THAT MADE THE FOLLOWING STATEMENTS       *
**********************************************************************
        EXEC SQL DECLARE XLIM.EMPTABLE TABLE
        ( EMPNO                 CHAR(5) NOT NULL,
          EMPNAME               CHAR(30) NOT NULL WITH DEFAULT,
          EMPDEPT               CHAR(3) NOT NULL WITH DEFAULT,
          EMPSALARY             DECIMAL(7,0) NULL
        ) END-EXEC.
**********************************************************************
* COBOL DECLARATION FOR TABLE XLIM.EMPTABLE                          *
**********************************************************************
  01  DCLEMPTABLE.
      10  EMPNO                 PIC X(5).
      10  EMPNAME               PIC X(30).
      10  EMPDEPT               PIC XXX.
      10  EMPSALARY             PIC S9(7) COMP-3.
**********************************************************************
* THE NUMBER OF COLUMNS DESCRIBED BY THIS DECLARATION IS 4           *
**********************************************************************
```

**Figure 12.1**   DCLGEN output for the XLIM.EMPTABLE employee table.

## 1.3 Current Data on XLIM.EMPTABLE

In this chapter, we will use Figure 12.2 as the input to our program. It contains the current data on the XLIM.EMPTABLE Employee table.

|     | Employee Number (EMPNO) | Name (EMPNAME) | Department Number (EMPDEPT) | Salary (EMPSALARY) |
| --- | --- | --- | --- | --- |
| 1. | 00005 | BAKER, C. | 003 | 0030000 |
| 2. | 00008 | RANDOLPH, R. | 005 | 0029000 |
| 3. | 00010 | RICHARDS, M. | 002 | Nulls |
| 4. | 00015 | DAVIS, L. | 006 | 0030000 |
| 5. | 00150 | ELLIOT, T. | 005 | 0031000 |
| 6. | 00170 | RABINOVITZ, M. | 003 | Nulls |
| 7. | 00190 | LEE, R. | 005 | 0030000 |

**Figure 12.2**   Current data on the XLIM.EMPTABLE employee table.

## 1.4 Program Logic: One-row Selection

If the selection criteria (WHERE clause) specifies a column(s) defined with a unique index, then at most only one row can be selected. In our example, we assume this case for the employee number column. The general program logic is shown in Figure 12.3.

```
WORKING-STORAGE SECTION.
    .....
    EXEC SQL
        INCLUDE member-name (from DCLGEN output)
    END-EXEC.
    EXEC SQL
        INCLUDE SQLCA
    END-EXEC.
    .....
PROCEDURE DIVISION.
    .....
*** Here set EMPNO to the correct value ***
    EXEC SQL
        SELECT EMPNAME,
               EMPSALARY
          INTO :EMPNAME,
               :EMPSALARY
          FROM XLIM.EMPTABLE
         WHERE EMPNO = :EMPNO
    END-EXEC.
    IF SQLCODE  EQUAL TO   ZEROS
        OK continue
    ELSE error routine.
```

**Figure 12.3**  Program logic: one-row selection.

The following apply:

1. At the beginning, we have to set the Cobol data-name EMPNO to the correct value. It will be used as the search criteria.

2. The column names in the SELECT statement (EMPNAME, EMPSALARY) are those of the table.

3. The INTO clause brings the data for the selected columns into the Cobol data-names specified (note the colon prefix). Thus, :EMPNAME and :EMPSALARY are the Cobol data-names generated by DCLGEN (see Fig. 12.1).

4. We check the SQLCODE field and if zero, we know the select was successful and we may continue or else we did not get any row.

### 1.5 Program Listing: One-row Selection

We will now print selected rows (one row per selection) from XLIM.EMPTABLE (Fig. 12.2). Selection is based on employee numbers coded in an in-line "card file", unless the salary value of the employee is nulls, where we bypass the row. Figure 12.4 is the program listing.

The following apply:

1. Lines 001400 to 002600 are the in-line card file that contains the employee numbers, and the print file.

2. Lines 002800 to 006800 are the various data-names such as counters and the print lines.

```
000100 IDENTIFICATION DIVISION.
000200 PROGRAM-ID. PROG1204.
000300*******************************************************************
000400*                                                                 *
000500*  1. THIS PROGRAM PRINTS SELECTED ROWS IN THE EMPLOYEE TABLE.  *
000600*                                                                 *
000700*  2. SELECTION IS BASED ON THE EMPLOYEE NUMBER.  IT IS THE      *
000800*     PRIMARY KEY (DEFINED WITH UNIQUE, CLUSTERED INDEX).         *
000900*                                                                 *
001000*******************************************************************
001100 ENVIRONMENT DIVISION.
001200 CONFIGURATION SECTION.
001300 INPUT-OUTPUT SECTION.
001400 FILE-CONTROL.
001500     SELECT SEARCH-FILE    ASSIGN TO  CARDIN.
001600     SELECT PRINT-OUTPUT   ASSIGN TO  LSTOUT.
001700 DATA DIVISION.
001800 FILE SECTION.
001900 FD  SEARCH-FILE
002000     BLOCK CONTAINS 0 RECORDS
002100     LABEL RECORDS OMITTED.
002200 01  SEARCH-RECORD               PIC X(80).
002300 FD  PRINT-OUTPUT
002400     BLOCK CONTAINS 0 RECORDS
002500     LABEL RECORDS OMITTED.
002600 01  PRINT-RECORD                PIC X(133).
002700 WORKING-STORAGE SECTION.
002800 01  W005-LINE-COUNT             PIC S9(8) COMP VALUE +99.
002900 01  W005-LINE-LIMIT             PIC S9(8) COMP VALUE +55.
003000 01  W005-LINE-SKIP              PIC 99.
003100 01  W005-SEARCH-EMPNO           PIC X(5).
003200 01  W005-SALARY-INDV            PIC S9(4) COMP.
003300 01  W005-END-OF-SEARCH-FILE     PIC X VALUE 'N'.
003400     88  W005-NO-MORE-SEARCH-CARDS    VALUE 'Y'.
003500 01  W005-DETAIL-LINE.
003600     05  FILLER                  PIC X(4).
003700     05  W005-DETAIL-EMPNO       PIC X(5).
003800     05  FILLER                  PIC X(4).
003900     05  W005-DETAIL-EMPNAME     PIC X(30).
004000     05  FILLER                  PIC X(2).
004100     05  W005-DETAIL-EMPDEPT     PIC XXX.
004200     05  FILLER                  PIC X(3).
004300     05  W005-DETAIL-EMPSALARY   PIC Z,ZZZ,ZZ9.
004400     05  W005-DETAIL-EMPSALARY-ALPHA
004500                     REDEFINES W005-DETAIL-EMPSALARY
004600                                 PIC X(9).
004700     05  FILLER                  PIC X.
004800     05  W005-DETAIL-SQLCODE     PIC ++++++++++.
004900     05  FILLER                  PIC X.
005000     05  W005-DETAIL-SQLCODE-NOTE  PIC X(3).
005100 01  W005-HEADER-LINE1.
005200     05  FILLER                  PIC X(3)  VALUE SPACES.
005300     05  FILLER                  PIC X(8)  VALUE 'EMPLOYEE'.
005400     05  FILLER                  PIC X(34) VALUE SPACES.
005500     05  FILLER                  PIC X(5)  VALUE 'DEPT.'.
005600     05  FILLER                  PIC X(18) VALUE SPACES.
005700     05  FILLER                  PIC X(6)  VALUE 'RETURN'.
005800 01  W005-HEADER-LINE2.
005900     05  FILLER                  PIC X(4)  VALUE SPACES.
006000     05  FILLER                  PIC X(6)  VALUE 'NUMBER'.
006100     05  FILLER                  PIC X(8)  VALUE SPACES.
006200     05  FILLER                  PIC X(4)  VALUE 'NAME'.
006300     05  FILLER                  PIC X(22) VALUE SPACES.
006400     05  FILLER                  PIC X(6)  VALUE 'NUMBER'.
006500     05  FILLER                  PIC X(4)  VALUE SPACES.
006600     05  FILLER                  PIC X(6)  VALUE 'SALARY'.
006700     05  FILLER                  PIC X(8)  VALUE SPACES.
006800     05  FILLER                  PIC X(4)  VALUE 'CODE'.
```

**Figure 12.4**  Program listing: one-row selection.

```
006900       EXEC SQL
007000            INCLUDE SQLCA
007100       END-EXEC.
007200       EXEC SQL
007300            INCLUDE EMPTABDL
007400       END-EXEC.
007500 PROCEDURE DIVISION.
007600       OPEN  INPUT SEARCH-FILE
007700            OUTPUT PRINT-OUTPUT.
007800       MOVE SPACES  TO  W005-DETAIL-LINE.
007900       PERFORM C120-READ-ONE-SEARCH-CARD.
008000       PERFORM C020-PROCESS-ALL-ROWS
008100            UNTIL W005-NO-MORE-SEARCH-CARDS.
008200       CLOSE SEARCH-FILE PRINT-OUTPUT.
008300       DISPLAY '*** END OF JOB PROG1204' UPON SYSOUT.
008400       GOBACK.
008500 C020-PROCESS-ALL-ROWS.
008600       PERFORM C100-FETCH-ONE-ROW.
008700       IF SQLCODE  EQUAL TO  ZERO
008800            PERFORM C040-LAYOUT-ROW-COLUMNS
008900       ELSE MOVE W005-SEARCH-EMPNO  TO  W005-DETAIL-EMPNO.
009000       MOVE SQLCODE     TO  W005-DETAIL-SQLCODE.
009100       IF SQLCODE  NOT EQUAL TO   ZERO
009200            MOVE '***'        TO  W005-DETAIL-SQLCODE-NOTE.
009300       PERFORM C060-PRINT-DETAIL-LINE.
009400       MOVE SPACES  TO  W005-DETAIL-LINE.
009500       PERFORM C120-READ-ONE-SEARCH-CARD.
009600 C040-LAYOUT-ROW-COLUMNS.
009700       MOVE EMPNO       TO  W005-DETAIL-EMPNO.
009800       MOVE EMPNAME     TO  W005-DETAIL-EMPNAME.
009900       MOVE EMPDEPT     TO  W005-DETAIL-EMPDEPT.
010000       IF W005-SALARY-INDV  LESS THAN  ZERO
010100            MOVE 'NULLS ***'  TO  W005-DETAIL-EMPSALARY-ALPHA
010200       ELSE MOVE EMPSALARY    TO  W005-DETAIL-EMPSALARY.
010300 C060-PRINT-DETAIL-LINE.
010400       IF W005-LINE-COUNT   GREATER THAN  W005-LINE-LIMIT
010500            PERFORM C080-PRINT-HEADER-LINES.
010600       WRITE PRINT-RECORD FROM W005-DETAIL-LINE
010700                 AFTER ADVANCING W005-LINE-SKIP LINES.
010800       ADD  1  TO  W005-LINE-COUNT.
010900       MOVE 1  TO  W005-LINE-SKIP.
011000 C080-PRINT-HEADER-LINES.
011100       WRITE PRINT-RECORD FROM W005-HEADER-LINE1
011200                 AFTER ADVANCING PAGE.
011300       WRITE PRINT-RECORD FROM W005-HEADER-LINE2
011400                 AFTER ADVANCING 2 LINES.
011500       MOVE  ZEROS  TO  W005-LINE-COUNT.
011600       MOVE  2      TO  W005-LINE-SKIP.
011700 C100-FETCH-ONE-ROW.
011800       EXEC SQL
011900            SELECT EMPNO,
012000                   EMPNAME,
012100                   EMPDEPT,
012200                   EMPSALARY
012300            INTO :EMPNO,
012400                 :EMPNAME,
012500                 :EMPDEPT,
012600                 :EMPSALARY:W005-SALARY-INDV
012700            FROM XLIM.EMPTABLE
012800               WHERE EMPNO = :W005-SEARCH-EMPNO
012900       END-EXEC.
013000 C120-READ-ONE-SEARCH-CARD.
013100       READ SEARCH-FILE INTO W005-SEARCH-EMPNO
013200            AT END, MOVE 'Y'  TO  W005-END-OF-SEARCH-FILE.
```

**Figure 12.4**  *(continued)*

3. Lines 006900 to 007100 generate the communication area data block shown in Figure 10.1.

4. Lines 007200 to 007400 include the DCLGEN output shown in Figure 12.1.

5. Lines 007600 to 008200 are the housekeeping routines and the main-loop control.

6. Lines 008500 to 009500 control the processing of rows selected from the employee number entered in the in-line card file. Since the employee number is a unique index, we actually select at most only one row.

   a. Line 008600 performs the attempt to select a single row.

   b. Lines 008700 to 008900 perform the laying out of the columns if there was a row selected; or else we only lay out the employee number from the original card file (so we can later print an error message).

   c. Lines 009000 to 009200 lay out the SQLCODE, plus the literal '***' if it is not zero. Note that an SQLCODE value of zeros will print as blanks because of line 004800.

   d. Lines 009300 to 009400 print out the detail line, then blank it out for the next row.

7. Lines 009600 to 010200 lay out the row columns (from lines 008700 to 008800) only if a row was selected.

   a. Lines 009700 to 009900 simply lay out the columns that will never contain nulls (see Fig. 12.1).

   b. Lines 010000 to 010200 check the W005-SALARY-INDV indicator variable to see if DB2 detected nulls (a negative value for W005-SALARY-INDV) for the EMPSALARY column (see line 012600). If so, we display the 'NULLS ***' literal, instead of the actual salary value.

8. Lines 010300 to 011600 are the routines to print the detail and header lines.

9. Lines 011700 to 012900 is the statement to select one row. Note that we use the INTO clause, which brings that single row selected into the data-names specified in the clause.

   a. Lines 011900 to 012200 specify the columns to be selected. Note that it is easy to code one row per line since the programmer can just copy the row definitions from the DCLGEN output (see Fig. 12.1). In addition, program maintenance becomes easier.

   b. Lines 012300 to 012600 specify the corresponding Cobol data-names that will get the value from the row. Note that each is prefixed with a colon.

   c. Line 012600 shows the use of the indicator variable for a column that may contain nulls; if not specified, there is an SQLCODE error if the column does contain nulls.

   d. Line 012800 is the selection criteria. We know that there will be at most only one row selected since EMPNO is defined with a unique index.

10. Lines 013000 to 013200 read the in-line card file to get the employee numbers used in the selection process.

### 1.6 Additional JCL Statements and In-line Card File

Assuming that we use "EDITJCL" in entry 3 of Figure 11.5 in Chapter 11, DB2 will generate most of the JCL statements for us. However, we still have to include those for the batch files.

For our program example, these are for the display output, the in-line "card file," and the print file. Thus:

```
//SYSOUT  DD  SYSOUT=*
//LSTOUT  DD  SYSOUT=*
//CARDIN  DD  *
 00015
 00010
 00600
 00008
/*
```

**1.6.1 The list of selected rows.**    Note that from the previous additional JCL statements, the employee numbers are not in sequence. The program will just do a random read of the input table as each input card is read. From the current data in XLIM.EMPTABLE (Fig. 12.2), we can see that we process in sequence, employee numbers '00015', '00010', and '00008'. Employee number 00600 does not exist in the table.

### 1.7 Output Listing: One-row Selection

Figure 12.5 is the output of the program in Figure 12.4.

| EMPLOYEE NUMBER | NAME | DEPT. NUMBER | SALARY | RETURN CODE |
|---|---|---|---|---|
| 00015 | DAVIS, L. | 006 | 30,000 | |
| 00010 | RICHARDS, M. | 002 | NULLS *** | |
| 00600 | | | | +100 *** |
| 00008 | RANDOLPH, R. | 005 | 29,000 | |

**Figure 12.5**    Output listing: one-row selection.

Note the following:

1. Employee number '00015' is printed out. SQLCODE is zero, hence the "RETURN CODE" column in the detail line shows spaces.
2. Employee number '00010' is printed out. Since the salary value is nulls, we print out 'NULLS ***' in the salary column.
3. Employee number '00600' is not in the table. The SQLCODE is 100, which we print out as +100.
4. Employee number '00008' is printed out. SQLCODE is zero.

## 2 PROCESSING MULTIPLE ROWS (BY USING A CURSOR)

In many cases, there are multiple rows that satisfy a particular selection criteria (that is, the column used in the WHERE clause is nonunique). *Since Cobol does not allow the programmer to bring all such rows "en masse" to the program, the only way to process this condition is by using a cursor to fetch the data, one row at a time. The style shown in Section 1 will not work.*

### 2.1 Defining the Cursor

The cursor name, which is not defined as a Cobol data-name, is defined in a DE-CLARE statement that has the SELECT statement subordinated to it. The DE-CLARE statement is nonexecutable code, and is coded either in the PROCEDURE DIVISION (preferably, for better documentation) or in the WORKING-STORAGE section. The subordinate SELECT statement (which is coded just like any other SE-LECT statement) identifies the subset of the input table(s) that will serve as the "temporary cursor table" (see Section 2.1.1) from which the program fetches data, one row at a time. Processing is then similar to that of a sequential file.

The format of the DECLARE statement is:

```
EXEC SQL
      DECLARE cursor-name CURSOR FOR
            SELECT EMPNAME, EMPSALARY
                FROM XLIM.EMPTABLE
                    WHERE EMPDEPT = :SEARCH-DEPT
END-EXEC.
```

The following apply:

1. Cursor-name is the programmer-defined cursor name. It is not a Cobol data-name.
2. The SELECT operand specifies the columns in the "temporary cursor table".
3. The WHERE operand specifies the rows in the "temporary cursor table". In our example, they are all rows where the value of the EMPDEPT column is equal to that of the Cobol SEARCH-DEPT data-name. If this operand is missing, all rows are used.

### 2.1.1 The "temporary cursor table".

The SELECT operand of the DE-CLARE cursor-name statement defines the group that serves as the "temporary cursor table" from which individual rows are later fetched. For instance, if we use Figure 12.2 as the original table and code the following:

```
EXEC SQL
      DECLARE EMPCSR CURSOR FOR
            SELECT EMPNO, EMPNAME, EMPSALARY
                FROM XLIM.EMPTABLE
                    WHERE EMPDEPT = '005'
END-EXEC.
```

```
         Employee
          Number          Name            Salary
         (EMPNO)        (EMPNAME)        (EMPSALARY)

1.        00005        BAKER, C.         0030000
2.        00008        RANDOLPH, R.      0029000
3.        00010        RICHARDS, M.      Nulls
4.        00015        DAVIS, L.         0030000
5.        00150        ELLIOT, T.        0031000
6.        00170        RABINOVITZ, M.    Nulls
7.        00190        LEE, R.           0030000
```

3 rows in the "temporary cursor table"

**Figure 12.6**  "Temporary Cursor Table".

We get Figure 12.6 as the "temporary cursor table".
Note that there are only three rows in this "temporary cursor table".

**2.1.2 The "conceptual temporary cursor table".**    If the program can use the original table (for instance, it does not care about the sequence of the rows being fetched), then this "temporary cursor table" is just a concept. DB2 will simply use the original table and point the cursor to the current row being processed.

This is in fact the case in Figure 12.6. As we said, only three rows can be fetched from the table.

**2.1.3 The "physical temporary cursor table".**    If the program requires rows fetched to be in a specific sequence, the ORDER BY clause is specified. If DB2 decides that using an existing index is more efficient than doing a sort, then DB2 will still use the original table as the "temporary cursor table"; otherwise, a sort is done.

In the latter, DB2 first selects the needed rows, then sorts them as the "temporary cursor table" in a temporary file. In short, it exists as a physical entity, independent of the original table. For instance, if we use Figure 12.2 as the input and code the following (we assume there is no index by EMPNAME):

```
EXEC SQL
      DECLARE EMPCSR CURSOR FOR
            SELECT EMPNO, EMPNAME, EMPSALARY
            FROM XLIM.EMPTABLE
            WHERE EMPDEPT = '005'
            ORDER BY EMPNAME
END-EXEC.
```

We get Figure 12.7 as the "temporary cursor table".

```
         Employee
          Number          Name            Salary
         (EMPNO)        (EMPNAME)        (EMPSALARY)

1.        00150        ELLIOT, T.        0031000
2.        00190        LEE, R.           0030000
3.        00008        RANDOLPH, R.      0029000
```

**Figure 12.7**  The physical "Temporary Cursor Table".

Note that Figure 12.7 shows a physical entity, implemented by DB2 in a temporary file.

## 2.2 Opening the Cursor to Start Processing

Before cursor processing starts, the program must execute the SQL statement OPEN cursor-name. This also brings the cursor to the first row of the "temporary cursor table". In Figure 12.6, this is the row belonging to employee number '00008'; in Figure 12.7, this is the row belonging to employee number '00150'.

The format is:

```
EXEC SQL
        OPEN cursor-name
END-EXEC.
```

## 2.3 FETCH Statement to Read One Row

For an open cursor, the FETCH statement gets one row at a time to the program. The format is:

```
EXEC SQL
        FETCH cursor-name
                INTO :data-name1, :data-name2 . . .
END-EXEC.
```

Note that SQLCODE is equal to 100 if there are no more rows ("no record found" condition).

## 2.4 Closing the Cursor at End of Processing

Once the program is finished with processing the "temporary cursor table" (or at any time), the CLOSE cursor-name statement is executed. The format is:

```
EXEC SQL
        CLOSE cursor-name
END-EXEC.
```

## 2.5 Basic Program Logic: Multiple Rows

The basic program logic is Figure 12.8.

The following apply:

1. The DECLARE cursor-name statement identifies the cursor, the columns selected, and the search criteria.
   a. The column-names in the SELECT clause (EMPNAME, EMPSALARY) are those of the table.
   b. Note that if the WHERE clause is missing (as we will show in the program example in Fig. 12.9), we are reading the whole table.
2. We set the Cobol data-name SEARCH-DEPT to the correct value since it is used as the search criteria.

```
WORKING-STORAGE SECTION.
    .....
    EXEC SQL
        INCLUDE member-name (from DCLGEN output)
    END-EXEC.
    .....
    EXEC SQL
        INCLUDE SQLCA
    END-EXEC.
    .....
PROCEDURE DIVISION.
    .....
    EXEC SQL
        DECLARE cursor-name CURSOR FOR
            SELECT EMPNAME,
                    EMPSALARY
              FROM XLIM.EMPTABLE
              WHERE EMPDEPT = :SEARCH-DEPT
    END-EXEC.
***  Here set SEARCH-DEPT to the correct value ***
    EXEC SQL
        OPEN cursor-name
    END-EXEC.
    PERFORM C200-PROCESS-EMPLOYEE-ROW UNTIL SQLCODE = 100.
    EXEC SQL
        CLOSE cursor-name
    END-EXEC.
    .....
C200-PROCESS-EMPLOYEE-ROW.
    EXEC SQL
        FETCH cursor-name
            INTO :EMPNAME,
                 :EMPSALARY
    END-EXEC.
    IF SQLCODE  EQUAL TO  ZEROS
        OK continue.
```

**Figure 12.8**  Program logic: multiple-row selection.

3. As part of the Main-loop routine, we open the cursor, perform the processing of all rows, then close the cursor.

4. The FETCH statement has the INTO clause, which brings the data for the selected columns into the Cobol data-names specified. Thus, :EMPNAME and :EMPSALARY are the Cobol data-names generated by DCLGEN (see Fig. 12.1).

5. We check the SQLCODE field and if zero, we know the FETCH was successful and we may continue; if the value is 100, then this is the "end of file" condition.

## 2.6 Program Example: Multiple-row Selection

We will use Figure 12.2 as the input.

### 2.6.1 Program listing: multiple-row selection.   We will now print all rows in the XLIM.EMPTABLE Employee table. Figure 12.9 is the program listing. The following apply:

1. Lines 001100 to 001800 define the print file.

2. Lines 002000 to 005100 are the various data-names such as counters and the print lines.

```
000100 IDENTIFICATION DIVISION.
000200 PROGRAM-ID. PROG1207.
000300****************************************************************
000400*                                                              *
000500*   1. THIS PROGRAM PRINTS ALL ROWS IN THE EMPLOYEE TABLE.     *
000600*                                                              *
000700****************************************************************
000800 ENVIRONMENT DIVISION.
000900 CONFIGURATION SECTION.
001000 INPUT-OUTPUT SECTION.
001100 FILE-CONTROL.
001200     SELECT PRINT-OUTPUT   ASSIGN TO  LSTOUT.
001300 DATA DIVISION.
001400 FILE SECTION.
001500 FD  PRINT-OUTPUT
001600     BLOCK CONTAINS 0 RECORDS
001700     LABEL RECORDS OMITTED.
001800 01  PRINT-RECORD                 PIC X(133).
001900 WORKING-STORAGE SECTION.
002000 01  W005-LINE-COUNT              PIC S9(8) COMP VALUE +99.
002100 01  W005-LINE-LIMIT              PIC S9(8) COMP VALUE +55.
002200 01  W005-LINE-SKIP               PIC 99.
002300 01  W005-SALARY-INDV             PIC S9(4) COMP.
002400 01  W005-END-OF-ROWS             PIC X VALUE 'N'.
002500     88  W005-NO-MORE-ROWS            VALUE 'Y'.
002600 01  W005-DETAIL-LINE.
002700     05  FILLER                   PIC X(4).
002800     05  W005-DETAIL-EMPNO        PIC X(5).
002900     05  FILLER                   PIC X(4).
003000     05  W005-DETAIL-EMPNAME      PIC X(30).
003100     05  FILLER                   PIC X(2).
003200     05  W005-DETAIL-EMPDEPT      PIC XXX.
003300     05  FILLER                   PIC X(3).
003400     05  W005-DETAIL-EMPSALARY    PIC Z,ZZZ,ZZ9.
003500     05  W005-DETAIL-EMPSALARY-ALPHA
003600                     REDEFINES W005-DETAIL-EMPSALARY
003700                                  PIC X(9).
003800 01  W005-HEADER-LINE1.
003900     05  FILLER                   PIC X(3)  VALUE SPACES.
004000     05  FILLER                   PIC X(8)  VALUE 'EMPLOYEE'.
004100     05  FILLER                   PIC X(34) VALUE SPACES.
004200     05  FILLER                   PIC X(5)  VALUE 'DEPT.'.
004300 01  W005-HEADER-LINE2.
004400     05  FILLER                   PIC X(4)  VALUE SPACES.
004500     05  FILLER                   PIC X(6)  VALUE 'NUMBER'.
004600     05  FILLER                   PIC X(8)  VALUE SPACES.
004700     05  FILLER                   PIC X(4)  VALUE 'NAME'.
004800     05  FILLER                   PIC X(22) VALUE SPACES.
004900     05  FILLER                   PIC X(6)  VALUE 'NUMBER'.
005000     05  FILLER                   PIC X(4)  VALUE SPACES.
005100     05  FILLER                   PIC X(6)  VALUE 'SALARY'.
005200     EXEC SQL
005300         INCLUDE SQLCA
005400     END-EXEC.
005500     EXEC SQL
005600         INCLUDE EMPTABDL
005700     END-EXEC.
```

**Figure 12.9**  Program listing: multiple-row selection.

**3.** Lines 005200 to 005400 generate the communication area data block shown in Figure 10.1 on page 62.

**4.** Lines 005500 to 005700 include the DCLGEN output shown in Figure 12.1.

**5.** Lines 005900 to 006600 implement the DECLARE statement that specifies the cursor name (EMPCSR), the columns selected, and usually also the WHERE

```
005800 PROCEDURE DIVISION.
005900     EXEC SQL
006000         DECLARE EMPCSR CURSOR FOR
006100             SELECT EMPNO,
006200                    EMPNAME,
006300                    EMPDEPT,
006400                    EMPSALARY
006500               FROM XLIM.EMPTABLE
006600     END-EXEC.
006700     EXEC SQL
006800         OPEN EMPCSR
006900     END-EXEC.
007000     OPEN OUTPUT PRINT-OUTPUT.
007100     MOVE SPACES  TO  W005-DETAIL-LINE.
007200     PERFORM C100-FETCH-ONE-ROW.
007300     PERFORM C020-PROCESS-ALL-ROWS
007400         UNTIL W005-NO-MORE-ROWS.
007500     EXEC SQL
007600         CLOSE EMPCSR
007700     END-EXEC.
007800     CLOSE PRINT-OUTPUT.
007900     DISPLAY '*** END OF JOB PROG1207' UPON SYSOUT.
008000     GOBACK.
008100 C020-PROCESS-ALL-ROWS.
008200     IF SQLCODE  EQUAL TO   ZERO
008300         PERFORM C040-LAYOUT-ROW-COLUMNS
008400         PERFORM C060-PRINT-DETAIL-LINE.
008500     PERFORM C100-FETCH-ONE-ROW.
008600 C040-LAYOUT-ROW-COLUMNS.
008700     MOVE EMPNO      TO  W005-DETAIL-EMPNO.
008800     MOVE EMPNAME    TO  W005-DETAIL-EMPNAME.
008900     MOVE EMPDEPT    TO  W005-DETAIL-EMPDEPT.
009000     IF W005-SALARY-INDV  LESS THAN   ZERO
009100         MOVE 'NULLS ***' TO  W005-DETAIL-EMPSALARY-ALPHA
009200     ELSE MOVE EMPSALARY    TO  W005-DETAIL-EMPSALARY.
009300 C060-PRINT-DETAIL-LINE.
009400     IF W005-LINE-COUNT  GREATER THAN  W005-LINE-LIMIT
009500         PERFORM C080-PRINT-HEADER-LINES.
009600     WRITE PRINT-RECORD FROM W005-DETAIL-LINE
009700             AFTER ADVANCING W005-LINE-SKIP LINES.
009800     ADD  1  TO  W005-LINE-COUNT.
009900     MOVE 1  TO  W005-LINE-SKIP.
010000 C080-PRINT-HEADER-LINES.
010100     WRITE PRINT-RECORD FROM W005-HEADER-LINE1
010200                         AFTER ADVANCING PAGE.
010300     WRITE PRINT-RECORD FROM W005-HEADER-LINE2
010400                         AFTER ADVANCING 2 LINES.
010500     MOVE  ZEROS  TO  W005-LINE-COUNT.
010600     MOVE  2      TO  W005-LINE-SKIP.
010700 C100-FETCH-ONE-ROW.
010800     EXEC SQL
010900         FETCH EMPCSR
011000             INTO :EMPNO,
011100                  :EMPNAME,
011200                  :EMPDEPT,
011300                  :EMPSALARY:W005-SALARY-INDV
011400     END-EXEC.
011500     IF SQLCODE = 100
011600         MOVE 'Y' TO  W005-END-OF-ROWS.
```

**Figure 12.9**   *(continued)*

clause as the row selection criteria. However, there is no WHERE clause and we are in fact selecting all rows.

**6.** Lines 006700 to 006900 open the cursor.

7. Lines 007000 to 007400 are the housekeeping routines and the Main-loop control.

8. Lines 007500 to 007700 close the cursor.

9. Lines 008100 to 008500 control the processing of each row as we select each one in sequence.

  a. Lines 008200 to 008400 perform the laying out and printing of the columns if there was a row selected; if not (negative SQLCODE value), there is nothing to process.

  b. Line 008500 fetches another row from the table.

10. Lines 008600 to 009200 lay out the row columns (from line 008200, only if a row was selected).

  a. Lines 008700 to 008900 simply lay out the columns that will never contain nulls (see Fig. 12.1).

  b. Lines 009000 to 009200 check the W005-SALARY-INDV indicator variable to see if DB2 detected nulls (a negative value for W005-SALARY-INDV) for the EMPSALARY column (see line 011300). If so, we display the 'NULLS***' literal instead of the actual salary value.

11. Lines 009300 to 010600 are the routines to print the detail and header lines.

12. Lines 010800 to 011400 implement the statement to fetch one row. Note that we use the INTO clause, which brings the row selected into the data-names specified in the SELECT clause of the DECLARE cursor-name statement (lines 005900 to 006600).

  a. Lines 011000 to 011300 specify the Cobol data-names that will get the value from the row. Note that each is prefixed with a colon.

  b. Line 011300 shows the use of the indicator variable for a column that may contain nulls; if not specified, there is an SQLCODE error if the column does contain nulls.

13. Lines 011500 to 011600 set the "end of row" switch once SQLCODE becomes 100.

**2.6.2 Additional JCL statements to be included.**    Assuming that we use "EDITJCL" in entry 3 of Figure 11.5 in Chapter 11, DB2 will generate most of the JCL statements for us. However, we still have to include those for the batch files.

For our program example, these are for the display output and print file. Thus:

```
//SYSOUT  DD  SYSOUT=*
//LSTOUT  DD  SYSOUT=*
```

**2.6.3 Output listing: multiple-row selection.**    Figure 12.10 is the output of the program in Figure 12.9.

Note the following:

1. All seven rows are printed out.

2. For employee numbers '00010' and '00170', we print out 'NULLS***' in the salary column.

```
EMPLOYEE                                    DEPT.
 NUMBER           NAME                      NUMBER    SALARY

 00005       BAKER, C.                       003      30,000
 00008       RANDOLPH, R.                    005      29,000
 00010       RICHARDS, M.                    002      NULLS ***
 00015       DAVIS, L.                       006      30,000
 00150       ELLIOT, T.                      005      31,000
 00170       RABINOVITZ, M.                  003      NULLS ***
 00190       LEE, R.                         005      30,000
```

**Figure 12.10**   Output listing: multiple-row selection.

# 13

# UPInsdoe/DELETE Using the Current Cursor

## 1 UPDATE USING THE CURRENT CURSOR

*In most types of update, the programmer first selects a row before it is updated. This is because the row is printed out, verified, and so on before the update is made.* This type of processing uses many of the same cursor processing techniques shown in the previous chapter.

### 1.1 The DECLARE Statement

Since we are processing using a cursor, we must also code the DECLARE statement in the same manner as in Chapter 12. The format is:

```
EXEC SQL
    DECLARE cursor-name CURSOR FOR
        SELECT EMPNAME, EMPSALARY
        FROM XLIM.EMPTABLE
        WHERE EMPDEPT = :SEARCH-DEPT
        FOR UPDATE OF column-name1,
                      column-name2, . . . . .
END-EXEC.
```

The "FOR UPDATE OF . . . ." clause is an additional clause that specifies the column(s) to be updated. Note also that this statement merely defines the criteria for update; the actual update is done only with the UPDATE statement.

## 1.2 The OPEN/FETCH/CLOSE Cursor-name Statements

The "OPEN|FETCH|CLOSE cursor-name" statements function as explained in Chapter 12.

## 1.3 UPDATE/DELETE Using the Current Cursor

The UPDATE or DELETE statement, as with any other UPDATE or DELETE statement, may update or delete multiple rows if we use the "WHERE column-name = :data-name" clause and there are multiple rows with the value of data-name. We have seen this using SPUFI and we explain its use in programs in Chapter 14.

In this chapter, we deal with the common situation where we update/delete the same row we have just fetched, without updating/deleting any other row. This is done by coding the "WHERE CURRENT OF cursor-name" clause instead of the "WHERE column-name = :date-name" clause in the UPDATE/DELETE statement that updates or deletes the row brought into the program by the last FETCH statement.

### 1.3.1 Format of UPDATE using the current cursor.    The format of the statement is:

```
EXEC SQL
    UPDATE XLIM.EMPTABLE
        SET column1 = . . . .
            column2 = . . . .
    WHERE CURRENT OF cursor-name
END-EXEC.
```

The "WHERE CURRENT OF cursor-name" clause causes the update of the very same row brought into the program by the last FETCH statement.

### 1.3.2 UPDATE/DELETE using cursor and temporary cursor table.    In Chapter 12 we explained the difference between the conceptual and physical temporary cursor tables. When using the "WHERE CURRENT OF cursor-name" clause, only the conceptual temporary cursor table may be used. This means that the program must use the original table.

*If DB2 creates a physical temporary cursor table, then the "WHERE CURRENT OF cursor-name" clause cannot be used,* since the cursor would then be pointing to the former and not the original table. In this case, to update/delete rows in the original table, we have to use instead the "WHERE column-name = :data-name" clause. However, we cannot then guarantee that we are updating/deleting only one row (as we could if we update/delete using the current cursor), unless the value of column-name is unique.

## 1.4 SQLCODE for UPDATE/DELETE/INSERT Operations

Unlike the SELECT operation, we have to consider many values of SQLCODE in the program.

### 1.4.1 SQLCODE of 0 or 100.
As before, if SQLCODE is 0, then the statement had no error.

In an update/delete not using the WHERE CURRENT OF clause, this means there was no row updated or deleted. In an update using the WHERE CURRENT OF clause, this means that the corresponding FETCH statement resulted in the "end of rows" condition.

### 1.4.2 SQLCODE on too many pages for user.
Many installations limit the number of pages that a given user can own (lock) at any given time. This is the NUMLKTS parameter specified when DB2 is installed.

#### 1.4.2.1 SQLCODE if LOCKSIZE PAGE.
If the user has chosen LOCKSIZE PAGE and DB2 has determined that a user already owns lock on the maximum number of pages, it will not execute any further statement that will cause another page lock and instead generates an SQLCODE value of $-904$. The user should then either issue a COMMIT statement (SYNCPOINT command in CICS/VS) or ROLLBACK Statement (SYNCPOINT ROLLBACK command in CICS/VS) before continuing.

In most cases, the programmer should just commit, then continue, using the current input that caused the SQLCODE value of $-904$.

Note that this problem occurs only for page locking, if we choose LOCKSIZE PAGE, not LOCKSIZE ANY. In most situations, LOCKSIZE ANY is actually preferred, since we then allow DB2 to choose the lock size, usually starting with page lock, but with the possibility of promoting it to table space lock.

#### 1.4.2.2 SQLCODE if LOCKSIZE ANY.
On the other hand, if the user has chosen LOCKSIZE ANY and DB2 has determined that a user already owns lock on the maximum number of pages, on the next statement that would otherwise cause another page lock, it will simply promote the page lock to table space lock, with the user not even aware of it. Processing continues as usual.

Thus, in this case, there is no special SQLCODE to watch out for.

### 1.4.3 SQLCODE on deadlock condition.
The deadlock condition is very well known, even in nondatabase applications. In DB2, it can occur even more frequently, because there are so many users, each one having locks on pages scattered all over the table space and needing other pages that other users may have locks on.

Figure 13.1 shows the deadlock condition.

Depending on certain conditions, DB2 will choose which user will be sacrificed, and which one allowed to continue. For the program to be sacrificed, it will either automatically have its pages rolled back, with an SQLCODE of $-911$, or have an SQLCODE of $-913$, with the program itself doing the roll back.

PROGRAM ACTION                                                    DB2 ACTION

1. User A executes update on page1.     Update is allowed and DB2 notes that user
                                        A now has EXCLUSIVE lock on page1.

2. ..... (other activities).

3. User B executes update on page3.     Update is allowed and DB2 notes that user
                                        B now has EXCLUSIVE lock on page3.

4. ..... (other activities).

5. User A executes update on page6.     Update is allowed and DB2 notes that user
                                        A now has EXCLUSIVE lock on page6.

6. ..... (other activities).

7. User B executes update on page9.     Update is allowed and DB2 notes that user
                                        B now has EXCLUSIVE lock on page9.

8. ..... (other activities).

9. User A executes update on page3.     Update is disallowed since DB2 notes that
                                        user B has EXCLUSIVE lock on page3.  User
                                        A waits for the lock to be released.

10. ..... (other activities).

11. User B executes update on page1.    Update is disallowed since DB2 notes that
                                        user A has EXCLUSIVE lock on page1.  User
                                        B waits for the lock to be released.

12. This is a deadlock condition.       Both user A and B cannot continue until
                                        locks are released.  DB2 sacrifices
                                        either user A or user B.

**Figure 13.1**   The deadlock condition.

## 1.5 Program Logic: Update the Current Row

The logic is Figure 13.2.
     Note the following:

1. The DECLARE cursor-name statement identifies the cursor, the columns read
   into the program, the search criteria, and the FOR UPDATE OF clause that
   specifies the column(s) that are updated.
   a. The column names in the SELECT clause (EMPNAME, EMPSALARY) are
      those of the table. These are the columns we want read into the program.
   b. Any column name in the FOR UPDATE OF clause does not have to appear
      as a column name in the SELECT clause. Those in the former are simply
      the columns we want updated.
      1) If the column to be updated is simply replaced with new values indepen-
         dent of the current value, then there is no need to bring it first into the
         program for the update to be successful (although we may still have to
         do so for some other reasons, such as wanting to print the original
         value).

```
WORKING-STORAGE SECTION.
 . . . . .
    EXEC SQL
        INCLUDE member-name (from DCLGEN output)
    END-EXEC
    EXEC SQL
        INCLUDE SQLCA
    END-EXEC.
 . . . . .
PROCEDURE DIVISION.
 . . . . .
    EXEC SQL
        DECLARE cursor-name CURSOR FOR
            SELECT EMPNAME, EMPSALARY
                FROM XLIM.EMPTABLE
                WHERE EMPDEPT = :SEARCH-DEPT
                FOR UPDATE OF EMPSALARY
    END-EXEC.
*** Here set SEARCH-DEPT to the correct value ***
    EXEC SQL
        OPEN cursor-name
    END-EXEC.
    PERFORM C200-PROCESS-EMPLOYEE-ROW UNTIL SQLCODE = 100.
    EXEC SQL
        CLOSE cursor-name
    END-EXEC.
 . . . . .
C200-PROCESS-EMPLOYEE-ROW.
    EXEC SQL
        FETCH cursor-name
            INTO :EMPNAME, :EMPSALARY
    END-EXEC.
    IF  update condition is met
        move updating data to the columns to be updated
        EXEC SQL
            UPDATE XLIM.EMPTABLE
                SET EMPSALARY = :EMPSALARY
                WHERE CURRENT OF cursor-name
        END-EXEC.
```

**Figure 13.2**    Program logic: update the current row.

  2) If the original value of the column to be updated is needed in the pro-
     gram, then we have to bring it to the program before the update is made.

**2.** We set the Cobol data-name SEARCH-DEPT to the correct value. It will be
   used as the search criteria.

**3.** As part of the Main-loop routine, we open the cursor, process all rows, then
   close the cursor.

**4.** The FETCH statement has the INTO clause, which brings the data for the
   selected columns into the Cobol data-names specified. Thus, :EMPNAME and
   :EMPSALARY are the Cobol data-names generated by DCLGEN (see
   Fig. 12.1).

## 1.6 Program Example: Update the Current Row

We now run a program that reads "card images" from an in-line card file, which
contains department numbers and salary updating information. For each department
number read, we process corresponding departments in the XLIM.EMPTABLE
Employee table. For each row belonging to a department, we increase the salary

| | Employee<br>Number<br>(EMPNO) | Name<br>(EMPNAME) | Department<br>Number<br>(EMPDEPT) | Salary<br>(EMPSALARY) |
|---|---|---|---|---|
| 1. | 00005 | BAKER, C. | 003 | 0030000 |
| 2. | 00008 | RANDOLPH, R. | 005 | 0029000 |
| 3. | 00010 | RICHARDS, M. | 002 | Nulls |
| 4. | 00015 | DAVIS, L. | 006 | 0030000 |
| 5. | 00150 | ELLIOT, T. | 005 | 0031000 |
| 6. | 00170 | RABINOVITZ, M. | 003 | Nulls |
| 7. | 00190 | LEE, R. | 005 | 0030000 |

**Figure 13.3**  Current data on the XLIM.EMPTABLE employee table.

column by the salary updating information in the "card", except when the original salary value is NULLs, where no update is done.

Figure 13.3 is the data used as input to the update.

### 1.6.1 Program listing: update the current row.

The program shown in Figure 13.4 shows that for the SQLCODE, we only check for the "end of table" (SQLCODE 100) and deadlock conditions (SQLCODE −911 or −913). We are not concerned with the condition of number of pages going beyond the maximum allowed (SQLCODE −904) since we assume LOCKSIZE ANY.

The following apply:

1. Lines 001200 to 001800 pertain to the input file containing the deartment numbers and salary updating information.

2. Lines 002000 to 002600 are the various data-names such as counters and switches.

3. Lines 002700 to 002900 generate the communication area data block shown in Figure 10.1.

4. Lines 003000 to 003200 include the DCLGEN ouptut shown in Figure 12.1.

5. Lines 003400 to 004000 implement the DECLARE statement that specifies the cursor name (EMPCSR), the columns selected, the row selection criteria, and the clause 'FOR UPDATE OF "column-name"'.

   a. Line 003600 specifies the column we want read into the program. Note that in general, this column(s) is naturally the one(s) we want to process (say to print) in the program. It does not have to be the same column(s) that is updated (FOR UPDATE OF clause), although in our example it just happens to be the same.

   b. Line 003900 specifies the column to be updated.

6. Lines 004100 to 004700 are the housekeeping routines and the Main-loop control.

7. Lines 004800 to 007100 process each department read in the in-line card file.

   a. Lines 004900 to 005100 open the cursor.

   b. Line 005200 fetches the first row belonging to the department.

   c. Lines 005300 to 005500 display an error message if the department does not have a row in the table.

```
000100 IDENTIFICATION DIVISION.
000200 PROGRAM-ID. PROG1304.
000300**********************************************************************
000400*                                                                    *
000500*    1. THIS PROGRAM UPDATES ROWS VIA A CURSOR.                       *
000600*                                                                    *
000700**********************************************************************
000800 ENVIRONMENT DIVISION.
000900 CONFIGURATION SECTION.
001000 INPUT-OUTPUT SECTION.
001100 FILE-CONTROL.
001200      SELECT UPDATE-INPUT  ASSIGN TO  CARDIN.
001300 DATA DIVISION.
001400 FILE SECTION.
001500 FD  UPDATE-INPUT
001600      BLOCK CONTAINS 0 RECORDS
001700      LABEL RECORDS OMITTED.
001800 01  UPDATE-RECORD              PIC X(80).
001900 WORKING-STORAGE SECTION.
002000 01  W005-SALARY-INDV          PIC S9(4) COMP.
002100 01  W005-UPDATE-RECORD.
002200      05  W005-EMPDEPT          PIC X(3).
002300      05  FILLER                PIC XX.
002400      05  W005-SALARY-INCREASE  PIC S9(5).
002500 01  W005-END-OF-UPDATE-RECORDS PIC X VALUE 'N'.
002600      88  W005-NO-MORE-UPDATES       VALUE 'Y'.
002700      EXEC SQL
002800          INCLUDE SQLCA
002900      END-EXEC.
003000      EXEC SQL
003100          INCLUDE EMPTABDL
003200      END-EXEC.
003300 PROCEDURE DIVISION.
003400      EXEC SQL
003500          DECLARE EMPCSR CURSOR FOR
003600              SELECT EMPSALARY
003700                FROM XLIM.EMPTABLE
003800               WHERE EMPDEPT = :W005-EMPDEPT
003900               FOR UPDATE OF EMPSALARY
004000      END-EXEC.
004100      OPEN INPUT UPDATE-INPUT.
004200      PERFORM C120-READ-UPDATE-INPUT.
004300      PERFORM C020-PROCESS-EACH-DEPT
004400          UNTIL W005-NO-MORE-UPDATES.
004500      CLOSE UPDATE-INPUT.
004600      DISPLAY '*** END OF JOB PROG1304' UPON SYSOUT.
004700      GOBACK.
```

**Figure 13.4**   Program listing: update the current row.

   d. Line 005600 processes all rows otherwise.

   e. Lines 005700 to 006400 display an error message if the department processing is interrupted by DB2 due to a deadlock condition. If SQLCODE is −913, we do a rollback.

   f. Lines 006500 to 007000 execute after processing all rows for a department (SQLCODE now 100). It closes the cursor, then does a commit. Here, we commit for every department updated (that is, multiple rows belonging to the department).

**8.** Lines 007200 to 007500 process departments with at least one row until there are no more rows or DB2 determines a deadlock.

**9.** Lines 007700 to 007800 show that if the salary value contains NULLs (from line 009100), we don't do any update.

```
004800 C020-PROCESS-EACH-DEPT.
004900     EXEC SQL
005000         OPEN EMPCSR
005100     END-EXEC.
005200     PERFORM C100-FETCH-ONE-ROW.
005300     IF SQLCODE = 100
005400         DISPLAY 'PROG1304 -- DEPT ' W005-EMPDEPT
005500                     ' HAS NO TABLE DATA' UPON SYSOUT
005600     ELSE PERFORM C040-PROCESS-GOOD-DEPT.
005700     IF SQLCODE = (-911 OR -913)
005800         DISPLAY 'PROG1304 -- DEPT ' W005-EMPDEPT
005900                     ' BYPASSED DUE TO DEADLOCK' UPON SYSOUT
006000         IF SQLCODE = -913
006100             EXEC SQL
006200                 ROLLBACK
006300             END-EXEC
006400         ELSE NEXT SENTENCE
006500     ELSE EXEC SQL
006600             CLOSE EMPCSR
006700         END-EXEC
006800         EXEC SQL
006900             COMMIT
007000         END-EXEC.
007100     PERFORM C120-READ-UPDATE-INPUT.
007200 C040-PROCESS-GOOD-DEPT.
007300     PERFORM C060-PROCESS-EACH-DEPT-ROW UNTIL SQLCODE = 100
007400                                 OR SQLCODE = -911
007500                                 OR SQLCODE = -913.
007600 C060-PROCESS-EACH-DEPT-ROW.
007700     IF W005-SALARY-INDV  LESS THAN  ZERO
007800         NEXT SENTENCE
007900     ELSE PERFORM C080-UPDATE-THIS-ROW.
008000     PERFORM C100-FETCH-ONE-ROW.
008100 C080-UPDATE-THIS-ROW.
008200     ADD W005-SALARY-INCREASE TO EMPSALARY.
008300     EXEC SQL
008400         UPDATE XLIM.EMPTABLE
008500             SET EMPSALARY = :EMPSALARY
008600             WHERE CURRENT OF EMPCSR
008700     END-EXEC.
008800 C100-FETCH-ONE-ROW.
008900     EXEC SQL
009000         FETCH EMPCSR
009100             INTO :EMPSALARY:W005-SALARY-INDV
009200     END-EXEC.
009300 C120-READ-UPDATE-INPUT.
009400     READ UPDATE-INPUT INTO W005-UPDATE-RECORD
009500         AT END, MOVE  'Y'  TO W005-END-OF-UPDATE-RECORDS.
```

**Figure 13.4**   (*continued*)

10. Lines 008100 to 008700 execute the update.
    a. Line 008200 adds the salary updating data from the in-line card file to the original salary data from the row (from line 009100).
    b. Lines 008300 to 008700 update the current row (from line 008600). The column updated is EMPSALARY, which picks up the data in the data-name EMPSALARY (now containing the correct value).
11. Lines 008800 to 009200 fetch one row from the table. The EMPSALARY data from the row (from line 003600) are brought to the data-name EMPSALARY.
12. Lines 009300 to 009500 read the in-line card file for the department number and the corresponding salary updating information.

**1.6.2 Additional JCL statements to be included.**    Assuming that we use "EDITJCL" in entry 3 of Figure 11.5 in Chapter 11, DB2 will generate most of the JCL statements for us. However, we still have to include those for the batch files.

In this program example, these are:

```
//SYSOUT  DD  SYSOUT=*
//CARDIN  DD  *
005 00500
003 00700
/*
```

**1.6.3 Updated table: update the current row.**    Figure 13.5 is the updated table from the program in Figure 13.4.

| | Employee Number (EMPNO) | Name (EMPNAME) | Department Number (EMPDEPT) | Salary (EMPSALARY) |
|---|---|---|---|---|
| 1. | 00005 | BAKER, C. | 003 | 0030700 |
| 2. | 00008 | RANDOLPH, R. | 005 | 0029500 |
| 3. | 00010 | RICHARDS, M. | 002 | Nulls |
| 4. | 00015 | DAVIS, L. | 006 | 0030000 |
| 5. | 00150 | ELLIOT, T. | 005 | 0031500 |
| 6. | 00170 | RABINOVITZ, M. | 003 | Nulls |
| 7. | 00190 | LEE, R. | 005 | 0030500 |

**Figure 13.5**    Updated table: update the current row.

Note that for department numbers '005' and '003', we update all rows, except those with salary value of NULLs. All rows for department numbers '005' and '003' had their salary value updated by $500 and $700 respectively.

## 1.7 COMMIT Using Cursor Processing

Lines 006800 to 007000 in Figure 13.4 committed update changes. In our example, we did this for all rows belonging to a department. The programmer should issue the COMMIT statement when feasible to optimize concurrency. However, when processing using cursors, any commit or rollback automatically closes all open cursors.

**1.7.1 COMMIT with multiple open/close cursor.**    If there are too many updates between the OPEN/CLOSE of a single cursor, the program may be holding on to too many pages, with the ensuing problems of lower concurrency and deadlock potential. To avoid this problem, the programmer may be forced to commit changes even before he or she is finished with the temporary cursor table. This of course automatically closes the cursor.

If the program now opens another cursor, the DECLARE statement would still generate the same temporary cursor table and we would be processing what we processed before. However, the programmer may actually be able to continue normal processing (that is, access the correct row when we continue) by using the "trick" shown in the next section.

*This "trick" requires the rows to be in sequence.* If the search criteria (WHERE clause) specifies a clustered index, then the rows are always in sequence;

otherwise, the programmer has to specify the ORDER BY clause. However, in the
latter case DB2 creates a physical temporary cursor table, in which case the
"WHERE CURRENT OF cursor-name" clause cannot be used, since the cursor
would then be pointing to the former and not the original table. To update/delete
rows in the original table, we have to use instead the "WHERE column-
name = :data-name" clause. However, we cannot then guarantee that we are updat-
ing/deleting only one row (as we could if we update/delete using the current cursor),
unless the value of column-name is unique.

### *1.7.1.1. Program logic: COMMIT with multiple open/close cursor.*
Figure 13.6 shows the program logic.

```
WORKING-STORAGE SECTION.
    .....
    EXEC SQL
        INCLUDE SQLCA
    END-EXEC.
    EXEC SQL
        INCLUDE EMPTABDL
    END-EXEC.
PROCEDURE DIVISION.
    .....
    EXEC SQL
        DECLARE cursor-name CURSOR FOR
            SELECT EMPNO, EMPSALARY
                FROM XLIM.EMPTABLE
                WHERE EMPNO > :W005-EMPNO-UPDATED
                FOR UPDATE OF EMPSALARY
    END-EXEC.
    MOVE '00000' TO W005-EMPNO-UPDATED.
    PERFORM C020-PROCESS-ALL-ROWS UNTIL W005-NO-MORE-ROWS.
    GOBACK.
C020-PROCESS-ALL-ROWS.
    MOVE ZEROS TO W005-NUMBER-ROWS-UPDATED.
    EXEC SQL
        OPEN cursor-name
    END-EXEC.
    PERFORM C080-FETCH-ONE-ROW.
    PERFORM C040-PROCESS-GROUP-OF-ROWS UNTIL W005-NO-MORE-ROWS
                                  OR W005-NUMBER-ROWS-UPDATED = 3.
    EXEC SQL
        COMMIT
    END-EXEC
    EXEC SQL
        CLOSE cursor-name
    END-EXEC.
C040-PROCESS-GROUP-OF-ROWS.
    ADD W005-SALARY-INCREASE TO EMPSALARY.
    EXEC SQL
        UPDATE XLIM.EMPTABLE
            SET EMPSALARY = :EMPSALARY
            WHERE CURRENT OF cursor-name
    END-EXEC.
    ADD 1 TO W005-NUMBER-ROWS-UPDATED.
C080-FETCH-ONE-ROW.
    EXEC SQL
        FETCH cursor-name
            INTO :W005-EMPNO-UPDATED,
                 :EMPSALARY:W005-SALARY-INDV
    END-EXEC.
    IF SQLCODE = 100
        MOVE 'Y' TO W005-END-OF-ROWS.
```

**Figure 13.6**   Program logic: COMMIT with multiple open/close cursor.

The following apply:

1. The DECLARE cursor-name statement identifies the cursor, the column(s) read into the program, the search criteria, and the FOR UPDATE OF clause that specifies the column(s) that are updated.
   a. The column-names in the SELECT clause (EMPNAME, EMPSALARY) are those of the table.
   b. The column-names in the FOR UPDATE OF clause may be different from those in the SELECT clause.
   c. The WHERE clause makes sure that any OPEN cursor-name statement gets the row where the value of EMPNO is greater than the value of the data-name W005-EMPNO-UPDATED (originally set to '00000'). By putting the value of the last row fetched into W005-EMPNO-UPDATED, we can process the whole table correctly even with repeated open and close of the cursor.
2. The PROCESS-ALL-ROWS and PROCESS-GROUP-OF-ROWS paragraphs count the number of rows actually updated, then commit and close the cursor when we have reached the number we want (in this example, three rows).
3. The FETCH statement has the INTO clause, which brings the data for the selected columns into the Cobol data-names specified. The use of W005-EMPNO-UPDATED brings the employee number of the latest row fetched into this data-name.

*1.7.1.2 Program listing: COMMIT with multiple open/close cursor.* We will run a program that adds $500 to all salary columns, except when the original value is NULLs. We use Figure 13.5 as the input. The program listing is Figure 13.7.

```
000100 IDENTIFICATION DIVISION.
000200 PROGRAM-ID. PROG1307.
000300*******************************************************************
000400*                                                                 *
000500*    1. THIS PROGRAM UPDATES ROWS VIA A CURSOR.                    *
000600*                                                                 *
000700*    2. UPDATE IS VIA MULTIPLE OPEN/CLOSE OF CURSOR.               *
000800*                                                                 *
000900*******************************************************************
001000 ENVIRONMENT DIVISION.
001100 CONFIGURATION SECTION.
001200 INPUT-OUTPUT SECTION.
001300 DATA DIVISION.
001400 FILE SECTION.
001500 WORKING-STORAGE SECTION.
001600 01  W005-SALARY-INDV              PIC S9(4) COMP.
001700 01  W005-EMPNO-UPDATED            PIC X(5).
001800 01  W005-EMPNO-LOW-RANGE          PIC X(5).
001900 01  W005-NUMBER-ROWS-UPDATED      PIC S9(8) COMP.
002000 01  W005-SALARY-INCREASE          PIC S9(5) COMP-3  VALUE +500.
002100 01  W005-END-OF-ROWS              PIC X VALUE 'N'.
002200     88  W005-NO-MORE-ROWS             VALUE 'Y'.
002300     EXEC SQL
002400         INCLUDE SQLCA
002500     END-EXEC.
002600     EXEC SQL
002700         INCLUDE EMPTABDL
002800     END-EXEC.
```

**Figure 13.7**  Program listing: COMMIT with multiple open/close cursor.

```
002900 PROCEDURE DIVISION.
003000     EXEC SQL
003100         DECLARE EMPCSR CURSOR FOR
003200             SELECT EMPNO, EMPSALARY
003300                 FROM XLIM.EMPTABLE
003400                 WHERE EMPNO > :W005-EMPNO-UPDATED
003500                 FOR UPDATE OF EMPSALARY
003600     END-EXEC.
003700     MOVE '00000'  TO  W005-EMPNO-UPDATED.
003800     PERFORM C020-PROCESS-ALL-ROWS
003900                 UNTIL W005-NO-MORE-ROWS.
004000     DISPLAY '*** END OF JOB PROG1307' UPON SYSOUT.
004100     GOBACK.
004200 C020-PROCESS-ALL-ROWS.
004300     MOVE  ZEROS  TO  W005-NUMBER-ROWS-UPDATED.
004400     EXEC SQL
004500         OPEN EMPCSR
004600     END-EXEC.
004700     PERFORM C040-PROCESS-GROUP-OF-ROWS
004800                 UNTIL W005-NO-MORE-ROWS
004900                 OR SQLCODE = (-911 OR -913)
005000                 OR W005-NUMBER-ROWS-UPDATED = 3.
005100     IF SQLCODE = (-911 OR -913)
005200         DISPLAY 'PROG1307 -- EMPLOYEE ' W005-EMPNO-LOW-RANGE
005300             ' TO ' W005-EMPNO-UPDATED
005400             ' BYPASSED DUE TO DEADLOCK' UPON SYSOUT
005500         IF SQLCODE = -913
005600             EXEC SQL
005700                 ROLLBACK
005800             END-EXEC
005900         ELSE NEXT SENTENCE
006000     ELSE EXEC SQL
006100             CLOSE EMPCSR
006200         END-EXEC
006300         EXEC SQL
006400             COMMIT
006500         END-EXEC.
006600 C040-PROCESS-GROUP-OF-ROWS.
006700     PERFORM C080-FETCH-ONE-ROW.
006800     IF     SQLCODE        EQUAL TO       ZERO
006900     AND W005-SALARY-INDV   NOT LESS THAN   ZERO
007000         PERFORM C060-UPDATE-THIS-ROW.
007100 C060-UPDATE-THIS-ROW.
007200     IF W005-NUMBER-ROWS-UPDATED  EQUAL TO  ZERO
007300         MOVE W005-EMPNO-UPDATED  TO  W005-EMPNO-LOW-RANGE.
007400     ADD W005-SALARY-INCREASE TO EMPSALARY.
007500     EXEC SQL
007600         UPDATE XLIM.EMPTABLE
007700             SET EMPSALARY = :EMPSALARY
007800             WHERE CURRENT OF EMPCSR
007900     END-EXEC.
008000     ADD  1  TO  W005-NUMBER-ROWS-UPDATED.
008100 C080-FETCH-ONE-ROW.
008200     EXEC SQL
008300         FETCH EMPCSR
008400             INTO :W005-EMPNO-UPDATED,
008500                  :EMPSALARY:W005-SALARY-INDV
008600     END-EXEC.
008700     IF SQLCODE = 100
008800         MOVE 'Y' TO  W005-END-OF-ROWS.
```

**Figure 13.7**  *(continued)*

The following apply:

**1.** Lines 001600 to 002200 are the various data-names such as counters and switches.

a. Line 002000 shows the value of +500 which we will add to the salary column of all rows, except those with NULLs for values.

2. Lines 002300 to 002500 generate the communication area data block shown in Figure 10.1.

3. Lines 002600 to 002800 include the DCLGEN output shown in Figure 12.1.

4. Lines 003000 to 003600 implement the DECLARE statement that specifies the cursor name (EMPCSR), the columns selected, the row selection criteria, and the clause 'FOR UPDATE OF "column-name"'.
   a. Line 003200 specifies the column(s) we want read into the program. They do not have to be the same columns that are updated (FOR UPDATE OF clause).
   b. Line 003500 specifies the column(s) to be updated.

5. Line 003700 sets the proper value to W005-EMPNO-UPDATED. This makes sure that we initially fetch the first row in the table (from line 003400).

6. Line 004300 zeros out the update counter. We do a commit after updating three rows.

7. Lines 004700 to 005000 process each group for the three possible conditions.

8. Lines 005100 to 005900 display the range of bypassed rows if DB2 detected a deadlock.

9. Lines 006000 to 006500 do the close and commit if we have reached the end of rows or have updated three rows already.

10. Lines 006700 to 007000 show that we update only those rows where salary is not NULLs.

11. Lines 007200 to 008000 do the update.
    a. Line 007300 saves the first employee number in the group. It is used to display the range of bypassed rows if DB2 detects a deadlock (from lines 005100 to 005900).
    b. Line 007400 adds the value of +500 to the salary column.
    c. Line 008000 adds 1 to the count of updated rows.

12. Lines 008100 to 008800 fetch the row.
    a. Line 008400 is important since it places the employee number of the current row into W005-EMPNO-UPDATED. When we reopen the cursor the next time to process the next group, because of line 003400, we start at the first employee number after the last one fetched.

*1.7.1.3 Updated table: COMMIT with multiple open/close cursor.*
Figure 13.8 is the updated table from the program in Figure 13.7.

Note that all salary values from Figure 13.5 have increased by $500, except when the original value was NULLs.

*1.7.1.4 The first open: temporary cursor table.* Figure 13.9 is the group processed on the first open of the cursor. We process up to the fourth row (employee number 00015) since we do not include the row with NULLs value for salary.

|  | Employee<br>Number<br>(EMPNO) | Name<br>(EMPNAME) | Department<br>Number<br>(EMPDEPT) | Salary<br>(EMPSALARY) |
|---|---|---|---|---|
| 1. | 00005 | BAKER, C. | 003 | 0031200 |
| 2. | 00008 | RANDOLPH, R. | 005 | 0030000 |
| 3. | 00010 | RICHARDS, M. | 002 | Nulls |
| 4. | 00015 | DAVIS, L. | 006 | 0030500 |
| 5. | 00150 | ELLIOT, T. | 005 | 0032000 |
| 6. | 00170 | RABINOVITZ, M. | 003 | Nulls |
| 7. | 00190 | LEE, R. | 005 | 0031000 |

**Figure 13.8**    Updated table: COMMIT with multiple open/close cursor.

|  | Employee<br>Number<br>(EMPNO) | Salary<br>(EMPSALARY) |
|---|---|---|
| 1. | 00005 | 0030700 |
| 2. | 00008 | 0029500 |
| 3. | 00010 | Nulls |
| 4. | 00015 | 0030000 |
| 5. | 00150 | 0031500 |
| 6. | 00170 | Nulls |
| 7. | 00190 | 0030500 |

Temporary cursor table

**Figure 13.9**    Temporary cursor table. first open.

***1.7.1.5 The second open: temporary cursor table.***    Figure 13.10 is the group processed on the second open of the cursor. We process until the end of the table.

|  | Employee<br>Number<br>(EMPNO) | Salary<br>(EMPSALARY) |
|---|---|---|
| 1. | 00005 | 0030700 |
| 2. | 00008 | 0029500 |
| 3. | 00010 | Nulls |
| 4. | 00015 | 0030000 |
| 5. | 00150 | 0031500 |
| 6. | 00170 | Nulls |
| 7. | 00190 | 0030500 |

Temporary cursor table

**Figure 13.10**    Temporary cursor table. second open.

## 2 DELETE USING THE CURRENT CURSOR

*Just like that of update, in most types of delete, the programmer first selects the row before it is deleted. This is because the row is printed out, verified, and so on before the delete is made.* This type of processing uses the same cursor processing technique we saw in Section 1 of this chapter. The procedure is:

1. Code the usual DECLARE cursor statement in either the Procedure Division (preferred for better documentation), or working-storage section. Thus:

```
EXEC SQL
      DECLARE cursor-name CURSOR FOR
          SELECT EMPNAME, EMPSALARY
          FROM XLIM.EMPTABLE
          WHERE EMPDEPT = :SEARCH-DEPT
END-EXEC.
```

2. In the Procedure Division, code the DELETE statement after the corresponding FETCH statement. The format of the DELETE statement is:

```
EXEC SQL
      DELETE FROM table-name
            WHERE CURRENT OF cursor-name
END-EXEC.
```

3. As before, also code the OPEN, FETCH, and CLOSE cursor-name statements.

### 2.1 DELETE Using Cursor and Temporary Cursor Table

We explained earlier in this chapter (Section 1.3.2) that when using the "WHERE CURRENT OF current-name" clause, only the conceptual temporary cursor table may be used. This means that the program must use the original table.

*If DB2 creates a physical temporary cursor table, then the "WHERE CURRENT OF cursor-name" clause cannot be used,* since the cursor would then be pointing to the former and not the original table. In this case, to delete rows in the original table, we have to use instead the "WHERE column-name = :data-name" clause. However, we cannot then guarantee that we are deleting only one row (as we could if we delete using the current cursor), unless the value of column-name is unique.

### 2.2 Program Logic: Delete the Current Row

The program logic is Figure 13.11.
     The following apply:

1. The DECLARE cursor-name statement identifies the cursor, the columns read into the program, and the search criteria.
   a. The column-names in the SELECT clause (EMPNAME, EMPSALARY) are those of the table.
   b. The WHERE clause makes sure that any OPEN cursor-name statement gets the row where the value of EMPNO is greater than the value of the data-name W005-EMPNO-DELETED (originally set to '00000'). By putting the value of the last row fetched into W005-EMPNO-DELETED, we can process the whole table correctly even with repeated open and close of the cursor.
2. The PROCESS-ALL-ROWS and PROCESS-GROUP-OF-ROWS paragraphs count the number of rows actually deleted, then commit and close the cursor when we have reached the number we want (in this example, ten rows).

```
WORKING-STORAGE SECTION.
    .....
    EXEC SQL
        INCLUDE SQLCA
    END-EXEC.
    EXEC SQL
        INCLUDE EMPTABDL
    END-EXEC.
PROCEDURE DIVISION.
    .....
    EXEC SQL
        DECLARE cursor-name CURSOR FOR
            SELECT EMPNO, EMPSALARY
                FROM XLIM.EMPTABLE
                WHERE EMPNO > :W005-EMPNO-DELETED
    END-EXEC.
    MOVE '00000'  TO  W005-EMPNO-DELETED.
    PERFORM C020-PROCESS-ALL-ROWS UNTIL W005-NO-MORE-ROWS.
    GOBACK.
C020-PROCESS-ALL-ROWS.
    MOVE  ZEROS  TO  W005-NUMBER-ROWS-DELETED.
    EXEC SQL
        OPEN cursor-name
    END-EXEC.
    PERFORM C080-FETCH-ONE-ROW.
    PERFORM C040-PROCESS-GROUP-OF-ROWS UNTIL W005-NO-MORE-ROWS
                                    OR W005-NUMBER-ROWS-DELETED = 10.
    EXEC SQL
        COMMIT
    END-EXEC
    EXEC SQL
        CLOSE cursor-name
    END-EXEC.
C040-PROCESS-GROUP-OF-ROWS.
    EXEC SQL
        DELETE XLIM.EMPTABLE
            WHERE CURRENT OF cursor-name
    END-EXEC.
    ADD  1  TO  W005-NUMBER-ROWS-DELETED.
C080-FETCH-ONE-ROW.
    EXEC SQL
        FETCH cursor-name
            INTO :W005-EMPNO-DELETED,
                 :EMPSALARY:W005-SALARY-INDV
    END-EXEC.
    IF SQLCODE = 100
        MOVE 'Y'  TO  W005-END-OF-ROWS.
```

**Figure 13.11**  Program logic: delete the current row.

**3.** The FETCH statement has the INTO clause, which brings the data for the selected columns into the Cobol data-names specified. The use of W005-EMPNO-DELETED brings the employee number of the latest row fetched into this data-name.

### 2.3 Program Example: Delete the Current Row

We use the same data in Figure 13.8 as the input data for the delete.

**2.3.1 Program Listing: Delete the Current Row.**    We now delete all rows where the salary value is NULLs. Figure 13.12 is the program listing.

```
000100 IDENTIFICATION DIVISION.
000200 PROGRAM-ID. PROG1312.
000300*********************************************************************
000400*                                                                   *
000500*   1. THIS PROGRAM DELETES ROWS VIA A CURSOR.                      *
000600*                                                                   *
000700*   2. DELETE IS VIA MULTIPLE OPEN/CLOSE OF CURSOR.                 *
000800*                                                                   *
000900*********************************************************************
001000 ENVIRONMENT DIVISION.
001100 CONFIGURATION SECTION.
001200 INPUT-OUTPUT SECTION.
001300 DATA DIVISION.
001400 FILE SECTION.
001500 WORKING-STORAGE SECTION.
001600 01  W005-SALARY-INDV              PIC S9(4) COMP.
001700 01  W005-EMPNO-DELETED            PIC X(5).
001800 01  W005-EMPNO-LOW-RANGE          PIC X(5).
001900 01  W005-NUMBER-ROWS-DELETED      PIC S9(8) COMP.
002000 01  W005-END-OF-ROWS              PIC X VALUE 'N'.
002100     88  W005-NO-MORE-ROWS             VALUE 'Y'.
002200     EXEC SQL
002300         INCLUDE SQLCA
002400     END-EXEC.
002500     EXEC SQL
002600         INCLUDE EMPTABDL
002700     END-EXEC.
002800 PROCEDURE DIVISION.
002900     EXEC SQL
003000         DECLARE EMPCSR CURSOR FOR
003100             SELECT EMPNO, EMPSALARY
003200                 FROM XLIM.EMPTABLE
003300                 WHERE EMPNO > :W005-EMPNO-DELETED
003400     END-EXEC.
003500     MOVE '00000'  TO  W005-EMPNO-DELETED.
003600     PERFORM C020-PROCESS-ALL-ROWS
003700                         UNTIL W005-NO-MORE-ROWS.
003800     DISPLAY '*** END OF JOB PROG1312' UPON SYSOUT.
003900     GOBACK.
004000 C020-PROCESS-ALL-ROWS.
004100     MOVE ZEROS  TO  W005-NUMBER-ROWS-DELETED.
004200     EXEC SQL
004300         OPEN EMPCSR
004400     END-EXEC.
004500     PERFORM C040-PROCESS-GROUP-OF-ROWS
004600                 UNTIL W005-NO-MORE-ROWS
004700                    OR SQLCODE = (-911 OR -913)
004800                    OR W005-NUMBER-ROWS-DELETED = 10.
004900     IF SQLCODE = (-911 OR -913)
005000         DISPLAY 'PROG1312 -- EMPLOYEE ' W005-EMPNO-LOW-RANGE
005100             ' TO ' W005-EMPNO-DELETED
005200                 ' BYPASSED DUE TO DEADLOCK' UPON SYSOUT
005300         IF SQLCODE = -913
005400             EXEC SQL
005500                 ROLLBACK
005600             END-EXEC
005700         ELSE NEXT SENTENCE
005800     ELSE EXEC SQL
005900         CLOSE EMPCSR
006000         END-EXEC
006100         EXEC SQL
006200             COMMIT
006300         END-EXEC.
006400 C040-PROCESS-GROUP-OF-ROWS.
006500     PERFORM C080-FETCH-ONE-ROW.
006600     IF     SQLCODE         EQUAL TO    ZERO
006700        AND W005-SALARY-INDV LESS THAN  ZERO
006800             PERFORM C060-DELETE-THIS-ROW.
```

**Figure 13.12** Program listing: delete the current row.

```
006900 C060-DELETE-THIS-ROW.
007000     IF W005-NUMBER-ROWS-DELETED  EQUAL TO  ZERO
007100        MOVE W005-EMPNO-DELETED  TO  W005-EMPNO-LOW-RANGE.
007200     EXEC SQL
007300        DELETE XLIM.EMPTABLE
007400           WHERE CURRENT OF EMPCSR
007500     END-EXEC.
007600     ADD  1  TO  W005-NUMBER-ROWS-DELETED.
007700 C080-FETCH-ONE-ROW.
007800     EXEC SQL
007900        FETCH EMPCSR
008000           INTO :W005-EMPNO-DELETED,
008100                :EMPSALARY:W005-SALARY-INDV
008200     END-EXEC.
008300     IF SQLCODE = 100
008400        MOVE 'Y'  TO  W005-END-OF-ROWS.
```

**Figure 13.12**  (*continued*)

The following apply:

1. Lines 001600 to 002100 are the various data-names such as counters and switches.

2. Lines 002200 to 002400 generate the communication area data block shown in Figure 10.1.

3. Lines 002500 to 002700 include the DCLGEN output shown in Figure 12.1.

4. Lines 002900 to 003400 implement the DECLARE statement that specifies the cursor name (EMPCSR), the columns selected, and the row selection criteria.
   a. Line 003100 specifies the column(s) we want read into the program.

5. Line 003500 sets the proper value of W005-EMPNO-DELETED. This makes sure that we initially fetch the first row in the table (from line 003300).

6. Line 004100 zeros out the delete counter. We do a commit after deleting ten rows.

7. Lines 004500 to 004800 process each group for the three possible conditions.

8. Lines 004900 to 005700 display the range of bypassed rows if DB2 detected a deadlock.

9. Lines 005800 to 006300 do the close and commit if we have reached the end of rows or have deleted ten rows already.

10. Lines 006600 to 007600 show that we delete only those rows where salary is NULLs.
    a. Line 007100 saves the first employee number in the group. It is used to display the range of bypassed rows if DB2 detects a deadlock (from lines 004900 to 005700).
    b. Line 007600 adds 1 to the count of deleted rows.

11. Lines 007700 to 008400 fetch the row.
    a. Line 008000 is important since it places the employee number of the current row into W005-EMPNO-DELETED. When we reopen the cursor the next time to process the next group, because of line 003300, we start at the first employee number after the last one fetched.

**2.3.2 Additional JCL Statements to be included.**    Assuming that we use "EDITJCL" in entry 3 of Figure 11.5 in Chapter 11, DB2 will generate most of the JCL Statements for us. However, we still have to include additional JCL statements. In this example, this is the display output. Thus:

```
//SYSOUT  DD  SYSOUT=*
```

**2.3.3 Updated table: delete the current row.**    Figure 13.13 is the updated table from the program in Figure 13.6.

|     | Employee<br>Number<br>(EMPNO) | Name<br>(EMPNAME) | Department<br>Number<br>(EMPDEPT) | Salary<br>(EMPSALARY) |
|-----|-------------------------------|-------------------|-----------------------------------|-----------------------|
| 1.  | 00005                         | BAKER, C.         | 003                               | 0031200               |
| 2.  | 00008                         | RANDOLPH, R.      | 005                               | 0030000               |
| 3.  | 00015                         | DAVIS, L.         | 006                               | 0030500               |
| 4.  | 00150                         | ELLIOT, T.        | 005                               | 0032000               |
| 5.  | 00190                         | LEE, R.           | 005                               | 0031000               |

**Figure 13.13**   Updated table: delete the current row.

Note that we have deleted the two rows in Figure 13.8, where the salary is NULLs.

# — 14 —

# *UPDATE/DELETE/INSERT Without Using Current Cursor*

## 1 UPDATE/DELETE WITHOUT USING CURRENT CURSOR

We mentioned in the previous chapter that most update and delete operations use a cursor. However, a program may still do a noncursor update or delete in the same manner we did it in SPUFI in Chapter 9. We remember that in this case, all rows that meet the criteria (based on the WHERE clause) are updated. This is different from an update using the current cursor, where only the row we are currently processing is updated.

## 2 NONCURSOR UPDATE OF ONE OR MORE ROWS

The noncursor update using SPUFI and Cobol program are basically identical. The statement is issued at the point in the program we want the update done. The format is:

```
EXEC SQL
      UPDATE table-name
            SET column-name1 = expression1,
                column-name2 = expression2, . . . .]
                  [WHERE clause]
END-EXEC
```

The SET operand specifies the column(s) and the corresponding value(s) for the update; the WHERE clause specifies the criteria for selecting the rows to be updated and is very important because *all rows will be updated if it is missing*.

## 2.1 Current XLIM.EMPTABLE: Noncursor Update

Figure 14.1 is the input to the noncursor delete program.

| | Employee Number (EMPNO) | Name (EMPNAME) | Department Number (EMPDEPT) | Salary (EMPSALARY) |
|---|---|---|---|---|
| 1. | 00005 | BAKER, C. | 003 | 0031200 |
| 2. | 00008 | RANDOLPH, R. | 005 | 0030000 |
| 3. | 00015 | DAVIS, L. | 006 | 0030500 |
| 4. | 00150 | ELLIOT, T. | 005 | 0032000 |
| 5. | 00190 | LEE, R. | 005 | 0031000 |

**Figure 14.1**   Current XLIM.EMPTABLE: noncursor update.

## 2.2 Program Listing: Noncursor Update

For our program example, we read update cards containing both old and new department numbers. Rows which match the old department number are updated with the new department numbers. The program listing is Figure 14.2.

```
000100 IDENTIFICATION DIVISION.
000200 PROGRAM-ID. PROG1402.
000300*****************************************************************
000400*                                                               *
000500*   1. THIS PROGRAM DOES A NONCURSOR UPDATE.                    *
000600*                                                               *
000700*****************************************************************
000800 ENVIRONMENT DIVISION.
000900 CONFIGURATION SECTION.
001000 INPUT-OUTPUT SECTION.
001100 FILE-CONTROL.
001200      SELECT UPDATE-INPUT   ASSIGN TO   CARDIN.
001300 DATA DIVISION.
001400 FILE SECTION.
001500 FD  UPDATE-INPUT
001600     BLOCK CONTAINS 0 RECORDS
001700     LABEL RECORDS OMITTED.
001800 01  UPDATE-RECORD              PIC X(80).
001900 WORKING-STORAGE SECTION.
002000 01  W005-SALARY-INDV           PIC S9(4) COMP.
002100 01  W005-UPDATE-RECORD.
002200     05  W005-EMPDEPT           PIC X(3).
002300     05  FILLER                 PIC XX.
002400     05  W005-NEW-EMPDEPT       PIC X(3).
```

**Figure 14.2**   Program listing: noncursor update.

```
002500 01  W005-END-OF-UPDATE-RECORDS     PIC X VALUE 'N'.
002600     88  W005-NO-MORE-UPDATES                 VALUE 'Y'.
002700     EXEC SQL
002800         INCLUDE SQLCA
002900     END-EXEC.
003000     EXEC SQL
003100         INCLUDE EMPTABDL
003200     END-EXEC.
003300 PROCEDURE DIVISION.
003400     OPEN INPUT UPDATE-INPUT.
003500     PERFORM C040-READ-UPDATE-INPUT.
003600     PERFORM C020-PROCESS-EACH-DEPT
003700                           UNTIL W005-NO-MORE-UPDATES.
003800     CLOSE UPDATE-INPUT.
003900     DISPLAY '*** END OF JOB PROG1402' UPON SYSOUT.
004000     GOBACK.
004100 C020-PROCESS-EACH-DEPT.
004200     EXEC SQL
004300         UPDATE XLIM.EMPTABLE
004400             SET EMPDEPT = :W005-NEW-EMPDEPT
004500             WHERE EMPDEPT = :W005-EMPDEPT
004600     END-EXEC.
004700     IF SQLCODE = 0
004800         EXEC SQL
004900             COMMIT
005000         END-EXEC
005100     ELSE IF SQLCODE = 100
005200             DISPLAY 'PROG1402 -- DEPT ' W005-EMPDEPT
005300                     ' HAS NO TABLE DATA' UPON SYSOUT
005400     ELSE IF SQLCODE = (-911 OR -913)
005500         DISPLAY 'PROG1402 -- DEPT ' W005-EMPDEPT
005600                     ' BYPASSED DUE TO DEADLOCK' UPON SYSOUT
005700         IF SQLCODE = -913
005800             EXEC SQL
005900                 ROLLBACK
006000             END-EXEC.
006100     PERFORM C040-READ-UPDATE-INPUT.
006200 C040-READ-UPDATE-INPUT.
006300     READ UPDATE-INPUT INTO W005-UPDATE-RECORD
006400         AT END, MOVE  'Y'  TO W005-END-OF-UPDATE-RECORDS.
```

**Figure 14.2**   (*continued*)

The following apply:

1. Lines 001100 to 001800 describe the input file containing the old and new department numbers.

2. Lines 002000 to 002600 are the various data-names such as counters and switches.

3. Lines 002700 to 002900 generate the communication area data block shown in Figure 10.1.

4. Lines 003000 to 003200 include the DCLGEN output shown in Figure 12.1.

5. Lines 003400 to 004000 are the housekeeping routines, including the Main-loop routine.

6. Lines 004100 to 006000 process each department read from the in-line card file.

   a. Lines 004200 to 004600 update all rows with the same department number as that read from the card.

    b. Lines 004700 to 005000 commit the deletes.

    c. Lines 005100 to 005300 display an error message if the department does not have a row in the table.

    d. Lines 005400 to 006000 display an error message if the department processing is interrupted by DB2 due to a deadlock condition. IF SQLCODE is −913, we do a rollback.

  7. Lines 006200 to 006400 read the in-line card file for the department number of departments to be deleted.

## 2.3 Additional JCL Statement to Be Included

Assuming that we use "EDITJCL" in entry 3 of Figure 11.5 in Chapter 11, DB2 will generate most of the JCL statements for us. However, we still have to include those for batch files. In this example, these are for the display output and the card file. Thus:

```
//SYSOUT  DD  SYSOUT = *
//CARDIN  DD  *
003  045
005  046
/*
```

## 2.4 Output Table: Noncursor Update

Using Figure 14.1 as input, Figure 14.3 is the output of the program. Note that the original department numbers '003' and '005' have been changed to '045' and '046' respectively.

| | Employee Number (EMPNO) | Name (EMPNAME) | Department Number (EMPDEPT) | Salary (EMPSALARY) |
|---|---|---|---|---|
| 1. | 00005 | BAKER, C. | 045 | 0031200 |
| 2. | 00008 | RANDOLPH, R. | 046 | 0030000 |
| 3. | 00015 | DAVIS, L. | 006 | 0030500 |
| 4. | 00150 | ELLIOT, T. | 046 | 0032000 |
| 5. | 00190 | LEE, R. | 046 | 0031000 |

**Figure 14.3** Output table: noncursor update.

## 3 NONCURSOR DELETE

The style is similar for that of noncursor update. The format is:

```
EXEC SQL
      DELETE FROM table-name
            [WHERE clause]
END-EXEC
```

.   The WHERE clause specifies the criteria for selecting the row(s) to be deleted. Just like that of UPDATE, this clause is very important because *all rows will be deleted if it is missing*.

### 3.1 Program Listing: Noncursor Delete

For our program example, we read delete cards containing department numbers. Rows which match the department number are deleted. The input is Figure 14.3. The program listing is Figure 14.4.

The following apply:

1. Lines 001100 to 001800 describe the input file containing the department number of departments to be deleted.

2. Lines 002000 to 002400 are the various data-names such as counters and switches.

3. Lines 002500 to 002700 generate the communication area data block shown in Figure 10.1.

4. Lines 002800 to 003000 include the DCLGEN output shown in Figure 12.1.

5. Lines 003200 to 003800 are the housekeeping routines, including the Main-loop routine.

6. Lines 003900 to 005800 process each department read in the in-line card file.
   a. Lines 004000 to 004300 delete all rows with the same department number as that read from the card.
   b. Lines 004400 to 004700 commit the deletes.
   c. Lines 004800 to 005000 display an error message if the department does not have a row in the table.
   d. Lines 005100 to 005700 display an error message if the department processing is interrupted by DB2 due to a deadlock condition. If SQLCODE is −913, we do a rollback.

7. Lines 005900 to 006100 read the in-line card file for the department number of departments to be deleted.

```
000100 IDENTIFICATION DIVISION.
000200 PROGRAM-ID. PROG1404.
000300**********************************************************************
000400*                                                                    *
000500*   1. THIS PROGRAM DOES A NON-CURSOR DELETE.                         *
000600*                                                                    *
000700**********************************************************************
000800 ENVIRONMENT DIVISION.
000900 CONFIGURATION SECTION.
001000 INPUT-OUTPUT SECTION.
001100 FILE-CONTROL.
001200     SELECT DELETE-INPUT  ASSIGN TO  CARDIN.
001300 DATA DIVISION.
001400 FILE SECTION.
```

**Figure 14.4**  Program listing: noncursor delete.

```
001500 FD   DELETE-INPUT
001600      BLOCK CONTAINS 0 RECORDS
001700      LABEL RECORDS OMITTED.
001800 01   DELETE-RECORD                PIC X(80).
001900 WORKING-STORAGE SECTION.
002000 01   W005-SALARY-INDV             PIC S9(4) COMP.
002100 01   W005-DELETE-RECORD.
002200      05  W005-EMPDEPT             PIC X(3).
002300 01   W005-END-OF-DELETE-RECORDS   PIC X VALUE 'N'.
002400      88  W005-NO-MORE-DELETES         VALUE 'Y'.
002500      EXEC SQL
002600          INCLUDE SQLCA
002700      END-EXEC.
002800      EXEC SQL
002900          INCLUDE EMPTABDL
003000      END-EXEC.
003100 PROCEDURE DIVISION.
003200      OPEN INPUT DELETE-INPUT.
003300      PERFORM C040-READ-DELETE-INPUT.
003400      PERFORM C020-PROCESS-EACH-DEPT
003500                       UNTIL W005-NO-MORE-DELETES.
003600      CLOSE DELETE-INPUT.
003700      DISPLAY '*** END OF JOB PROG1404' UPON SYSOUT.
003800      GOBACK.
003900 C020-PROCESS-EACH-DEPT.
004000      EXEC SQL
004100          DELETE XLIM.EMPTABLE
004200              WHERE EMPDEPT = :W005-EMPDEPT
004300      END-EXEC.
004400      IF SQLCODE = 0
004500          EXEC SQL
004600              COMMIT
004700          END-EXEC
004800      ELSE IF SQLCODE = 100
004900              DISPLAY 'PROG1404 -- DEPT ' W005-EMPDEPT
005000                      ' HAS NO TABLE DATA' UPON SYSOUT
005100      ELSE IF SQLCODE = (-911 OR -913)
005200              DISPLAY 'PROG1404 -- DEPT ' W005-EMPDEPT
005300                      ' BYPASSED DUE TO DEADLOCK' UPON SYSOUT
005400          IF SQLCODE = -913
005500              EXEC SQL
005600                  ROLLBACK
005700              END-EXEC.
005800      PERFORM C040-READ-DELETE-INPUT.
005900 C040-READ-DELETE-INPUT.
006000      READ DELETE-INPUT INTO W005-DELETE-RECORD
006100          AT END, MOVE  'Y'  TO W005-END-OF-DELETE-RECORDS.
```

**Figure 14.4**  *(concluded)*

## 3.2 Additional JCL Statements to Be Included

Assuming that we use "EDITJCL" in entry 3 of Figure 11.5 in Chapter 11, DB2 will generate most of the JCL Statements for us. However, we still have to include those for batch files. In this example, these are for the display output and the deleting card file. Thus:

```
//SYSOUT  DD  SYSOUT=*
//CARDIN  DD  *
006
045
/*
```

### 3.3 Output Table: Noncursor Delete

Using Figure 14.3 as the input, Figure 14.5 is the output of the program. Note that department numbers '006' and '045' from Figure 14.3 have been deleted.

|   | Employee Number (EMPNO) | Name (EMPNAME) | Department Number (EMPDEPT) | Salary (EMPSALARY) |
|---|---|---|---|---|
| 1. | 00008 | RANDOLPH, R. | 046 | 0030000 |
| 2. | 00150 | ELLIOT, T. | 046 | 0032000 |
| 3. | 00190 | LEE, R. | 046 | 0031000 |

**Figure 14.5**  Output table: noncursor delete.

## 4 INSERT

The style is similar to those in Chapter 9. We can either insert a single row (as in Chapter 9, Section 1.5) or do a mass insert (as in Chapter 9, Section 1.7). The format for a single row insert is:

```
EXEC SQL
    INSERT INTO table-name
           [(column-name1, column-name2, ....]
           VALUES (string1, string2, ....,)
END-EXEC
```

The following apply:

1. The column list (column names) is optional. If it is not specified, the sequence of string values corresponds to the sequence of the columns of the table as created. If it is specified, columns and strings have a one-to-one correspondence and do not have to match the original sequence of the columns in the table.

2. If a column is missing in the column list and it was defined as "NOT NULL WITH DEFAULT" when the table was created, DB2 will generate the default value (zeroes for numeric columns, spaces for nonnumeric columns).

3. If a column is missing and it was defined as "NOT NULL", there is an error and the INSERT operation is not done.

### 4.1 Insert: No Cursor Required

Note that while there is a cursor version of update and delete, all insert operations are done without a cursor. Just like in SPUFI, we either insert one row or do a mass insert of multiple rows, where the input rows would then generally come from another table.

### 4.2 Program Listing: Insert One Row

For our program example, we insert rows based on data cards. The input is Figure 14.5. The program listing is Figure 14.6.

```
000100 IDENTIFICATION DIVISION.
000200 PROGRAM-ID. PROG1406.
000300**********************************************************************
000400*                                                                    *
000500*  1. THIS PROGRAM DOES A SINGLE ROW INSERT.                         *
000600*                                                                    *
000700**********************************************************************
000800 ENVIRONMENT DIVISION.
000900 CONFIGURATION SECTION.
001000 INPUT-OUTPUT SECTION.
001100 FILE-CONTROL.
001200     SELECT INSERT-INPUT  ASSIGN TO  CARDIN.
001300 DATA DIVISION.
001400 FILE SECTION.
001500 FD  INSERT-INPUT
001600     BLOCK CONTAINS 0 RECORDS
001700     LABEL RECORDS OMITTED.
001800 01  INSERT-RECORD                 PIC X(80).
001900 WORKING-STORAGE SECTION.
002000 01  W005-SALARY-INDV              PIC S9(4) COMP.
002100 01  W005-NUMBER-ROWS-INSERTED     PIC S(8) COMP.
002200 01  W005-INSERT-RECORD.
002300     05  W005-EMPNO                PIC X(5).
002400     05  FILLER                    PIC XX.
002500     05  W005-EMPNAME              PIC X(30).
002600     05  FILLER                    PIC XX.
002700     05  W005-EMPDEPT              PIC X(3).
002800     05  FILLER                    PIC XX.
002900     05  W005-EMPSALARY            PIC S9(7).
003000 01  W005-END-OF-INSERT-RECORDS    PIC X VALUE 'N'.
003100     88  W005-NO-MORE-INSERTS          VALUE 'Y'.
003200 01  W005-FIRST-RECORD-POINTER     PIC S9(8) COMP.
003300 01  W005-LAST-RECORD-POINTER      PIC S9(8) COMP.
003400 01  W005-RECORD-COUNT             PIC S9(8) COMP VALUE ZERO.
003500     EXEC SQL
003600         INCLUDE SQLCA
003700     END-EXEC.
003800     EXEC SQL
003900         INCLUDE EMPTABDL
004000     END-EXEC.
004100 PROCEDURE DIVISION.
004200     OPEN INPUT INSERT-INPUT.
004300     PERFORM C060-READ-INSERT-INPUT.
004400     PERFORM C020-PROCESS-ALL-ROWS
004500                         UNTIL W005-NO-MORE-INSERTS.
004600     CLOSE INSERT-INPUT.
004700     DISPLAY '*** END OF JOB PROG1406' UPON SYSOUT.
004800     GOBACK.
```

**Figure 14.6**  Program listing: insert one row.

The following apply:

1. Lines 001100 to 001800 are the input file containing the data to be inserted.
2. Lines 002000 to 003400 are the various data-names such as counters and switches.
3. Lines 003500 to 003700 generate the communication area data block shown in Figure 10.1.
4. Lines 003800 to 004000 include the DCLGEN output shown in Figure 12.1.
5. Lines 004200 to 004800 are the housekeeping routines.

```
004900 C020-PROCESS-ALL-ROWS.
005000     MOVE ZEROS  TO  W005-NUMBER-ROWS-INSERTED.
005100     MOVE W005-RECORD-COUNT  TO  W005-FIRST-RECORD-POINTER.
005200     PERFORM C040-PROCESS-ROW-GROUP
005300                       UNTIL W005-NO-MORE-INSERTS
005400                           OR W005-NUMBER-ROWS-INSERTED = 10
005500                           OR SQLCODE = (-911 OR -913).
005600     IF SQLCODE = 0
005700         EXEC SQL
005800             COMMIT
005900         END-EXEC
006000     ELSE IF SQLCODE = (-911 OR -913)
006100         COMPUTE W005-LAST-RECORD-POINTER
006200                       = W005-RECORD-COUNT - 1
006300         DISPLAY 'PROG1406 -- INPUT ' W005-FIRST-RECORD-POINTER
006400              ' TO ' W005-LAST-RECORD-POINTER
006500              ' BYPASSED DUE TO DEADLOCK' UPON SYSOUT
006600         IF SQLCODE = -913
006700             EXEC SQL
006800                 ROLLBACK
006900             END-EXEC.
007000 C040-PROCESS-ROW-GROUP.
007100     MOVE W005-EMPNO    TO  EMPNO.
007200     MOVE W005-EMPNAME  TO  EMPNAME.
007300     MOVE W005-EMPDEPT  TO  EMPDEPT.
007400     IF W005-EMPSALARY  NUMERIC
007500         MOVE 0  TO  W005-SALARY-INDV
007600         MOVE W005-EMPSALARY  TO  EMPSALARY
007700     ELSE MOVE -1  TO  W005-SALARY-INDV.
007800     EXEC SQL
007900         INSERT INTO XLIM.EMPTABLE
008000                 (EMPNO,
008100                  EMPNAME,
008200                  EMPDEPT,
008300                  EMPSALARY)
008400         VALUES (:EMPNO,
008500                 :EMPNAME,
008600                 :EMPDEPT,
008700                 :EMPSALARY:W005-SALARY-INDV)
008800     END-EXEC.
008900     IF SQLCODE = 0
009000         ADD 1  TO  W005-NUMBER-ROWS-INSERTED.
009100     PERFORM C060-READ-INSERT-INPUT.
009200 C060-READ-INSERT-INPUT.
009300     READ INSERT-INPUT INTO W005-INSERT-RECORD
009400         AT END, MOVE 'Y' TO W005-END-OF-INSERT-RECORDS.
009500     IF NOT W005-NO-MORE-INSERTS
009600         ADD 1 TO W005-RECORD-COUNT.
```

**Figure 14.6**  *(continued)*

6. Lines 004900 to 009100 process each input card.

a. Line 005100 marks the first record number in the group.

b. Lines 005200 to 005500 process the input under three conditions.

c. Lines 005600 to 005900 commit the insertions.

d. Lines 006000 to 006900 display an error message if the processing is interrupted by DB2 due to a deadlock condition. If SQLCODE is $-913$, we do a rollback.

e. Lines 007100 to 007300 lay out columns which will never have null values.

f. Lines 007400 to 007700 lay out the salary column. We indicate via an indicator variable whether or not we want DB2 to use nulls (if the input is not numeric).

g. Lines 007800 to 008800 do the insert of one row.

h. Lines 008900 to 009000 add 1 to the count on a successful insertion.

**7.** Lines 009200 to 009600 read the in-line card file for the input data.

### 4.3 Additional JCL Statements to Be Included

Assuming that we use "EDITJCL" in entry 3 of Figure 11.5 in Chapter 11, DB2 will generate most of the JCL for us. However, we still have to include those for batch files. In this example, these are for the display output and the input card file. Thus:

```
//SYSOUT  DD  SYSOUT=*
//CARDIN  DD  *
00600 LIM,P.              005  0034000
00763 WARNER,P.           006  0031500
/*
```

### 4.4 Output Table: Insert One Row

Using Figure 14.5 as the input, Figure 14.7 is the output of the program in Figure 14.6.

|     | Employee Number (EMPNO) | Name (EMPNAME) | Department Number (EMPDEPT) | Salary (EMPSALARY) |
| --- | --- | --- | --- | --- |
| 1. | 00008 | RANDOLPH, R. | 046 | 0030000 |
| 2. | 00150 | ELLIOT, T. | 046 | 0032000 |
| 3. | 00190 | LEE, R. | 046 | 0031000 |
| 4. | 00600 | LIM, P. | 005 | 0034000 |
| 5. | 00763 | WARNER, P. | 006 | 0031500 |

**Figure 14.7**   Output table: insert one row.

Note that we have added the data for employee numbers '00600' and '00763'.

### 4.5 Mass Insert from a Table

The programmer may do a mass insert of rows from current tables. The style is similar to that of Chapter 9, Sections 1.7 and 1.8.

# 15

# *Basic Logical Design: Preliminary Phase*

## 1 LOGICAL AND PHYSICAL DESIGN

Designing a database is broken up into logical and physical design.

### 1.1 Logical Design

Logical design is done first and produces the final tables and the columns they contain. It is based primarily on how the various users will be accessing information. This chapter and the next one deal with logical design.

### 1.2 Physical Design

Physical design is the actual implementation of the tables in physical devices. Here, we decide such things as which devices should hold which tables, whether they should be split into several devices, and so on. The primary goal of physical design is efficiency. Physical design is explained in Chapter 17.

## 2 PHASES IN THE LOGICAL DESIGN PROCESS

The logical design of a database is done in two phases.

1. *The preliminary phase* is explained in this chapter. In it, the user builds a rough but basically complete picture of the database. All the entities that comprise the database are identified (except maybe the subordinate entities, which should then "naturally" appear during the normalization process done in the final phase, as shown in the next chapter), including their properties and possible keys. The user produces a preliminary set of tables, subject to revision in the next phase.

2. *The final phase* is explained in the next chapter. It uses the output from the preliminary phase, cleans it up and finalizes it. It is here that the process of normalization is done to produce the final tables.

## 3 THE PRELIMINARY DESIGN PHASE

This phase is always used when designing a database from scratch. The most important activity here is the identification of the entities and their properties and how they relate to each other. From these, the tables that comprise the database are identified and laid out.

### 3.1 Identify the Entities

The entities are the first to be identified. Each one is a distinguishable object such as an employee, an inventory item, a car, infrared light, and so on. Naturally, the designer is only interested in those entities that are relevant to the database.

For each entity defined, there will be a unique row in the database that represents that entity and nothing else. *Entities of the same type (an entity type) generate one preliminary table in the database, such as a Vendor table, an Employee table, a Department table*.

#### 3.1.1 Classes of entities.    There are three classes of entities.

*3.1.1.1 Kernel entities.    Kernel entities* are independent entities. They represent the data that are the core of the database and do not depend on other entities for their existence. *The Employee entity and Department entity are kernel entities in the Personnel database*. They produce two kernel tables, the Employee table and Department table, respectively.

*It is only in a kernel table that a row does not depend for its existence on other factors. It is there simply because the corresponding entity (employee, inventory item, etc.) exists*. Thus, a department must be in the department table, even if there is currently no employee in that department.

Figure 15.1 shows the two kernel entities in the Personnel database. The primary key for the Employee table is employee number while that of the Department table is the department number.

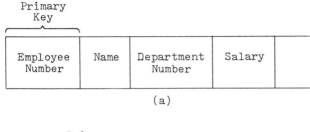

**Figure 15.1A**   The employee table: a kernel table in the personnel database.

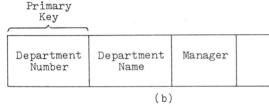

**Figure 15.1B**   The department table: a kernel table in the personnel database.

***3.1.1.2 Association entities.***    *An association entity* represents the relationship among two or more entities. *The Item-ordered entity is an association entity of the Inventory item and Purchase order entities (both of which are themselves kernel entities).* We have an item ordered only if a customer ordered it and it is an inventory item.

The Item-ordered association entity produces the Item-ordered association table. *Unlike rows in a kernel table, a row in an association table exists only if there are corresponding rows in the tables it is associated with.* One combination of "input source" rows produces one "output association" row. One row in the Purchase order table (the purchase order) and one row in the Inventory table (the item being ordered) produces one row in the Item-ordered table.

Figure 15.2 shows two kernel tables and an association table in the Purchase Order database. The association table has a primary key that is a combination of the primary keys of the two entities it is associated with.

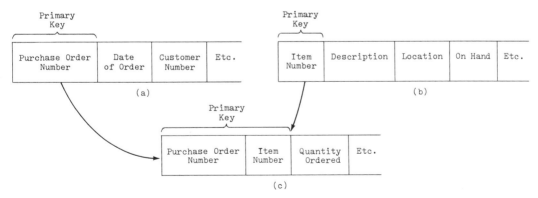

**Figure 15.2**   (a) The purchase order table: a kernel table in the purchase order database. (b) The inventory item table: a kernel table in the purchase order database. (c) The item-ordered table: an association table in the purchase order database.

A typical Item-ordered table would be Figure 15.3.

The Purchase order number is associated with the Purchase order table; the Item number is associated with the Inventory item table.

| Purchase Order Number | Item Number | Item Ordered | Etc. |
|---|---|---|---|
| 000001 | 00250 | 6 | --- |
| 000001 | 00367 | 10 | --- |
| 000001 | 02497 | 150 | --- |
| 000002 | 00367 | 15 | --- |

**Figure 15.3**  Example of an item-ordered table.

**3.1.1.3 Subordinate entities.**    *A subordinate entity* is one that qualifies or describes another entity and only exists because of it. *In a Course database, the Offering entity is a subordinate entity of the Course kernel entity.* An offering (course and section number) only exists if the course is being offered that semester; naturally, the course itself remains in the Course table. The Offering subordinate entity produces the Offering subordinate table.

*Unlike rows in a kernel table, but like rows in an association table, a row in a subordinate table exists only if there is a corresponding row in the table it is subordinated to.* However, unlike rows in an Association table, one or more rows in a subordinate table correspond to a single row in the table it is subordinated to. For instance, one or more sections are offered for a single course.

Figure 15.4 shows the Course kernel table and the Offering subordinate table in the Course database. The subordinate table has a primary key of which the major component is the primary key of the table it qualifies.

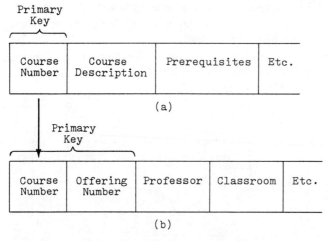

**Figure 15.4A**  The course table: a kernel table in the course database.

**Figure 15.4B**  The offering table: a subordinate table in the course database.

A typical Offering table is Figure 15.5.

## 3.2 Entity Relationships

The process in identifying the relationships of entities aids in identifying the tables (and the columns) that comprise the database.

| Course Number | Offering Number | Schedule | Etc. |
|---|---|---|---|
| 0001 | 01 | M, W | --- |
| 0001 | 02 | T, Th | --- |
| 0002 | 01 | W, F | --- |

**Figure 15.5**  Example of an offering table.

### 3.2.1 One-to-one relationship.

A one-to-one relationship exists if for one value of the former there exists only one value of the latter. An example is department number and department name. One specific department number only has one specific department name.

*A one-to-one relationship is implemented by having both data as separate columns in the same table.* In our example, the department number and department name are together in one table (if normalized to the third normal form, as shown in Chapter 16, they are in the Department table).

### 3.2.2 One-to-many/many-to-one relationship.

A one-to-many or many-to-one (which is simply the reverse of the former) relationship exists if for one value of the former there exists none, one, or many values of the latter.

A good example is the relationship between departments and employees. One specific department can have none, one, or many employees, while an employee can only belong to one department (at least, we hope so!).

*A one-to-many/many-to-one relationship is implemented by having both form separate tables.* As shown in Figure 15.6, the departments are in one table, the employees in another. However, the "many" group (department) is identified in the "one" group (employee). Thus, in the Employee table (Fig. 15.6A), the department number for that employee is identified.

*In the situation shown in Figure 15.6, the department number in the Department table is a primary key. The same department number in the Employee table is a foreign key. For the two tables, the Department table is the primary table, while the Employee table is a foreign table.*

### 3.2.3 Many-to-many relationship.

A many-to-many relationship exists if for one value of the former there exists none, one, or many values of the latter; in addition, for one value of the latter there exists none, one, or many values of the former.

A good example is the relationship between purchase orders and inventory items. One specific purchase order can have none, one, or many items, while a specific item can appear in none, one, or many purchase orders.

*A many-to-many relationship is defined with the association entity!* It is implemented as in Section 3.1.1.2.

## 3.3 Identify the Properties of Entities

An entity has certain properties. The Employee entity has the properties of employee number, name, annual salary, and so on. Each property may do any of three things:

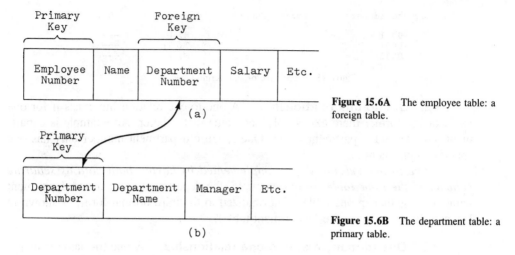

Figure 15.6A   The employee table: a foreign table.

Figure 15.6B   The department table: a primary table.

1. Identify an entity. For instance, the employee number identifies an employee.
2. Refer to another related entity. The department number of the Employee entity refers to the employee's department.
3. Stand by itself only. For instance, the salary of an employee.

*Properties are implemented as columns of the table.*

### 3.3.1 Importance in identifying the properties.

It is important to identify the properties of entities. In most cases this is basically common sense. In a Personnel database, such data as employee number, name, address, social security number, salary, and department assignment are all properties of the Employee entity. The department name is a property of the Department entity.

The designer has to be careful in putting properties where they rightly belong. For instance, the part location is a property of the Inventory entity only, not the Item-ordered entity. On the other hand, the quantity ordered is a property of the Item-ordered entity, not the Purchase order or Inventory entity.

### 3.3.2 The primary key property.

The primary key is the property that uniquely identifies the row belonging to an entity. The following apply:

1. A *kernel entity* usually has a primary key. For instance, the employee number for the employee record, the department number for the department record.
2. An *association entity* has for its primary key the primary keys of the tables it is associated with. (See Fig. 15.2.)
3. A *subordinate entity* has for its major primary key the primary key of the table it qualifies, and an additional minor primary key. (See Fig. 15.4.)

**3.3.3 DB2 and primary keys.**    Although most tables have a primary key, DB2 does not require one for a table. This is because a row can always be identified by the value of any one or more columns.

*If a user wants a primary key that works like the primary key he is used to (say, like one in a KSDS VSAM dataset, tape file, etc.), he defines an index that is both UNIQUE and CLUSTER. In addition, no one is granted UPDATE permission on the column(s) that comprise the index.*

# — 16 —

# *Basic Logical Design: Final Phase*

## 1 THE FINAL PHASE APPROACH

The final phase uses the output from the preliminary phase, cleans it up and finalizes it. A few details not detected in the latter are detected here; for instance, missing properties (columns).

Note that when an existing database is modified (especially if only to a minor degree), often the designer skips the preliminary phase and goes directly to the final phase.

### 1.1 Output of the Final Phase

The output of this phase are final, "clean" tables. Such tables are those implemented in the physical devices.

## 2 NORMALIZATION

Normalization is the tool used in the final phase. It is the process of reducing a more complex table into one or more simpler ones. With increasing normalization, data redundancy decreases.

## 2.1 The Ideal Table

Normalization to the highest degree is ideal since the whole table becomes stream-lined. We will achieve what we desire in a table, that is: *all nonkey columns belong to the key, the whole key, and nothing but the key.* Figure 16.1 shows this ideal table.

However, in the next sections, we will learn that sometimes, we will gladly forego achieving this ideal table for the sake of efficiency.

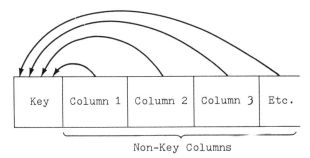

Non-Key Columns

**Figure 16.1**   The ideal table.

## 2.2 Levels of Normal Forms

In relational database theory, there are five normal forms. However, the fifth is very theoretical and has no importance to the practicing programmer. To us, therefore, the highest normal form is the fourth, which produces the simplest table.

For relational database systems, *only the first normal form is mandatory.*

## 2.3 Normalize to What Degree?

Since further normalization produces simpler tables, with a corresponding reduced amount of redundancy, the initial goal is to normalize all tables up to the fourth form, thus producing the simplest tables.

However, producing simpler and simpler tables really means breaking up a current larger table into two or more simpler ones. Because of the reduced amount of redundancy, updates are more efficient. In addition, SELECT operations may also become more efficient if most of the access involves only one of the resulting indi-vidual tables.

On the other hand, it may actually promote inefficiency if in most access the resulting simpler tables have to be joined (put back together in their original form) to get the data needed.

It is usually advisable, therefore, to *normalize to the highest form until the re-sulting inefficiency becomes intolerable.*

## 2.4 The First Normal Form

*This normal form is mandatory.* A table is in first normal form if it has only two dimensions, rows and columns. It is commonly called a "flat" table. In Figure 16.2,

Primary
Key

| Order Number | Date | (Items Ordered) | | |
|---|---|---|---|---|
| | | Item No. | Units | Price |
| 000007 | 01/19/88 | 0083005 | 50 | 006075 |
| | | 0007548 | 10 | 004600 |
| | | 0643222 | 25 | 015000 |
| 000450 | 01/21/88 | 0007548 | 15 | 004600 |
| | | 1038876 | 10 | 016400 |

**Figure 16.2**  A table violating first normal form.

we have a table with three dimensions, the third one being the repeating group, "items ordered", which varies from order to order. We have three such occurrences for order number '000007' and two such occurrences for order number '000450'.

**2.4.1 Transforming to first normal form.**    We transform Figure 16.2 to Figure 16.3 to satisfy first normal form. It is done in the following steps:

1.  Retain all nonrepeating columns in the old table. In Figure 16.2, this is the order number and the date.
2.  Put all columns belonging to a variable repeating group (and only those) into a new table. Use the key of the old table (order number) as the major key of the resulting table; use the "key" of that group (item number) as the minor key.
3.  The resulting tables are Figure 16.3A (purchase order table, with order number as the primary key) and Figure 16.3B (Item-ordered table, with item number within order number as the primary key).

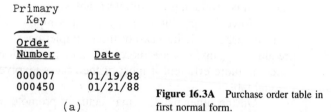

Primary
Key

| Order Number | Date |
|---|---|
| 000007 | 01/19/88 |
| 000450 | 01/21/88 |

(a)

**Figure 16.3A**  Purchase order table in first normal form.

Note that the original table now has only two rows and two columns. The rest of the data are in Figure 16.3B.

Note that Figure 16.3B uses the order number as the major key and the item number as the minor key.

## 2.5 The Second Normal Form

*This normal form is optional.* In the second normal form, a table must be of the first normal form; in addition, each column that is not part of the key must have a value

```
              Primary
                Key
        ┌─────────────────────┐
   Order
   Number      Item No.    Units      Price

   000007      0083005      50       006075
   000007      0007548      10       004600
   000007      0643222      25       015000
   000450      0007548      15       004600
   000450      1038876      10       016400
                   (b)
```

**Figure 16.3B**  Item-ordered table in first normal form.

that depends on the entire key, not just a part of the key. Thus, *violation of second normal form occurs if a column depends only on part of the key.*

Figure 16.4 shows a violation of this. The key is a combination of the item number and the warehouse number. However, the warehouse location depends only on the warehouse number, thus on part of the key, not the whole key.

```
              Primary
                Key
        ┌──────────────────┐          Dependency on part of the key
    Item        Warehouse
   Number        Number          Location              Other Columns

   00001          001         QUEENS, NEW YORK           . . . . .

   00001          002         NEW JERSEY                 . . . . .

   00001          003         WASHINGTON, DC             . . . . .

   00002          001         QUEENS, NEW YORK           . . . . .

   00002          003         WASHINGTON, DC             . . . . .
```

**Figure 16.4**  A table violating second normal form.

**2.5.1 Problems with a table not in second normal form.**    For Figure 16.4, we can see several potential problems:

1. The warehouse location is repeated in every row for an item stored in that warehouse (thus very redundant). In the first five rows, both "QUEENS, NEW YORK" and WASHINGTON, DC" appear twice.

2. If the location of the warehouse changes, every row referring to an item stored in that warehouse must be updated. There is therefore extra processing on update.

3. If a warehouse does not have any item at all, information on that warehouse (warehouse number, location) disappears from the database. "WASHINGTON, DC" disappears if it does not carry any item at all.

4. Because of redundancy, the data might become inconsistent, with different rows showing different warehouse locations for the same warehouse. DB2 however avoids this problem, since it can simultaneously update all rows with the same value in a column, via the WHERE clause. For instance, if ware-

house number '003' is moved from "WASHINGTON, DC" to "BROOKLYN, NEW YORK", we can code:

```
UPDATE table-name
    SET WAREHOUSENAME = 'BROOKLYN, NEW YORK'
        WHERE WAREHOUSENO = '002';
```

**2.5.2 Transforming to the second normal form.**    Figure 16.4 can be transformed into Figure 16.5A (Item table, with item number as the key) and Figure 16.5B (Warehouse table, with warehouse number as the key).

```
                Primary
                  Key
          ┌──────────────────┐
  Item      Warehouse
 Number      Number        Other Columns

 00001        001          . . . . .
 00001        002          . . . . .
 00001        003          . . . . .
 00002        001          . . . . .
 00002        003          . . . . .
              (a)
```

**Figure 16.5A**   Item table in second normal form.

```
              Primary
                Key
          ┌──────────────┐
          Warehouse
           Number          Location

            001            QUEENS, NEW YORK
            002            NEW JERSEY
            003            WASHINGTON, DC
              (b)
```

**Figure 16.5B**   Warehouse table in second normal form.

The following apply:

1.  All problems discussed in Section 2.5.1 are solved.
2.  The Warehouse table is streamlined. There are no duplicates.
3.  However, if we need to recreate the old table in any processing step, there is a performance penalty since we now have to join the two new tables together.

**2.5.3 Should we go to the second normal form?**   *As mentioned before, we should go to the second normal form unless any resulting decrease in performance is intolerable.*

## 2.6 The Third Normal Form

*This normal form is optional.* In the third normal form, a table must be of the second normal form; in addition, each column that is not part of the key must have a value that depends only on the key and not on some other column. Thus, *violation of third normal form occurs if a column depends on a nonkey column.*

```
Primary
  Key                                Dependency on a nonkey
~~~~~~~~~
Employee      Department      Department
Number          Number          Name            Other Columns

00005            003          Data Processing      .....

00008            005          Administration       .....

00010            002          Accounts Payable     .....

00015            006          Finance              .....

00150            005          Administration       .....

00170            003          Data Processing      .....

00190            005          Administration       .....
```

**Figure 16.6**   A table violating third normal form.

Figure 16.6 shows a violation of this. The employee number is the key but department name depends not on it but on the department number.

### 2.6.1 Problems with a table not in third normal form.   For Figure 16.6, we can see several potential problems:

1. The department name is repeated in every row. It is therefore very redundant. In the seven rows, "Data Processing" appears twice while "Administration" appears three times.
2. If the department name changes, every row referring to that department must be updated. There is therefore extra processing on update.
3. If a department currently has no employee, all department information (department number, department name) disappears from the database.
4. Because of redundancy, the data might become inconsistent, with different rows showing different department names for the same department. However, DB2 avoids this problem, since it can simultaneously update all rows with the same value in a column via the WHERE clause. For instance, if department number '005' is changed from "Administration" to "Management", we can code:

```
UPDATE table-name
    SET DEPTNAME = 'Management'
    WHERE DEPTNO = '005';
```

### 2.6.2 Transforming to the third normal form.   Figure 16.6 can be transformed into Figure 16.7A (Employee table, with employee number as the key) and Figure 16.7B (Department table, with department number as the key).

```
Primary
  Key
┌──────┴──────┐
Employee     Department
Number       Number        Other Columns

00005          003          .....
00008          005          .....
00010          002          .....
00015          006          .....
00150          005          .....
00170          003          .....
00190          005          .....
              (a)
```

**Figure 16.7A**  Employee table in third normal form.

```
          Primary
            Key
      ┌───────┴───────┐
      Department       Department
       Number           Name

         002          Accounts Payable
         003          Data Processing
         005          Administration
         006          Finance
              (b)
```

**Figure 16.7B**  Department table in third normal form.

The following apply:

1. All problems discussed in Section 2.6.1 are solved.
2. The second table (Department) is streamlined. There are no duplicates.
3. However, if we need to recreate the old table in any processing step, there is a performance penalty since we now have to join the two new tables together.

**2.6.3 Should we go to the third normal form?**   *As mentioned before, we should go to the third normal form unless any resulting decrease in performance is intolerable.*

**2.6.4 The key, the whole key, and nothing but the key.**   *For a table that meets the third normal form, all nonkey columns belong to the key, the whole key, and nothing but the key.*

## 2.7 The Fourth Normal Form

*This normal form is optional.* In the fourth normal form, a table must be of the third normal form; in addition, no row contains two or more independent multivalued facts about an entity (employee, department, and so on).

Figure 16.8 shows a violation of this. Both programming language and program development software can have multiple values for a single employee and one has nothing to do with the other. Employee number 00005, for instance, knows how to program in ANS Cobol and PL/I, and knows how to use TSO/ISPF, CMS, and LIBRARIAN.

```
                      Primary
                       Key
                  ┌──────────────────────────┐
Employee        Programming          Program
Number          Language             Development

00005           ANS Cobol           TSO/ISPF

00005           ANS Cobol           CMS

00005           ANS Cobol           LIBRARIAN

00005           PL/I                TSO/ISPF

00005           PL/I                CMS

00005           PL/I                LIBRARIAN

00010           ANS Cobol           CMS
```

**Figure 16.8**  A table violating fourth normal form.

**2.7.1 Problems with a table not in fourth normal form.**   For Figure 16.8, we can see these potential problems:

1. There is too much redundancy. Both ANS Cobol and PL/I are entered three times, one for each program development software.
2. If the programmer learns a new language, there would also be an entry for each program development software.

**2.7.2 Transforming to the fourth normal form.**   Figure 16.8 can be transformed into Figures 16.9A and 16.9B. From one original table, we now have the programming language table (with programming language within employee number as the key) and the Program Development table (with program development software within employee number as the key).

```
               Primary
                Key
           ┌──────────────────┐
Employee        Programming
Number          Language

00005           ANS Cobol
00005           PL/I
00010           ANS Cobol

              (a)
```

**Figure 16.9A**  Programming language table in fourth normal form.

```
               Primary
                Key
           ┌──────────────────┐
Employee        Program
Number          Development

00005           CMS
00005           LIBRARIAN
00005           TSO/ISPF
00010           CMS

              (b)
```

**Figure 16.9B**  Program development table in fourth normal form.

You can see that redundancy has been eliminated.

**2.7.3 Should we go to the fourth normal form?**  *As mentioned before, we should go to the fourth normal form unless any resulting decrease in performance is intolerable.*

## 2.8 The Fifth Normal Form

The fifth normal form is a theoretical concept and is not discussed in this book. It has no meaning to the practicing programmer.

# 17

# *Physical Design*

## 1 SIZE OF A DATA ROW

There is a difference between the size of the row as seen by the user and its size as implemented on disk.

### 1.1 Size of a Data Row as Seen by the User

The size of a row as seen by the user is simply the sum of the length of all columns, and nothing more. For variable-length columns, use the maximum length for the column.

### 1.2 Size of a Data Row on Disk (Physical Record)

The size of a row as implemented on disk (physical record) is based on the following:

1. Six bytes for the record prefix.
2. For each fixed-length column, the number of bytes allocated to the column.
3. For each variable-length column, the number of bytes its current value contains, plus two additional bytes overhead.

**4.** For each column that may contain nulls (whether fixed-length or variable-length), one additional byte overhead.

Note that the record prefix and overhead for columns are transparent to the application program.

## 2 NUMBER OF DATA ROWS IN A PAGE

If the physical record is 4,056 bytes or less, then it is more efficient to place it in a 4K page (BUFFERPOOL BP0, BP1, or BP2 when the table space is created); otherwise, the user must use the 32K page size.

### 2.1 Overhead in Page

Each page uses a 22-byte header and two bytes additional overhead per row as a directory pointer to the row.

### 2.2 Maximum Number of Data Rows in Page

DB2 allows a maximum of 127 rows per page.

### 2.3 Record Size that Wastes Disk Space

Because of constraints, there are two record sizes that waste disk space.

**2.3.1 Waste if physical size slightly greater than 2,035 bytes.**  Since 22 bytes of a page is always a header, the data (including the two bytes directory pointer per row) can use only up to 4,074 bytes (4,096 − 22). Divided by two, this results in 2,037 bytes. Taking off two bytes for the directory pointer, a physical record size of slightly more than 2,035 bytes wastes space since there is still only one row that can fit in a page, with the rest remaining unused.

**2.3.2 Waste if physical size smaller than 30 bytes.**  In addition, 127 (maximum number of rows per page) multiplied by 32 results in 4,064 bytes, just less than 4,074 bytes. Taking off two bytes for the directory pointer, a physical record size of less than 30 bytes also wastes space since the extra unused space can never be utilized.

## 3 COMPUTATION FOR SPACE NEEDED FOR A TABLE

Assume the following:

**1.** $R$ is the number of rows in the table.
**2.** $S$ is the average physical record size + two bytes for the directory pointer.

**3.** *P* is the percentage of free space (PCTFREE P clause when creating or modifying the table space).

**4.** FREEPAGE is 0.

The computation follows.

### 3.1 Compute for Percentage of Initially Usable Space

This is percentage of space used by DB2 in the initial mass load of rows or on reorganization.

$$\text{let } u = \text{percentage of initially usable space}$$

$$u = (100 - P)/100$$

### 3.2 Compute for Number of Data Rows Per Page

$$\text{let } a = \text{number of rows per page}$$

$$a = 4{,}074 * u/S \text{ (discard any remainder)}$$

$$(\text{if } a > 127, \text{ use } 127 \text{ as the maximum})$$

### 3.3 Compute for Number of Pages for Table

$$\text{let } tp = \text{total number of pages for table}$$

$$tp = R/a \text{ (round off to nearest integer)}$$

### 3.4 Compute for Final Total Pages for Table

$$\text{let } ftp = \text{final total pages for table}$$

$$ftp = tp + 2$$

### 3.5 Compute for Table Size in Kilobytes

$$\text{let total space} = \text{table size in kilobytes}$$

$$\text{total space} = fpt * 4$$

### 3.6 Computation Example

Assume the following:

**1.** *R* (the number of rows in the table) = 10,000

**2.** *S* = 350 (the average physical record size + two bytes for the directory pointer).

**3.** *P* [the percentage of free space (PCTFREE P clause when creating or modifying the table space)] = 20.

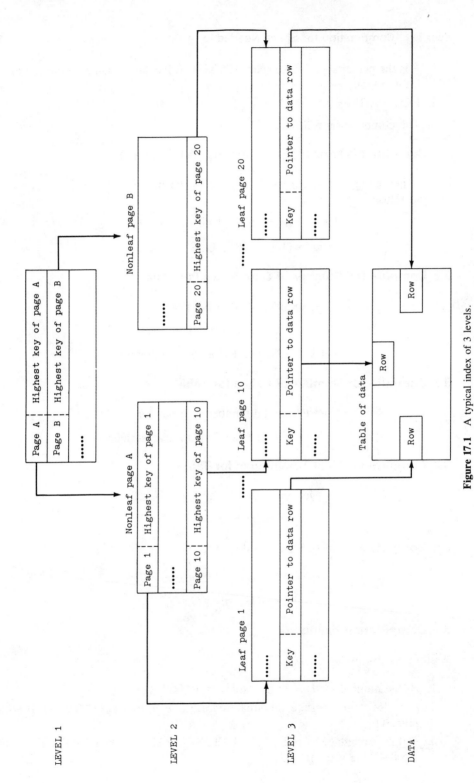

**Figure 17.1** A typical index of 3 levels.

LEVEL 1

LEVEL 2

LEVEL 3

DATA

The computation is as follows:

$$u \text{ (initially usuable space)} = (100 - 20)/100$$
$$= .8$$
$$a \text{ (number of rows per page)} = 4{,}074 * .8/350$$
$$= 9 \text{ (remainder discarded)}$$
$$tp \text{ (total number of pages for table)} = 10{,}000/9$$
$$= 1112$$
$$\text{(round off to nearest integer)}$$
$$ftp \text{ (final total pages for table)} = 1112 + 2$$
$$= 1114$$
$$\text{total space} = 1114 * 4$$
$$= 4{,}456K$$

## 4  THE PHYSICAL INDEX

An index is created if we want DB2 to maintain pointers to data in a table. It is implemented in a data set of its own, independent of the data set for the data.

### 4.1  The Leaf Pages

Figure 17.1 is a typical index of three levels. The index pages that point directly to the data are leaf pages. These are the index pages (three such pages in Fig. 17.1) of level 3. Each data row will have a corresponding entry in a leaf page.

### 4.2  Nonleaf Pages

Nonleaf pages are index pages that point to lower-level index pages, rather than data pages. The first nonleaf index page (which is level 2 in Fig. 17.1) is created if there is more than one leaf page. Each leaf and nonleaf index page will have one entry in the higher-level index page, the entry being the page number and the highest key in that page.

### 4.3  Root Page

The root page is simply the highest-level nonleaf index page. There is only one root page.

# 18

# Subquery and Union

## 1 SUBQUERY

A subquery (SELECT) is a query that is subordinated to a higher-level function (SELECT, UPDATE, DELETE). It is often called a nested query, although strictly speaking, a nested query is one where the higher-level function is also a SELECT.

While there is no limit to the level of subqueries, a five-level subquery is the practical limit, since beyond that the code is hard to interpret. In addition, performance naturally becomes progressively slower with each level.

### 1.1 Use of a Subquery

*A subquery is used if we access data from one table based on a condition found in another table.* For instance, we select employee records (data in the Employee table) for employees involved in a specific project (a condition found in the Project table). The Employee table does not contain any data on projects, but contains employee numbers whose value can be matched to the value of employee numbers in the Project table that correspond to the project we are interested in.

The selection of employee records is then the higher-level function, while the selection of employees working in a specific project is the subquery.

| Employee Number (EMPNO) | Name (EMPNAME) | Department Number (EMPDEPT) | Salary (EMPSALARY) |
|---|---|---|---|
| 00005 | BAKER, C. | 003 | 0030000 |
| 00008 | RANDOLPH, R. | 005 | 0029000 |
| 00010 | RICHARDS, M. | 002 | 0031000 |
| 00015 | DAVIS, L. | 006 | 0030000 |
| 00150 | ELLIOT, T. | 005 | 0031000 |
| 00170 | RABINOVITZ, M. | 003 | 0031000 |
| 00190 | LEE, R. | 005 | 0030000 |

**Figure 18.1**   The XLIM.EMPTABLE employee table.

| PROJNO | EMPNO |
|---|---|
| 001 | 00010 |
| 001 | 00150 |
| 001 | 00190 |
| 002 | 00005 |
| 002 | 00015 |

**Figure 18.2**   The XLIM.PROJTABLE project table.

## 1.2 Example of Subquery Using IN

Let us illustrate a subquery using Figures 18.1 and 18.2.

A subquery may of course be used either in application programs or in SPUFI or QMF. An example of one used in SPUFI implements the previous problem, where we extract the employee number and name of employees working on project number '001'. Thus:

```
SELECT XLIM.EMPTABLE.EMPNO, EMPNAME
    FROM XLIM.EMPTABLE
        WHERE XLIM.EMPTABLE.EMPNO IN
            (SELECT DISTINCT XLIM.PROJTABLE.EMPNO
            FROM XLIM.PROJTABLE
            WHERE PROJNO = '001');
```

Figure 18.3 as follows will be selected.

| Employee Number (EMPNO) | Name (EMPNAME) |
|---|---|
| 00010 | RICHARDS, M. |
| 00150 | ELLIOT, T. |
| 00190 | LEE, R. |

**Figure 18.3**   Output of subquery using IN.

Only those employees working in project number '001' are selected.

## 1.3 Rules of the Subquery

The following rules apply:

1. The subquery is implemented by having a SELECT clause subordinated to the WHERE clause of the higher-level function (which may be SELECT, UPDATE, or DELETE).

2. This subquery is enclosed in parentheses.

3. The subquery is generally done first. For instance, in the previous example, distinct employee numbers working in project number '001' are initially selected. These are employee numbers '00010', '00150', and '00190'.

4. The higher-level function follows. Because of IN, we only select employees that were themselves selected in step 3. Thus, the employee number and name of employee numbers '00010', 00150', and '00190' are generated in the final output.

## 1.4 Other Subquery Examples

The following are other subquery examples.

### 1.4.1 Subquery example using comparison operator.    Assume we have the following Manager table. We want to identify those managers whose salary is less than 30 percent above the average for all employees in the company.

Suppose the average salary is $25,000 (computed from AVG(XLIM. EMPTABLE.EMPSALARY) FROM XLIM.EMPTABLE). Therefore, we want to select manager records where the salary is less than $32,500 ($25,000 multiplied by 1.3).

Given the XLIM.MANAGERTAB Manager table in Figure 18.4:

| EMPNO | EMPNAME | EMPSALARY | |
|-------|----------|-----------|---|
| 00130 | DEAVER, S. | 0032300 | **Figure 18.4**  The XLIM.MANAGERTAB |
| 20017 | JONES, L. | 0034000 | table. |
| 30135 | NOLAN, R. | 0032100 | |

Then the statement:

```
SELECT XLIM.MANAGERTAB.EMPNO, XLIM.MANAGERTAB.EMPNAME,
       XLIM.MANAGERTAB.EMPSALARY
    FROM XLIM.MANAGERTAB
    WHERE (XLIM.MANAGERTAB.EMPSALARY / 1.3) <
          (SELECT AVG(XLIM.EMPTABLE.EMPSALARY)
           FROM XLIM.EMPTABLE);
```

Will generate the output in Figure 18.5.

| EMPNO | EMPNAME | EMPSALARY | |
|-------|----------|-----------|---|
| 00130 | DEAVER, S. | 0032300 | **Figure 18.5**  Output of subquery using |
| 30135 | NOLAN, R. | 0032100 | "<". |

The following apply:

1. Because the AVG built-in function is without the optional GROUP BY clause, the subquery returns only one value, the average employee salary for the whole Employee table.

2. The rows finally selected are those where the value of EMPSALARY in XLIM.MANAGERTAB is less than 30 percent above the average salary that the subquery generated.

### 1.4.2 Subquery example using comparison operator with ANY|ALL.
Assume that in addition to the previous example, we want to identify those managers whose salary is less than the average salary of any department.

Suppose that for the departments, the average salaries are $30,000, $32,200, and $29,000 (computed from AVG(EMPTABLE.EMPSALARY) FROM XLIM.EMPTABLE GROUP BY EMPTABLE.EMPDEPT). Therefore, we want to select manager records where the salary is less than any of the preceding amounts.

Using the same Figure 18.4 as input, with the statement:

```
SELECT XLIM.MANAGERTAB.EMPNO, XLIM.MANAGERTAB.EMPNAME,
            XLIM.MANAGERTAB.EMPSALARY
    FROM XLIM.MANAGERTAB
    WHERE XLIM.MANAGERTAB.EMPSALARY < ANY
        (SELECT AVG(XLIM.EMPTABLE.EMPSALARY)
            FROM XLIM.EMPTABLE
            GROUP BY XLIM.EMPTABLE.EMPDEPT);
```

will generate the output in Figure 18.6.

| EMPNO | EMPNAME | EMPSALARY |
|-------|---------|-----------|
| 30135 | NOLAN, R. | 0032100 |

**Figure 18.6**  Output of subquery using ANY.

The following apply:

1. Because the AVG built-in function includes the optional GROUP BY clause, the subquery returns multiple values, the average employee salary for each department in the whole Employee table.
2. ANY means the expression must compare in the specified way (in this example, less than) to any of the values the subquery returns.
3. ALL (instead of ANY) means the expression must compare in the specified way (in this example, less than) to all of the values the subquery returns.
4. The row finally selected is one where salary is $32,100, which is less than $32,200, one of the department salary subtotals. If ALL were specified, instead of ANY, there would be no row selected since $32,100 is still greater than $29,000 and $30,000, two of the department salary subtotals.

### 1.4.3 Subquery example using EXIST|NOT EXIST.
The EXIST operand specifies that if at least one row in the subquery meets the condition (that is, true), then the higher-level query is done. For instance, extract all rows from the Sales employee view (all salesmen) if the total gross sales of one (of the two sales divisions existing) is greater than $100M.

The statement would be:

```
SELECT EMPNO, EMPNAME, . . .
    FROM XLIM.SALESEMPVIEW
    WHERE EXISTS
        (SELECT SUM(SALES)
            FROM XLIM.SALESTABLE
            GROUP BY SALESDIV
            HAVING SUM(SALES) > 100000000);
```

This subquery version is useful in the referential integrity problems in Chapter 21 where we delete, update, or insert rows in one table depending on whether its key exists in another related table.

## 1.5 Subquery in UPDATE and DELETE

As mentioned before, subqueries may also be used in UPDATE and DELETE operations and in much the same way. The only difference is that the table used in the subquery is different from that updated or deleted.

In fact, the mass update of rows from one table to another is really a subquery, with the subquery selecting the rows extracted from the source table.

## 1.6 The Correlated Subquery

In most subqueries, DB2 executes the subquery once, then uses the result in the WHERE clause of the higher-level query to generate the output.

However, if we have a problem such as listing all employees whose salary is greater than the average salary in the department, this style will not work. DB2 has to calculate the average department salary for every row in the higher-level query SELECT. It really means the subquery has to be reevaluated once for each row in the higher-level query.

This is the correlated subquery and is used when there is computation and the result may be different for each row.

**1.6.1 Example of correlated subquery.** Using Figure 18.1, the following code will select rows where the salary is greater than the average salary for the department.

```
SELECT EMPNO, EMPNAME, EMPDEPT, EMPSALARY
    FROM XLIM.EMPTABLE THISROW
        WHERE EMPSALARY >
            (SELECT AVG(EMPSALARY)
                FROM XLIM.EMPTABLE
                WHERE EMPDEPT = THISROW.EMPDEPT);
```

The result is Figure 18.7.

| Employee Number (EMPNO) | Name (EMPNAME) | Department Number (EMPDEPT) | Salary (EMPSALARY) |
|---|---|---|---|
| 00010 | RICHARDS, M. | 002 | 0031000 |
| 00015 | DAVIS, L. | 006 | 0030000 |
| 00150 | ELLIOT, T. | 005 | 0031000 |
| 00170 | RABINOVITZ, M. | 003 | 0031000 |
| 00190 | LEE, R. | 005 | 0030000 |

**Figure 18.7**  Output of correlated subquery.

Note that employee numbers '00005' and '00008' are not in the output since their salary is not greater than the average for the department.

The following apply:

1. The WHERE clause in the subquery identifies the current row of the higher-level query SELECT statement.

2. Here, we select a row if the salary is greater than the average salary for the department.

3. THISROW correlates the subquery to the higher-level query. In the "WHERE EMPDEPT = THISROW.EMPDEPT" clause, "THISROW.EMPDEPT" contains the department number of the current employee row that we will include, if its salary is indeed greater than the average salary for the department (which the subquery computes).

### 1.7 Subqueries Versus Joins

Each level of subquery is a separate operation and the more levels there are, the slower is the performance. In comparison, a Join operation is only one operation.

Thus, a Join operation is usually faster than a subquery. While there are situations that can only be solved with a subquery, *a Join should be used instead of a subquery if both will produce the same results*.

**1.7.1 Join version of subquery example.**    For instance, the subquery example in Section 1.2 (extract the employee number and name of employees working on project number '001'), using the same Figures 18.1 and 18.2, can be accomplished via a join. In fact, any subquery using IN can generally be done with a join. Thus:

```
SELECT XLIM.EMPTABLE.EMPNO, EMPNAME
   FROM XLIM.EMPTABLE, XLIM.PROJTABLE
      WHERE XLIM.EMPTABLE.EMPNO = XLIM.PROJTABLE.EMPNO
                AND PROJNO = '001';
```

This also extracts the employee number and name.

Note, however, that we assume that XLIM.EMPTABLE.EMPNO is defined with a unique index. If not unique, there will be duplicates generated in the output. There is no problem with duplicates for XLIM.PROJTABLE.EMPNO, since an employee appears only once in a project.

## 2 UNION OF TABLES

The union of tables merges two or more tables vertically, with each such table initially preselected (via the SELECT statement) and generating an interim table. All interim tables must have identical column formats from left to right, which are then combined vertically. If we preselect five rows from the first table and seven rows from the second, the final output will have twelve rows, unless there are duplicates, which are eliminated during the union process.

Note that this is different from the join operation where we horizontally concatenate rows from two or more tables.

### 2.1 Union of Tables: Format

The format is:

```
SELECT statement1
    FROM table-name1
        WHERE clause
            (other clauses)
UNION
    SELECT statement2
        FROM table-name2
        WHERE clause
        (other clauses)
    [ORDER BY clause]
```

Note the following:

1. Each SELECT generates the interim table that will be part of the union process. The columns selected must match in format for all SELECTs.
2. All interim tables are later combined to produce the final table.
3. The ORDER BY clause may be coded after the last SELECT statement to specify the sequence of the output table. This clause specifies the column number (1, 2, 3, and so on), not the column name.

### 2.2 Union of Tables: Example

Assume that we want all employee numbers of all personnel in department number '005' as well as those working in project '001'. We thus do a union of the tables in Figures 18.1 and 18.2. The statement is:

```
SELECT EMPNO
    FROM XLIM.EMPTABLE
        WHERE EMPDEPT = '005'
UNION
    SELECT EMPNO
        FROM XLIM.PROJTABLE
            WHERE PROJNO = '001'
    ORDER BY 1;
```

```
Employee
 Number
(EMPNO)

 00008
 00010
 00150
 00190          Figure 18.8   Output of UNION.
```

The result is Figure 18.8.

It is in sequence by EMPNO. EMPNO values of '00008', '00150', and '00190' are generated from department number '005' of the Employee table. EMPNO values of '00010', '00150', and '00190' are generated from project number '001' of the Project table. Note that duplicates are eliminated.

# 19

# *Efficiency Techniques*

## 1 INTRODUCTION

There are two classes of efficiency techniques. One is in the coding of SQL statements, the other in the management of DB2 resources.

## 2 EFFICIENCY IN CODING SQL STATEMENTS

Often, several versions of SQL statements produce identical results to the user. However, they differ in how fast they execute. Some very important techniques follow, grouped into basic or advanced techniques.

### 2.1 Basic SQL Efficiency Techniques

Basic efficiency techniques are those that are either inherent to DB2 or else very obvious.

**2.1.1 Select Only Those Columns Needed.**   Do not use the "SELECT *" option if you do not need all columns, since DB2 is sensitive to the number of columns being selected. It is more efficient to specify the columns such as "SE-LECT EMPNO, EMPSALARY". This is especially important if there is a sort operation (which may be triggered by ORDER BY clause, and so on).

In addition, "SELECT *" may make a program obsolete if a column is later added or deleted from the original table.

### 2.1.2 Use "BETWEEN" Instead of ">= AND <=".

The phrase "WHERE data-name BETWEEN range1 AND range2" is more efficient than "WHERE data-name >= range1 AND data-name <= range2". For example:

```
WHERE EMPNO BETWEEN '0005' AND '0020'
```

is more efficient than

```
WHERE EMPNO >= '0005' AND EMPNO <= '0020'
```

### 2.1.3 Avoid Numeric Conversions.

Try to specify the same data type and precision when comparing a numeric column value to a program variable or literal. DB2 will not use an index if the variable or literal has a greater precision than the data in the column.

For instance, if salary has a precision on 0 (defined as DECIMAL(9,0), then:

```
WHERE SALARY > 30000.00
```

will not use an index even if the salary column was defined as an index and it would have been otherwise more efficient to use that index, rather than do a table space scan.

### 2.1.4 Avoid Character String Padding.

Try to use the same data length when comparing a fixed-length CHAR column value to a program variable or literal. DB2 will not use an index if the variable or literal value is longer than the column length. For instance, WHERE EMPNO = '00050b' (b is blanks) will not use an index if EMPNO was defined as CHAR(5).

### 2.1.5 Avoid the Use of LIKE Predicates Beginning With % or _.

The "%" and "_" characters specify a character string that is similar to the column value of rows to be selected. When used in the middle or at the end of a character string, they produce efficient results. An example is "WHERE data-name LIKE 'AS%ET%' ".

However, when used at the beginning of a character string, they may prevent DB2 from using any indexes that might be defined on the data-name column. This is especially critical for large tables. Thus, avoid something like '%BLE'.

### 2.1.6 Avoid an Arithmetic Expression in a Predicate.

DB2 will not use an index for a column if the column is in a predicate that includes an arithmetic expression. An example is:

```
EXEC SQL
      . . . . . .
            WHERE data-name > :variable1 + 1
END-EXEC
```

Go around this problem by recording the preceding example as:

```
ADD 1 TO :variable1
EXEC SQL
      . . . . .
            WHERE data-name > :variable1
END-EXEC
```

**2.1.7 Redundant Predicate.**    The more predicates that can be specified, the easier it is for the DB2 Optimizer to make an intelligent decision on how best to access the data. For instance, on a join operation of the Employee table and Department table, where the join is made on the department number '005', the following predicate:

```
WHERE XLIM.EMPTABLE.EMPNO = XLIM.DEPTABLE.EMPNO
    AND XLIM.EMPTABLE.EMPNO = '005'
```

is complete and will work. However, the following predicate is even better.

```
WHERE XLIM.EMPTABLE.EMPNO = XLIM.DEPTABLE.EMPNO
    AND XLIM.EMPTABLE.EMPNO = '005'
    AND XLIM.DEPTABLE.EMPNO = '005'
```

Note that the last line is redundant. However, it may potentially allow DB2 to find an even more efficient path to the data.

## 2.2 Advanced SQL Efficiency Techniques

Advanced efficiency techniques are those where the user has a choice between several alternatives, including deciding whether an index should be defined or not. A discussion on situations where DB2 will probably use or not use an existing index starts on page 169 of this chapter.

**2.2.1 SELECT: Indexonly Direct Search Is Fastest Access.**    The fastest data access is when DB2 does a single direct search of an index entry only, with no access to the data row. This happens if the column(s) selected are defined with a single index which is also the criteria for row selection (WHERE clause) that use the "=" operand. In the following example, EMPNO is defined with an index.

```
SELECT EMPNO FROM XLIM.EMPTABLE
    WHERE EMPNO = '00030';
```

This statement is used to check if employee number '00030' does exist in the table (SQLCODE would be 0). Since the data are available in index entries, DB2 does not access the data rows. If we frequently have this type of access, an index on the column would promote efficiency.

**2.2.2 SELECT: Indexonly Scan Is Fast Access.**    A relatively fast data access is when DB2 does a scan on multiple index entries, still with no access to the data row. This happens if the column(s) selected are defined with a single index which is also the criteria for row selection (WHERE clause) that does not use the "=" operand. In the following example, EMPNO is defined with an index.

```
SELECT EMPNO FROM XLIM.EMPTABLE
    WHERE EMPNO < '00030';
```

Since the data are still available in index entries, DB2 does not access the data rows. If we frequently have this type of access, an index on the column would promote efficiency. Another example of this is:

```
SELECT EMPNO FROM XLIM.EMPTABLE
    WHERE EMPNO IN ('00030', '00040', 00120');
```

**2.2.3 SELECT: Index Lookup Is Fast Access.**    Another relatively fast data access is when DB2 does a single direct search of an index entry, then searches for the corresponding data row. The situation is similar to the previous Section 2.2.1, but the select includes a column(s) that is not part of the index and is therefore available only in the data row itself. In the following example, EMPNO is defined with an index.

```
SELECT EMPNO, EMPNAME FROM XLIM.EMPTABLE
    WHERE EMPNO = '00030';
```

Unlike Section 2.2.1, EMPNAME has to be read from the data row.

**2.2.4 SELECT: Index Scan Is Slow Access.**    An index scan is one where DB2 uses an index but still accesses all data rows. It is relatively slow and is done if the search criteria (column-name in the WHERE clause) has no index, but another index is used. In the following example, EMPSALARY is not defined with an index, although EMPNO is and DB2 uses the latter.

```
SELECT EMPNO, EMPNAME FROM XLIM.EMPTABLE
    WHERE EMPSALARY < 30000;
```

**2.2.5 SELECT: Table Space Scan Is Slowest Access.**    A table space scan is done when DB2 accesses all data rows without using an index. It is the slowest type of access and is done if DB2 cannot use an index and all data rows have to be accessed. In the following example, the table has no index at all.

```
SELECT EMPNO, EMPNAME FROM XLIM.EMPTABLE
    WHERE EMPSALARY < 30000;
```

**2.2.6 Index Access Faster than Sort.**    If the data has to be in a specific sequence because it is requested by the statement (say, by the ORDER BY clause), or is deemed necessary by DB2 itself because of the operation (say, a merge scan join), DB2 will generally use an index if available. Otherwise, a sort is done. Sort is always inefficient and it uses virtual storage.

**2.2.7 Efficient SQL Statement: Join Operation.**    A join operation is done in different ways, depending on the presence of an index.

*2.2.7.1 Fastest Join: Nested Loop.*    If there are indexes for both tables on the common column used in the join, DB2 generally uses them. This is the "nested loop" join, the fastest join. No extra sort is done to execute the join, but may be done on the output if the ORDER BY clause is specified and it identifies a column(s) that has no index.

*2.2.7.2 Slowest Join: Merge Scan.*    If there are no indexes, DB2 does a "merge scan" join where there is an index scan or table space scan for all tables, with possibly an extra sort operation.

*2.2.7.3 Join With Partial Useful Index.*    If one table has an index on the common column and the other has none, it is more efficient if the left table is the one without the index. DB2 then does a table space scan for that table, but does it only once. And for each row from that table, DB2 does an index look-up on the table with the index.

Assuming that DEPTNO has an index in the Department table but has no index in the Employee table, we can code:

```
WHERE XLIM.EMPTABLE.DEPTNO = XLIM.DEPTABLE.DEPTNO
       AND XLIM.EMPTABLE.DEPTO = '003';
```

Here we specify the DEPTNO column of XLIM.EMPTABLE, which then becomes the controlling table in the join (the left table). It will do a table space scan on the table, and do a look-up on XLIM.EMPTABLE (which has the index).

The other way around (using AND XLIM.DEPTABLE.DEPTNO = '003') is inefficient. DB2 does an index look-up on XLIM.DEPTABLE (because it has the index), but for each row from it, does a table space on XLIM.EMPTABLE. As a result, the less efficient table space scan is repeated many times.

**2.2.8 Other Efficient SQL Statements.**    The following are a few more efficient techniques.

*2.2.8.1 Example Where Correlated Subquery Is Superior.*    If an index is available for a subquery, a correlated subquery using EXIST is faster than a regular subquery using IN. For example, we want to get information on employees working on projects:

```
SELECT EMPNO, EMPNAME, EMPSALARY
    FROM XLIM.EMPTABLE THISROW
        WHERE EMPNO EXISTS
            (SELECT EMPNO FROM XLIM.PROJTABLE
                WHERE THISROW.EMPNO = EMPNO);
```

If EMPNO in XLIM.PROJTABLE has an index, a single direct indexonly access is done on it per row in XLIM.EMPTABLE. The alternative, using the regular subquery with IN, is inefficient.

```
SELECT EMPNO, EMPNAME, EMPSALARY
    FROM EMPTABLE
        WHERE EMPNO IN
            (SELECT EMPNO FROM PROJTABLE);
```

Because of the syntax of IN, there is an indexonly scan on XLIM.PROJTABLE per row in XLIM.EMPTABLE. The single direct indexonly access in the previous subquery is faster.

***2.2.8.2 Union "Trick" to Utilize an Index.***    In the following statement, DB2 will not use an index even if column-name3 and column-name4 are both defined with indexes. In a compound condition, it will use an index only if the column-name is the same throughout the condition.

```
SELECT column-name1, column-name2, . . . .
    FROM XLIM.EMPTABLE
        WHERE column-name3 = 'value1'
        AND column-name4 = 'value2';
```

To have DB2 use both indexes, a trick is to place column-name3 and column-name4 in separate SELECT statements, then do a UNION on the same table. Thus:

```
SELECT column-name1, column-name2, . . . .
    FROM XLIM.EMPTABLE
        WHERE column-name3 = 'value1'
    UNION
SELECT column-name1, column-name2, . . . .
    FROM XLIM.EMPTABLE
        WHERE column-name4 = 'value2';
```

Here, DB2 will use both indexes in the two separate SELECTs and spite of the UNION and the ensuing sort operation, this "trick" will execute faster.

***2.2.8.3 If Possible, Use Join Instead of Subquery.***    This is discussed in Chapter 18, Section 1.7.

## 3 EFFICIENCY TECHNIQUES IN DB2 RESOURCE MANAGEMENT

Techniques in DB2 resource management offer greater efficiency than those for SQL statements. This is because proper resource management affects the whole installation.

Often, there has to be a trade-off in resource management, since conserving resources in one area may promote inefficiency in other areas. The user will have to choose the method where the efficiency gained is greater than the efficiency lost. Important techniques follow.

### 3.1 Optimize the Speed of the DB2 Subsystem

We accomplish this in three ways. First, we reduce the number of I/O operations by reducing the number of seeks of the disk heads to get data rows. Second, we reduce the time needed to perform I/O operations. Third, we reduce the amount of processor resources used. Examples follow.

**3.1.1 Putting rows in sequence.**    If an application reads rows in a given sequence, physically putting the rows in that sequence promotes efficiency. This is because on a succeeding read (except after reading the last row in a page), the next row requested will be on the same page. DB2 does not have to read another page (thus no further I/O) to get the next piece of data.

A good example of this type of application is a weekly payroll system. Many organizations do this for nonmanagerial employees. The employee rows are updated with the week's number of work hours, then processed once more to print the payroll checks. Since processing of the rows is best done in sequence, in a batch run with the input data sorted in the same sequence as the data rows, then a clustered index is useful.

Note that a clustered index is not helpful for applications where the next row requested is not on the same page. This is the case for most online applications where processing is random. For instance, an inquiry on available stock will use item numbers that are usually not in sequence.

As mentioned before, with a clustered index, rows are placed in sequence at the initial mass load of rows or at reorganization.

**3.1.2 Define indexes.**    If an index is defined for a column, the DB2 Optimizer will decide if such an index offers a faster access to the data. If so, it will be used instead of doing a table space scan.

*3.1.2.1 When is an index useful?*    In DB2, an index has four uses. *First, a UNIQUE index guarantees uniqueness for a column(s) value.* DB2 will not allow a duplicate value on an insert or update operation.

*Second, a UNIQUE, CLUSTER index implements a primary key.* The values for the column(s) that comprise the index are therefore unique and in physical sequence. In addition, no UPDATE permission is granted for the column(s).

*Third, a CLUSTER index is mandatory for a partitioned table space.* See the next chapter.

*Fourth, an index promotes efficiency.* While DB2 will decide for itself when to use an existing index, it will probably use one in the examples below. Assume that indexes have been defined for column-name1 and column-name2.

1. In the case "WHERE column-name1 simple-operator value", as in WHERE EMPNO > '00300';
   a. The simple operators are =, <, >, <=, >=, ⌐>, ⌐<.
   b. WHERE NOT column-name1 [<|>] value.
2. If column-name1 is in the following clauses:
   a. ORDER BY column-name1.
   b. GROUP BY column-name1.
   c. Column-name1 BETWEEN value1 AND value2.
   d. Column-name1 LIKE pattern, except when the pattern starts with a "%" or "_".
   e. DISTINCT column-name1.
3. The clause "WHERE column-name1 IN (value1, value2, . . . . .)" as in WHERE EMPNO IN ('00100', '00400').
   a. Note that this is equivalent to WHERE EMPNO = '00100' OR EMPNO = '00400';
4. If 3a above is actually coded.
   a. Thus, column-name1 is repeated with OR, and the operand is "=".
5. In a join of two or more tables using identical columns.
   a. WHERE column-name1 = column-name2 where both columns are say, department numbers, etc.

DB2 will not use an index on the following:

1. The simple operator ⌐=.
2. WHERE NOT column-name1 = value.
3. If column-name1 has a different length than the literal or data-name it is checked against.
4. If WHERE has an arithmetic expression.
   a. To have the index considered, recode the statement to do the arithmetic outside the SQL statement and use the result in it. See Section 2.1.6 in this chapter.
5. Union operations.

It goes without saying that any efficiency gained with indexes is greater for larger tables that are used in read-only access.

***3.1.2.2 Trade-off when defining indexes.*** Note that each index requires disk space in addition to the table space of the data it corresponds to. In addition, each data insertion, deletion, or update (for the latter, only if the column being changed has an index) also requires a corresponding update to the indexes, thus making data update less efficient. Unlike VSAM files, the update to indexes is automatically done even with online applications and cannot be postponed to a later time (say, an overnight reconstruction of indexes).

Note also that the presence of an index does not guarantee it will be used for an SQL statement. The DB2 Optimizer will decide, for each SQL statement, if an index offers a faster access to the data.

*3.1.2.3 Maximum number of indexes for a table.*    While there is no theoretical limit, in practice we try to define indexes only if they are useful, since each update of a row now takes that much longer. Most tables will have at most three to five indexes.

### 3.1.3 Use the RUNSTAT utility.

[Author's note: This is explained in more detail in Chapter 22.] The RUNSTAT utility collects statistics about DB2 objects (table space and/or index) and stores the information in the DB2 catalog. The information is used by the DB2 Optimizer during the BIND process to choose the most efficient path in accessing data. Without up-to-date data from RUNSTAT, an inefficient access path may be selected, resulting in unnecessary I/O operations.

Run this utility on the following:

1. After the initial mass load of rows into a table.
2. After a table is reorganized (REORG utility).
3. After a large number of insertions and deletions.

Statistics generated by RUNSTAT will be used on the next BIND operation. For applications using the table space and/or index that were previously bound, the programmer may do a rebind to reconstruct a more efficient plan.

### 3.1.4 Use the STOSPACE utility.

[Author's note: This is explained in more detail in Chapter 22.] STOSPACE also updates the DB2 catalog with actual space allocated for table spaces, indexes, and storage groups. These are also useful in tuning the database.

### 3.1.5 Use the REORG utility.

[Author's note: This is explained in more detail in Chapter 22.] One type of information provided by the RUNSTAT utility is data clustering. For a table with a large number of insertions and deletions, the information may point out the drastic spreading of data rows (especially if defined with a clustered index). The REORG utility will fix the problem and reclaim free space for new insertions.

After running REORG, the user should also run RUNSTAT, then possibly do a rebind operation for applications that use the table space and/or index.

### 3.1.6 Reduce OPEN/CLOSE operations.

DB2 recognizes table spaces and indexes (but not tables) as files and if they are frequently used, specify CLOSE NO in the CREATE|ALTER TABLESPACE and CREATE|ALTER INDEX statements. This will cause the file to be left open when not in use, avoiding the repeated open and close during the day.

If they are infrequently used, specify CLOSE YES in the CREATE|ALTER TABLESPACE and CREATE|ALTER INDEX statements. This will reduce the unnecessary allocation of virtual storage.

### 3.1.7 Allocate enough buffer pools.

The user may allocate many buffers of each buffer pool size (BP0, BP1, BP2, and BP32K). The more buffer pools there are, the more pages can be held in the buffers, increasing the odds that the page a user wants may already be in the buffer, thus saving on I/O.

## 3.2 Improve the Utilization of Disk Devices

There are five ways to do this.

### 3.2.1 Specify the proper PCTFREE parameter.

The PCTFREE parameter of the CREATE|ALTER TABLESPACE and CREATE|ALTER INDEX statements can reduce access time to a table space.

When data rows are initially loaded or a table is reorganized, PCTFREE reserves a percentage of each page as free space, to be used for the latter insertion of data. If there is no free space available, new data are inserted in another page which may be in a distant location.

For tables requiring frequent insertions, assign a value to PCTFREE greater than the default of 5 percent. For those with very few insertions, the value may be set to zero to save storage space.

### 3.2.2 Use fast devices.

Assign the most frequently used data to the faster DASD devices available. You may use a partitioned table space where the data may be split into different devices.

### 3.2.3 Specify proper primary/secondary allocations.

In general, the primary allocation (PRIQTY operand in the CREATE TABLESPACE statement) should be enough to handle the anticipated storage needs. The secondary allocation should be just enough to allow the applications to run until the data can be reorganized. When data go into the secondary allocation, it is time to reorganize.

### 3.2.4 Place large tables in partitioned table spaces.

Partitioning the table space allows the data, especially the more frequently-used ones, to be spread to different volumes. In addition, if some devices are faster than others, partitioning allows the frequently-used data to be placed in the faster devices.

In addition, a partitioned table space is semi-independent of the other partitions such that certain utilities (for instance, REORG) may process it separately without affecting the other.

**3.2.5 Use incremental image copies.**  For very large tables in which the number of pages updated is less than 1 percent, an incremental image copy may be faster than a full image copy. We are concerned with the percentage of pages having updated records. We are not concerned with the number of records updated.

The MERGECOPY utility may be used later to generate a full image copy. As a general rule, if more than 10 percent of the pages contain updated records, use full image copy.

### 3.3 Improve Virtual Storage Utilization

There are two ways to do this.

**3.3.1 Reduce the number of open data sets.**  The following are guidelines:

1. Each table space is a file and DB2 will use virtual storage for each one opened. For small tables, we conserve virtual storage by putting multiple tables per table space. Note that for tables of 250 pages or more, it is better to place each one in a separate table space.
2. Each index is a file and DB2 will also use virtual storage for each one opened (which is the case if the corresponding table is being used). Using fewer indexes conserves virtual storage.
3. Specify CLOSE YES in the CREATE TABLESPACE statement for infrequently-used tables. DB2 will reclaim virtual storage that the table space used.

**3.3.2 Reduce the use of DB2 sort (for large tables).**  DB2 sort uses virtual storage. If an index is available instead, and DB2 uses it, then it is a more efficient method.

### 3.4 Optimize Concurrency

There are five ways to do this.

**3.4.1 Specify the proper LOCKSIZE parameter.**  For a heavily-used table (say, one used in online applications), locking by page optimizes concurrency, since many users can then access data. In this case the user may specify either LOCKSIZE ANY (generally the better choice, since DB2 then starts with page locking, with a possible promotion to table space locking if needed) or LOCKSIZE PAGE in the CREATE TABLESPACE statement.

When that same table space is accessed by only one user (say, an overnight batch run to apply payments), then the program issues the "EXEC SQL LOCK TABLE . . . . END-EXEC" statement (see page 196) to override the original DB2 rules.

Note that for an infrequently-used table space, locking by table space may be more efficient since we avoid the overhead of processing multiple page locks.

**3.4.2 Use the LOCK TABLE statement when appropriate.**   This is explained in detail on page 195. In two of the three examples shown, there is an efficiency gain.

**3.4.3 Increase the number of subpages.**   The SUBPAGES parameter of the CREATE INDEX statement controls the number of subpages for the index. Using 16 allows the most number of users and may promote greater efficiency, especially for frequently-used indexes.

**3.4.4 Issue COMMIT and ROLLBACK when appropriate.**   Chapter 10 explains this in more detail. Here, let it suffice to say that when a COMMIT or ROLLBACK is issued, pages locked by users are unlocked and therefore accessible to other users.

**3.4.5 Control duration of locks on resources.**   The ACQUIRE and RELEASE parameters of the BIND process allows the user to determine when table spaces are to be locked and released.

The ACQUIRE(USE)/RELEASE(COMMIT) specification allows DB2 to lock the resource only when first used and to release it as soon as possible (at commit or rollback). This allows maximum concurrency. Note, however, that an application will have to wait in mid-run if resources are not available. ACQUIRE(ALLOCATE)/ RELEASE(DEALLOCATE) guarantees an application will not start until all resources needed are available. However, this reduces concurrency.

## 3.5 Validate During the BIND|REBIND Process

The VALIDATE option of the BIND and REBIND subcommand may specify that validity checking be deferred until execution time. This should, however, be avoided since it degrades run performance. Instead, ensure that all privileges are granted before BIND.

## 3.6 On Page Locking Use Cursor Stability, Not Repeatable Read

In Chapter 11, Figure 11.8, the BIND panel, the programmer may choose to enter CS (cursor stability) or RR (repeatable read) for the isolation level. These two have a bearing on the locking of pages on read-only operations. This is in addition to locking which results from an update operation (UPDATE, INSERT, DELETE).

Note that CS and RR are effective only if locking is by page (LOCKSIZE PAGE|ANY). The rules on CS and RR are as follows:

1. With CS, a page lock starts when a user first reads any row in a page. It ends when that user reads a row in another page. This allows greater concurrency compared to RR since locks are of shorter duration and more pages are avail-

able to more users. However, if the program later on reads the same row, it could have been modified in the meantime by another user.

2. With RR, a page lock also starts when a user first reads any row in a page. However, it ends only on the next commit point. This allows repeatable reads, which means that since nobody else can update (but can read) the locked pages, the rows can be read again with the assurance that the value will not have changed. However, this reduces concurrency and should be used only if the program really requires it.

Figure 19.1 shows the difference between cursor stability and repeatable read. Note that CS promotes a shorter lock duration.

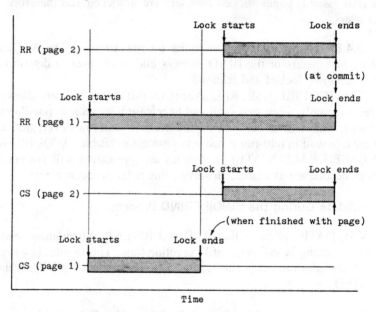

**Figure 19.1**    CS versur RR on read-only operations

# 20

# *Creating and Dropping DB2 Objects*

## 1 THE ROLE OF THE SYSTEM ADMINISTRATOR AND DBA

All DB2 objects used in SQL statements must have been previously created. All objects mentioned in this chapter, except for synonyms, this being created by a user authorized access to a table or view, are created by the system administrator or the DBA. In addition, while a view is usually created for a user (who has no access authorization to the original table) by the DBA, a user allowed access to the original tables may create a view from them.

The creation of objects is best done when system usage is slow, possibly at night so they do not take resources from the daily production jobs.

The general format of the statement is:

```
CREATE object object-name
       options
```

## 2 CREATING A STORAGE GROUP

This function is usually done by the system administrator. If the user prefers that DB2 itself manages the disk space for data, a storage group is used. Each one is a set of identical DASD volumes that will physically contain tables and indexes. For most situations, this is the better and easier choice over self-management.

One good example for self-management is if a table is quite volatile, meaning its size may increase or decrease significantly via the insertion or deletion of data. A user who manages his or her own table space and index can more easily change space allocation when needed. The user then allocates space via the VSAM DEFINE CLUSTER facility, deallocates space via DELETE CLUSTER, and adds secondary volumes for expansion via ALTER ADDVOLUMES.

### 2.1 Example of Creating a Storage Group

An example of creating a storage group is:

```
CREATE STOGROUP storagegroup-name
        VOLUMES (volume1, volume2, ...)
        VCAT [CAT1|CAT2]
        PASSWORD password;
```

The following apply:

1. Storagegroup-name is eight characters long and is the name of the storage group.
2. There is a maximum of 133 DASD volumes.
3. The VSAM ICF catalog and password (if required) are specified.
4. Each storage group will have a one-row entry in the SYSIBM.SYSSTOGROUP table in the DB2 catalog.

## 3 CREATING A DATABASE

This function is usually done by the system administrator. A specific database contains the data for an application or group of related applications. For instance, we have the Personnel database, the Accounts Receivable database, and so on.

### 3.1 Example of Creating a DataBase

An example of creating a database is:

```
CREATE DATABASE database-name
        STOGROUP storagegroup-name
        BUFFERPOOL BP1;
```

The following apply:

1. Database-name is up to eight characters long.
2. Storagegroup-name is the default storage group for the database; if none is specified, the SYSDEFLT storage group is the default. Every table space or in-

dex belonging to this database will default to this storage group, unless another one is specified when the table space or index is created.

3. DB2 has three types of 4K buffer pools: BP0, BP1, BP2. In this statement, BP1 becomes the default buffer pool (instead of BP0, which is the default if no buffer pool is specified) for tables and indexes within this database. A 32K buffer pool, BP32K, should be used only for tables where a row cannot fit in a 4K buffer pool.

4. Each database will have a one-row entry in the SYSIBM.SYSDATABASE table in the DB2 catalog.

## 4 CREATING A TABLE SPACE

This function is done by the DBA who owns the database on which this table space is a member. A table space is a VSAM ESDS that contains one or more tables.

### 4.1 Simple Versus Partitioned Table Space

The DBA and user must decide whether to have a simple or partitioned table space. In the former, one or more tables are physically implemented in one data set. In the latter, a single table is physically implemented in several data sets.

A partitioned table space is very useful for large tables. First, a load or reorganization of rows may be done selectively by partition, saving both time in doing so and leaving other partitions to be used in the meantime. Secondly, the 5 percent or 10 percent of heavily accessed rows may be placed into several faster devices, thus promoting efficiency.

While a table space may be up to 64 gigabytes long, each partition in a table space may only be as large as 4 gigabytes.

### 4.2 Creating a Simple Table Space

The format is:

```
CREATE TABLESPACE tablespace-name
      IN database-name
      USING storagegroup-name
      PRIQTY n
      SECQTY m
      ERASE [YES|NO]
      LOCKSIZE [TABLESPACE|PAGE|ANY]
      BUFFERPOOL BP1
      CLOSE [YES|NO]
      DSETPASS password
      PCTFREE p
      FREEPAGE n;
```

The following apply:

1. Tablespace-name is up to eight characters long.
2. Database-name specifies the database where this table space belongs; if none is specified, the default DSNDB04 database is used.
3. Storagegroup-name is the storage group used. If none is specified, the default storage group for the database is used (see Section 3).
4. The primary space allocation is nK; the secondary is mK. The primary allocation should be enough to minimize any access to data in the secondary allocation. There is a maximum of 64 gigabytes for a table space.
5. ERASE YES means the space is set to hexadecimal zeroes when the table space is dropped (released for reuse by DB2), and is primarily a security measure; the default is NO, in which case the data are potentially accessible, although not through DB2.
6. LOCKSIZE informs DB2 whether locking is specifically by TABLESPACE, by PAGE of a table, or ANY.
   a. If TABLESPACE, all tables and indexes in that table space are locked by a user from the time the table space is acquired either at allocation, ACQUIRE(ALLOCATE) at BIND, or at first use, ACQUIRE(USE) at BIND. Other users may or may not be able to access data in that table space depending on the lock mode. The lock is released either at deallocation, RELEASE(DEALLOCATE) at BIND, or at commit or rollback, RELEASE(COMMIT) at BIND. Locking by table space is useful only for table spaces that have a low level of concurrency or when you want to avoid the classical deadlock problem, as explained later.
   b. If PAGE, only pages that contain rows accessed by a user are locked, leaving other pages available to other users. Locking by page is useful for tables that have a high level of concurrency.
      1) If a user attempts to lock to more pages than the maximum allowed (NUMLKTS parameter for the DB2 subsystem), DB2 will not execute the statement and instead generates an SQLCODE value of $-904$. The user should then either issue a COMMIT (SYNCPOINT in CICS/VS) or ROLLBACK (SYNCPOINT ROLLBACK in CICS/VS) before it continues.
      2) In addition, the classical deadlock problem occurs if one user who has a lock on page A tries to access data on page B, which is locked to another user who is in turn trying to access data on page A. Both cannot continue and DB2 will sacrifice one user (generally the one with the smaller number of locks) by automatically doing a rollback, then issuing an SQLCODE of $-911$ or issuing an SQLCODE of $-913$, with the program doing the rollback itself or terminating the execution.
   c. If ANY, DB2 decides on the locking starting off with PAGE locking. If the user attempts to lock to more pages than the maximum allowed

(NUMLKTS parameter for the DB2 subsystem), DB2 will escalate the locking to TABLESPACE.

7. BUFFERPOOL has the same use as that for creating the database, and will override the latter specification if they are different. Again, we should choose a 4K buffer pool size (BP0, BP1, BP2) if the data row can fit in it. For table space defined with indexes, the buffer pool for the table space might be different from that of the index so there is less contention for buffer pool between the two.

8. CLOSE YES informs DB2 to close the table space when no longer in use and is the default; NO may be more efficient for a table accessed by many users since repeated open and close operations are avoided.

9. DSETPASS is the password.

10. PCTFREE p states that p percent of every page is left free at initial load or reorganization to absorb future insertions. The default is 5 percent. A volatile table may have a larger p value, say 20 percent, 30 percent, and so on.

11. FREEPAGE n specifies that after every n pages during initial load or reorganization, a completely blank page is generated for future insertions. PCTFREE is more useful than FREEPAGE and this option is generally left at the default of 0, unless the row length is such that only one row can fit in a page. At no instance should this be 16 or greater in an MVS/XA system, since this is the number of pages prefetched in certain situations.

12. Each table space will have a one-row entry in the SYSIBM.TABLESPACE table in the DB2 catalog.

## 4.3 Creating a Partitioned Table Space

The format is:

```
CREATE TABLESPACE tablespace-name
     IN database-name
     USING storagegroup-name1
     PRIQTY n1
     SECQTY m1
     ERASE [YES|NO]
     NUMPARTS a
(PART 1 USING storagegroup-name2
 PRIQTY n2
 SECQTY m2
 PART 2 USING storagegroup-name3
 PRIQTY n3
 SECQTY m3
 PART 3 . . . .)
     LOCKSIZE [TABLESPACE|PAGE|ANY]
     BUFFERPOOL BP1
     CLOSE [YES|NO]
     DSETPASS password
     PCTFREE p
     FREEPAGE n;
```

Most operands work the same way as for the simple table space. In addition, the following apply:

1. Storagegroup-name1 is the default for the table space. It and its primary and secondary allocations will be used for any partition that is not specified (no PART specification).
2. NUMPARTS a specifies that there are a partitions, which is from 1 to 16.
3. A part (such as PART 1) may specify that it is implemented in a specific storage group, not the default storage group. This has its own primary and secondary space allocation.
4. PART 2 is specified for the second partition.
5. PART 3 or other partitions (if any), if not specified, will use the default as per storage group, allocation, and so on.

*Note that a partitioned table space must have a corresponding clustered index, which will specify how the rows are distributed in the various partitions.* See Section 7.3 for an example.

### 4.4 Number of Tables In a Table Space

The decision of whether to place only one table or multiple tables in a table space depends largely on the size of the table. An exception is a partitioned table space, which by definition has only one logical table in the table space.

**4.4.1 One Table in Table Space.**    Locking cannot be done by table, only by table space or page within a table. Therefore, if a user, because of processing needs, locks a table space, all tables within that table space are locked, even those not currently used by that user. This causes a problem for the users of the other tables in that table space who will find it harder to access data from them.

In general (see also the following Section 4.4.2), putting only one table in a table space is the better choice. An added reason for its use is that data reorganization (more critical for a clustered index) and data recovery are done by table space, not by table. For a partitioned table space (which by definition is one table in a table space), both data reorganization and recovery may even be done by partition. In general, a table with 250 pages or more is best placed in a table space of its own.

**4.4.2 Multiple tables in a table space.**    On the other hand, a table with 20 pages or less is considered a small table and many such related tables may be placed together in a single table space. There is a saving of virtual storage since there is then only one table space that is opened, and each one requires 1.75K of virtual storage. In addition, the LOAD utility can place related rows in such table into a single page, thus making certain operations such as join more efficient.

## 5 CREATING TABLES

This function is done by the DBA who owns the database on which this table is a member. All tables must be created first before they can be used in SQL statements (SELECT, UPDATE, and so on). This is normally done by the database administrator (DBA). The format is:

```
CREATE TABLE table-name
        (column-name1 data-type(length)
        [NULL|NOT NULL[WITH DEFAULT]]
        FIELDPROC module1, . . . . .
        column-namen data-type(length)
        [NULL|NOT NULL[WITH DEFAULT]]
        FIELDPROC module2)
        EDITPROC module3
        VALIDPROC module4
        IN tablespace-name;
```

The following apply:

1. Table-name is of the format [owner-userid.]table-description, table-description being such names as EMPTABLE and DEPTABLE (up to 18 characters long). If the owner-userid is specified, then it is the owner of the table; else DB2 uses the TSO-userid of the table creator as the owner. In general though, the DBA specifies the owner-userid.

2. All columns-names are identified, from left to right and each one can have 18 characters. Each column entry is separated from the others by a comma, and together they are enclosed within parentheses.

3. The data types and length are:
   a. CHAR(n). Character of n bytes.
   b. VARCHAR(n). Variable-length character of n bytes maximum. This varies the length of the column in the physical device only but will take on the maximum length when used in the program. This option should be used only if the maximum length is at least 18 bytes and there is a large variation of length from row to row (say, 20 bytes). Otherwise, CHAR (which does not require any buffer-to-physical device conversion) is more efficient. Note that each column defined as VARCHAR carries a two-byte length prefix in the physical device.
   c. SMALLINT. Halfword binary integer. Value of $-32768$ to $+32767$.
   d. INTEGER. Fullword binary integer. Value of $-2,147,483,648$ to $2,147,483,647$.
   e. DECIMAL(p, s). Packed decimal of p digits; s digits after the decimal point, 15 digits maximum.
   f. GRAPHIC(n). Fixed length of double-byte characters of n characters.
   g. FLOAT. A floating point number of 64 bits.

4. The default for a column is NULL. During an INSERT operation, DB2 may accept the row even without any data for that column. A column that can contain a NULL value has a one-byte prefix in physical storage which contains X'00' for a column value of nulls and X'FF' otherwise. If it is also VARCHAR, then it will further have the two-byte prefix in front of the extra byte.

   a. If defined as NOT NULL (say, for the record key), the field must have data on every insert operation.

   b. If defined as NOT NULL WITH DEFAULT, DB2 inserts default values if no value is provided during an INSERT operation. It is zeroes for numeric data and spaces for nonnumeric. For VARCHAR, the empty string is the default.

5. EDITPROC, VALIDPROC, and FIELDPROC are explained in the section on table exit routines.

6. IN identifies the table space to which the table belongs.

7. Each table will have a one-row entry in the SYSIBM.SYSTABLES table in the DB2 catalog.

8. Each column will have a one-row entry in the SYSIBM.SYSCOLUMNS table in the DB2 catalog.

### 5.1 The Table Owner

The owner-userid or the TSO-userid (if the former is not specified) is the owner of the table. He or she has complete authorization on use of the table (INSERT, UPDATE, and so on) and may also grant authorization for access to others (see Granting Authorization in the next chapter).

### 5.2 Significance of NULL/NOT NULL WITH DEFAULT

The columns and their default values (if any) have some bearing on how a row may be processed. The designer must therefore be very careful about whether NULL or NOT NULL WITH DEFAULT is defined for a column.

   **5.2.1 Example #1: NULL more appropriate.** If NULL is defined for a numeric column, any row with a NULL value will not be included in the computation when using the column in the built-in function. We can see this when using AVG(EMPSALARY) in Figure 20.1.

| Employee Number (EMPNO) | Name (EMPNAME) | Department Number (EMPDEPT) | Salary (EMPSALARY) |
|---|---|---|---|
| 00008 | RANDOLPH, R. | 005 | 0029000 |
| 00150 | ELLIOT, T. | 005 | NULL |
| 00190 | LEE, R. | 005 | 0030000 |

**Figure 20.1**   Table example: NULL more appropriate

The value of AVG(EMPSALARY) is 0029500 (59000/2), which is what we want. The row with the NULL value is not used in the computation.

On the other hand, if NOT NULL WITH DEFAULT had been specified for salary, the second row would have defaulted to zeroes and the average salary would then be 0019667 as rounded (59000/3).

### 5.2.2 Example #2: NOT NULL WITH DEFAULT more appropriate.    In the following example, NOT NULL WITH DEFAULT is more appropriate. Assume that in Figure 20.2, the country code column is defined as NOT NULL WITH DEFAULT. For the third row (student named CRUZ, W.), the data reverted to spaces.

| Student number | Name | Country code |
|---|---|---|
| 1200045 | JONES, S. | 01 |
| 1400036 | DAVIS, R. | 25 |
| 3860994 | CRUZ, W. | (spaces) |
| 5049927 | CHOU, M. | 30 |

**Figure 20.2**  Table example: NOT NULL WITH DEFAULT more appropriate

We can see how this style is appropriate when we join this table with Figure 20.3 to determine the country to which students belong to.

| Country code | Country |
|---|---|
| (spaces) | UNKNOWN |
| 01 | UNITED STATES |
| 02 | CANADA |
| 03 | MEXICO |
| 25 | ENGLAND |
| 30 | CHINA |

**Figure 20.3**  Country table with space in a column

Note that the first row has the country code set to spaces with the country name of 'UNKNOWN'.

Now we do the join of Figures 20.2 and 20.3. We code (in pseudocode):

```
SELECT STUDENTNO, STUDENTNAME, COUNTRY
       FROM Student-table, Country-table
       WHERE the country code are equal;
```

The result is Figure 20.4.

| Student number | Name | Country |
|---|---|---|
| 1200045 | JONES, S. | UNITED STATES |
| 1400036 | DAVIS, R. | ENGLAND |
| 3860994 | CRUZ, W. | UNKNOWN |
| 5049927 | CHOU, M. | CHINA |

**Figure 20.4**  Output of join using NULL input

Note that all students are shown, showing "UNKNOWN" for the country of the student named "CRUZ W.". This resulted because the join was done on the value of spaces. We will therefore always generate "UNKNOWN" for the country if the country code is indeed unknown.

Note that if the country code was defined as NULL, then on the join operation the row for "CRUZ W." will not appear. This is because the join operation will not include any null value on the column(s) used in the join.

## 5.3 Table Exit Routines

The user may optionally specify Assembler program modules when creating a table. These routines are automatically called into execution on certain operations of the table.

The user must use these options only with the full knowledge of the system programmer. The Assembler modules are considered extensions of DB2 and are capable of manipulating registers and certain DB2 data blocks. The Assembler modules have an impact on DB2 and MVS operations and may therefore cause problems if used improperly. These modules cannot issue SQL statements.

### 5.3.1 The VALIDPROC operand.

The VALIDPROC operand of CREATE (or ALTER) TABLE specifies the routine that will take control before a row is inserted, updated, or deleted. This routine is primarily used to validate the data, indicating to DB2 whether or not the row should be inserted, updated, or deleted. If VALIDPROC NULL is specified in the ALTER TABLE statement, the routine is dropped.

### 5.3.2 The EDITPROC operand.

The EDITPROC operand of CREATE TABLE specifies a routine that will take control every time a row is selected, inserted, or updated. This routine is primarily used to compress or encrypt the data. This routine cannot be dropped once specified.

### 5.3.3 The FIELDPROC operand.

The FIELDPROC operand of CREATE (or ALTER) TABLE specifies for each nonnumeric column not defined as "NOT NULL WITH DEFAULT" a routine for every type of access to the column. This routine is primarily used to encode or decode column data, as for instance when sorting data in collating sequence different from the standard IBM collating sequence. Just like EDITPROC, this routine cannot be dropped once specified.

## 6 CREATE A VIEW

Although a view is also generally created by the DBA (who owns the database on which this view is a member) for a user who has no authorized access to the original table(s), it may also be created by a user authorized to access the table(s) used in that view. The format is:

```
CREATE VIEW view-name
    [(column-name1, column-name2, . . . .)]
        AS SELECT statement;
```

The following apply:

1. The format of view-name is the same as table-name in Section 5. Thus, the view also has an owner.

**2.** The optional column names list is coded if you want column names different from those originally defined for the table. They will have to be coded if the view contains columns that are the result of a computed function, including the DB2 built-in function (SUM, AVG, and so on).

**3.** The SELECT statement is the same one used to retrieve data. It defines the table(s), column(s), and row(s) that will form the view.

**4.** Defining a view only generates a definition in the DB2 catalog. Unlike a table, a view has no physical representation on disk.

**5.** Each view will have a one-row entry in the SYSIBM.SYSVIEWS table in the DB2 catalog.

# 7 CREATE AN INDEX

This function is done by the DBA who owns the database on which this index is a member. We create one for a table, never for a view. The reasons for creating an index were discussed in the previous chapter.

Each index entry carries the key plus a four-byte pointer for every row it points to. The pointer consists of a page number and the row within the page.

## 7.1 When Are Index Entries Created?

If the table has data, index entries are generated after the index is created. An exception is a clustered index, where index entries are generated only on a mass load or when the table space is reorganized.

In addition, any insert, delete, or update (where the index is changed) will modify the index.

## 7.2 Format of CREATE INDEX for Table in Simple Table Space

The format is:

```
CREATE [UNIQUE] INDEX index-name
    ON table-name (column-name1 [ASC|DESC], . . .
                    column-namen [ASC|DESC])
    USING STOGROUP storage-group-name1
    SUBPAGES x
    CLUSTER
    BUFFERPOOL BP0|BP1|BP2|BP32
    FREEPAGE p
    PCTFREE n
    CLOSE YES|NO;
```

The following apply:

1. We mentioned before that we create an index only for a table, never for a view.
2. STOGROUP, BUFFERPOOL, CLOSE, and DSETPASS are the same as those used when creating the table space.
3. UNIQUE is specified if there should be no duplicate values for the specified column(s); often associated with record keys.
4. The column names for one index need not be contiguous. Ascending sequence is the default. The suggested maximum length for an index is 40 bytes. In addition, if the column is defined as VARCHAR, DB2 will use the maximum length as the length of the column.
5. SUBPAGES x allows the index to be broken up into x subpages. It is useful in improving concurrency since locks can be held by subpages instead of pages. However, too many subpages increase processing overhead. The default is 4, the maximum 16.
6. CLUSTER is specified if the rows are to be physically sequenced by the index. Note that a table can only have one index that is defined as CLUSTER.
7. BUFFERPOOL may only specify BP0, BP1, or BP2, which are 4K in size. A 32K buffer pool size is not allowed for an index. The buffer pool specified here might be different from that of the table space so there is less contention for buffer pool between the two.
8. PCTFREE p works in the same manner as for the table space. The default for an index is 10 percent.
9. FREEPAGE n works in the same manner as for the table space. The default is 0.
10. CLOSE YES (the default) will deallocate the data set for the index when the program terminates, thus freeing resources. It is useful, especially for infrequently-used indexes. For frequently-used indexes, CLOSE NO avoids repeated open and close processing.
11. Each index will have a one-row entry in the SYSIBM.SYSINDEXES table in the DB2 catalog.

An example is:

```
CREATE UNIQUE INDEX EMPNOIDX
    SUBPAGES 8
    PCTFREE 15
    ON XLIM.EMPTABLE (EMPNO) CLUSTER;
```

## 7.3 Format of CREATE INDEX for Partitioned Table Space

The format is:

```
CREATE [UNIQUE] INDEX index-name
    ON table-name (column-name1 [ASC|DESC], . . .
            column-namen [ASC|DESC])
```

```
USING STOGROUP storage-group-name1
SUBPAGES x
CLUSTER
(PART 1 VALUES (value1)
USING STOGROUP storage-group-name2,
PART 2 VALUES (value2)
USING STOGROUP storage-group-name3,
PART 3 VALUES (value3))
BUFFERPOOL BP0|BP1|BP2|BP32
FREEPAGE p
PCTFREE n
CLOSE YES|NO;
```

The operands are mostly the same as those previously explained in Section 7.2. The other operands are:

1. The CLUSTER operand is mandatory for one index in the table space; this is the one that specifies how rows are spread among the various partitions. Note that any other index in this table space cannot be clustered.

2. The number of partitions must equal the number of PART operands, each PART operand specifying the range of values of the index to be placed in the partition.

   a. Value1 is the maximum value in PART 1 if the index is defined as ascending (ASC); otherwise, it is the lowest value. Value2 and value3 work in the same manner.

   b. If the storagegroup is specified, the index partition is placed there; otherwise, it is placed in the default.

   c. The other partitions have their own specification of range of values and possible storage groups.

3. In addition to the one-row entry in SYSIBM.SYSINDEXES, there is a one-row entry per partition in SYSIBM.SYSINDEXPART.

   An example is:

```
CREATE UNIQUE INDEX EMPNOIDX
    ON XLIM.EMPTABLE (EMPNO)
    NUMPARTS 3
    USING STOGROUP STGRP1
    SUBPAGES 8
    CLUSTER
    (PART 1 VALUES ('299999')
        USING STOGROUP STGRP2,
    PART 2 VALUES ('599999')
        USING STOGROUP STGRP3,
    PART 3 VALUES ('999999'))
    BUFFERPOOL BP0
    FREEPAGE 15
    PCTFREE 0
    CLOSE YES|NO;
```

Since the index is in ascending sequence, the first partition contains the index values '000000' to '299999', the second partition contains the index values '300000' to '599999', and so on.

## 8 CREATING A SYNONYM

An authorized user, who is not an owner, of a table or view may find it convenient to refer to the table with his or her own name. This is done by defining a synonym for the table or view. Using a synonym is however not advisable because of potential problems in maintenance. The format is:

```
CREATE SYNONYM synonym
      FOR authorization-id.table-name|view-name;
```

An example is:

```
CREATE SYNONYM LIMTABLE
      FOR XQYZ.EMPLOYEETABLE
```

The person who executed this statement may now use "LIMTABLE" when refering to the "XQYZ.EMPLOYEETABLE" table.

### 8.1 Dropping a Synonym

The format is:

```
DROP SYNONYM synonym;
```

## 9 DROPPING DB2 OBJECTS

The DBA may drop objects he or she has created. This has to be done with care since such objects and those subordinated to it are lost.

### 9.1 Dropping a Table Space

The statement is:

```
DROP TABLESPACE tablespace-name;
```

Note that all tables and indexes in that table space are dropped.

### 9.2 Dropping a Table or View

When a table is dropped, the definition as well as its data are lost. This statement must therefore be used with extreme care. When a view is dropped, however, there is no loss of data since it really has no data by itself. The format is:

```
DROP TABLE table-name|VIEW view-name;
```

# 10 ALTERING TABLE SPACES AND TABLES

The format to change a table space specification is:

```
ALTER TABLESPACE tablespace-name
        BUFFERPOOL . . .
        LOCKSIZE . . .
        CLOSE . . .
        FREEPAGE . . .
        PCTFREE . . .
        DSETPASS . . . ;
```

The preceding operands will alter the corresponding entry in the current table space.

## 10.1 Altering a Table

The format to change a table specification is:

```
ALTER TABLE tablespace-name
    ADD (column1 data-type [NULL|NOT NULL WITH DEFAULT]
    FIELDPROC module1 , . . . .
    columnm data-type [NULL|NOT NULL [WITH DEFAULT],)
    VALIDPROC [module2|NULL];
```

The following apply:

1. Each column is appended to the right of the rightmost column of the table.
2. The column cannot be defined as NOT NULL.
3. Records are not changed until values are inserted in the new columns; to prevent potential performance problems on insertion, the table should have enough free space allocated for expansion.
4. FIELDPROC and VALIDPROC are as explained in the CREATE TABLE statement.

# 21

# *Other Advanced Topics*

## 1 THE LOCKING MECHANISM

To satisfy typical data processing needs, DB2 allows multiple users to access the same data at essentially the same time. This is known as concurrency, and the greater the level of concurrency, the more users can simultaneously access the data.

However, such concurrency has to be controlled; otherwise, certain problems occur. The control mechanism is locking, which is how a DB2 resource is associated with a current user (the owner of the lock) and how that affects access permission for other users.

### 1.1 Purposes of Locking

DB2's locking mechanism accomplishes several goals. These are:

1. *Prevent access to uncommitted data.* Without locking, if user A updates certain data, user B can immediately access such data in their updated form. This may cause data inconsistency if user A, as in some situations, later decides (after user B has accessed the updated data) that his or her update should be rolled

back or be disregarded. By locking updated data until the one who did the update decides that such update is final and is to be committed, DB2 helps guarantee data integrity.

2. *Allow repeatable reads*. Without locking, if user A reads the same data twice (naturally at different points in time), there is a possibility that another user may have updated those data in between the two reads. This makes the data inconsistent to user A. With locking, if user A indicates the repeatable-read option, pages read by him or her cannot be updated (but may be read) by other users until such time that user A indicates that such pages be unlocked (presumably after user A is finished with them).

## 1.2 The Lock Owner

If a resource (table space, page of table, index subpage) has no current owner (that is, currently not in use), the first user who accesses it becomes the lock owner and will not relinquish such ownership until the lock is released. Other users may be allowed to access the same resource but only under certain situations (see Lock Compatibility, Section 1.5.1).

## 1.3 Object and Size of Locked Resource

The object and size of the locked resource depends on whether it is data or an index.

### 1.3.1 Locked object and size for data.    For data, locking is done by pages within a table or a whole table space. The following apply:

1. To get page locking, the user specifies LOCKSIZE [PAGE|ANY] in the CREATE|ALTER TABLESPACE statement. ANY is preferable, and DB2 will then generally start with page locking, and just upgrade it to table space locking if the user attempts to lock more pages than the installation limit for a user (NUMLKTS operand at DB2 installation). PAGE will always use page locking and if the NUMLKTS limit is already reached, DB2 will not execute the statement but instead issue the SQLCODE value of $-904$, where the user may then do a commit or rollback.

2. To get table space locking:
   a. The program issues the "EXEC SQL LOCK TABLE . . . END-EXEC " statement for a table space originally locked by page.
   b. The user specifies LOCKSIZE TABLESPACE in the CREATE|ALTER TABLESPACE statement.

### 1.3.2 Locked object and size for index.    Index locking follows the locking of the data it corresponds to. If the latter is by table space, the whole index is also locked. If it is by page, index locking is by subpage within a page.

**1.3.3 No locking by table, only table space.**    Note that there is no such thing as locking by table, since to DB2, a table is not a file. If a user locks a table space, all tables and indexes within that table space are locked.

**1.3.4 Locking diagrams.**    Figure 21.1 shows locking by page within a table.

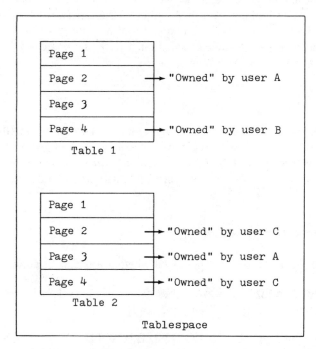

Figure 21.1   Locking by page.

Note that different users are concurrent lock owners and a user may own locks on several pages. From the discussion on Lock Compatibility (Section 1.5.1), we learn that other users may be allowed to access the same page but only under certain situations.

Figure 21.2 shows locking by table space.

Note that there is only one lock owner.

## 1.4 Duration of Locks

The duration of a lock (how long it is owned by a user) is determined by certain factors.

**1.4.1 Duration of page lock.**    A page lock is acquired when a page is first accessed. It is released in several ways:

1. When the user issues an SQL COMMIT statement (batch program) or a CICS SYNCPOINT command (CICS application program).

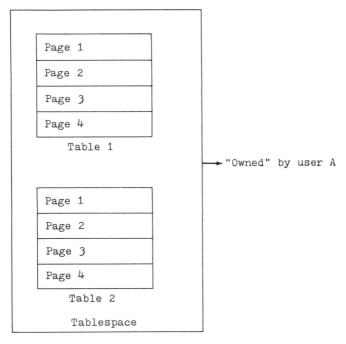

**Figure 21.2**    Locking by table space.

2. When the user issues an SQL ROLLBACK statement (batch program) or a CICS SYNCPOINT ROLLBACK command (CICS application program).

3. When the batch program normally terminates or the task normally terminates (CICS application program).

4. When the cursor goes to another page, if processing is done by cursor (by using the clause WHERE CURRENT OF), the program indicates cursor stability (CS) option, and the page is not updated.

**1.4.2 Duration of table space lock.**    The duration of a table space lock is more complex.

*1.4.2.1 Acquiring table space lock.*    A table space lock is acquired in several ways.

1. When choosing ACQUIRE(USE) during BIND/REBIND, the lock is acquired on the first access of any data in that table space. Note that acquiring the lock will fail if any other user currently owns a lock on any part of the table space.

2. When choosing ACQUIRE(ALLOCATE) during BIND/REBIND, the lock is acquired when the application plan is allocated (at program start). Note also that acquiring the lock will fail if any other user currently owns a lock on any part of the table space. ACQUIRE(ALLOCATE) makes sure that all locks needed by the plan are available before a program runs, and thus reduces the

problem of deadlocks. However, if the duration is longer, there is less concurrency, and thus it is inherently inefficient.

***1.4.2.2 Releasing Table Space Lock.***    A table space lock is released in several ways:

1. ACQUIRE(USE)/RELEASE(COMMIT) options of BIND/REBIND:
   a. When the user issues an SQL COMMIT statement (batch program) or a CICS SYNCPOINT command (CICS application program).
   b. When the user issues an SQL ROLLBACK statement (batch program) or a CICS SYNCPOINT ROLLBACK command (CICS application program).
2. ACQUIRE(USE)/RELEASE(DEALLOCATE) option of BIND/REBIND:
   a. When the plan is deallocated. This is done when the batch program normally terminates or the task normally terminates (CICS application program).
3. ACQUIRE(ALLOCATE)/RELEASE(DEALLOCATE) option of BIND/RE-BIND:
   a. When the plan is deallocated. This is done when the batch program normally terminates or the task normally terminates (CICS application program).
   b. Note that for ACQUIRE(ALLOCATE), RELEASE(COMMIT) is not allowed.

## 1.5 Mode of Locking for Page Locks

The following are the modes of page locks, by order of increasing control of resources. This means that a SHARE(S) page lock allows other concurrent users, while an EXCLUSIVE(X) page lock does not allow any concurrent user. The modes are:

1. The SHARE(S) page lock. It is issued if the owner gets it via a read-only statement. The SQL statement does not, and has no intention, to update.
2. The UPDATE(U) page lock. It is issued if the owner intends to do an update (DECLARE . . . CURSOR . . . FOR UPDATE OF); locking is by page, and the option is cursor stability.
3. The EXCLUSIVE(X) page lock. It is issued if the owner gets it via an updating statement, such as INSERT, UPDATE, and DELETE.

### 1.5.1 Lock compatibility for page locks.    We mentioned before that under certain situations, a user may access pages owned by another user. This is known as lock compatibility and Figure 21.3 illustrates it.

Note the following:

1. If the owner has an S lock, another user may also have an S lock (may do a read-only operation), or even a U lock (indicate the intention to update, though cannot yet do an update), but cannot have an X lock (cannot execute an updating statement).

| Mode of lock for owner | Mode of lock for others | | |
|---|---|---|---|
| | SHARE(S) | UPDATE(U) | EXCLUSIVE(X) |
| SHARE(S) | Yes | Yes | No |
| UPDATE(U) | Yes | No | No |
| EXCLUSIVE(X) | No | No | No |

**Figure 21.3**   Compatibility of page lock modes.

2. If the owner has a U lock, another user may only have an S lock, and can therefore read it. No other function is allowed.

3. If the owner has an X lock, no other user can access the data.

## 1.6 The LOCK TABLE Statement

The LOCK TABLE statement may be issued by an application program to specifically lock the table space (not just the table) specified. It will temporarily override any LOCKSIZE parameter specified for the table space. It has several uses, and we illustrate three of them.

**1.6.1 LOCK TABLE for online table used in batch.**   A table that is heavily used, especially in online applications, is generally defined (at the CREATE|ALTER TABLESPACE statement) with a page lock so there is maximum concurrency. However, when that table space is used in an overnight batch run (say, to apply payments to an Accounts Receivable table), it is more efficient to lock the whole table space so there is no additional processing overhead in the locking and unlocking of individual pages. The LOCK TABLE statement in that batch program is used. There is no problem with concurrency here since there is only one program accessing the table at this time.

**1.6.2 LOCK TABLE to process table space as is.**   If a program wants to freeze all the data "as is," without fear that part of them may be changed during their processing, it may issue the LOCK TABLE statement. Specifying the repeatable-read option (which is valid only on page locks) still allows other users to change pages the program has not yet processed. The LOCK TABLE statement guarantees the data will remain "as is" during the processing.

**1.6.3 LOCK TABLE in applications using multiple tables.**   If an application uses multiple tables from different table spaces, of which only one such table needs to be processed with the repeatable-read option, the use of the option at BIND applies to all tables in the application. This means that the rest of the tables, which should be processed with the more efficient cursor-stability option are still processed with repeatable read.

A more efficient solution is to specify cursor stability at BIND, then issue the LOCK TABLE statement for the specific table that is processed with repeatable read. Assuming that this table space has only one table, we guarantee that only the table that requires it is processed in the less efficient style.

**1.6.4 Format of the LOCK TABLE statement.** The format of the statement is:

```
EXEC SQL
  LOCK TABLE table-name IN [SHARE|EXCLUSIVE] MODE
END-EXEC
```

The program chooses SHARE if it wants others to be able to read (but not update) data, EXCLUSIVE if it wants no one else to access the data. Note again that although the statement specifies a table, it is the whole table space that is locked.

## 2 GRANTING AUTHORIZATION

There are several levels of authorization, depending on what activity is to be performed.

### 2.1 No Authorization Needed for Non-DB2 Activities

If the activity is outside DB2, there is naturally no need for any authorization by DB2. For instance, a programmer does not need authorization to code a program, even if it issues SQL statements, since coding is only under TSO or whatever text editor/time-sharing software is being used. However, a programmer needs authorization to bind a program (prepare it for execution) and another authorization to execute it.

### 2.2 Authorization for DB2 Activities

For any activity under DB2, the user must have authorization. This book deals only with authorization for running applications, thus excluding authorization to administer the database.

Let it suffice to say at this point that such administrative authorization is for the system administrator, who is authorized to control and access all DB2 resources; for the database administrator, who is authorized to create table spaces, tables, indexes, and so on for applications; and for the system operator, who is authorized to issue system operator commands to run DB2.

The application programmer mostly deals with the database administrator, who takes care of such functions as creating table spaces, granting access authorization to users, and so on.

**2.2.1 Authorization for access of DB2 data.**   The system administrator is automatically authorized to access all data in the installation; the database administrator is likewise automatically authorized to do so, but only for the database he or she controls. Specific authorization for other users is as follows.

*2.2.1.1 Automatic SPUFI access for table/view owner.*   The table or view owner is the owner-userid specified when the table/view is created or if missing, it is the TSO-userid of the creator. He or she has all privileges to access the table or view. For that owner, the SQL statement does not require a user-id since DB2 will append it. This authorization allows the user to access data via SPUFI. There is a separate authorization for application programs.

*2.2.1.2 Explicit SPUFI access for nonowners.*   Nonowners who need to access tables or views can only do so if granted specific privileges. This will allow access via SPUFI (additional authorization is required for access in application programs). The general format is:

```
GRANT privilege(s)|ALL
  ON table-name|view-name
  TO authorization-id(s)|PUBLIC;
```

The following apply:

1. Privileges are:
   a. Row access (SELECT, INSERT, DELETE, UPDATE (column-namel, . . . .), and so on). Note that an update by a specific authorization-id can be restricted to specific columns.
   b. Create indexes for table columns (CREATE INDEX).
   c. Alter the table (ALTER TABLE table-name).
2. If ALL is specified, then all privileges are granted.
3. There may be multiple authorization-ids granted privilege in a single GRANT statement. If PUBLIC is specified, then all users are authorized.
4. All nonowners must specify the owner-userid when specifying the table or view name.

**2.2.2 Authorization for preparing programs for execution.**   There are several of them.

*2.2.2.1 BINDADD authorization.*   The system administrator has BINDADD authorization, and may pass it to a DBA or a programmer, in which case they are authorized to create and BIND plans (prepare programs for execution) and execute them.

In most cases, however, to control the use and naming of plans (each plan name must be unique for the installation), only the system administrator or the DBA create the plan, then just grant authorization to programmers and system operators.

**2.2.2.2. Explicit authorization for programmers.**    Programmers (assuming no BINDADD authorization) have to be authorized by the system administrator or the DBA to BIND or REBIND an existing plan to prepare the corresponding application program(s) for execution. If the programmer also wants to test (execute) the program, he or she must further be authorized to execute the plan. The format of the authorization is:

```
GRANT [BIND,] [EXECUTE]
  ON plan-name
  TO authorization-id(s)|PUBLIC;
```

The following apply:

1. BIND (that is, bind and rebind) and EXECUTE authorization may be given separately, with some users only allowed BIND, others EXECUTE, others both.
2. As before, there may be multiple authorization-ids granted privilege in a single GRANT statement. If PUBLIC is specified, then all users are authorized.

**2.2.3 authorization for executing application programs.**    Users who have BINDADD authorization are automatically authorized to create, bind, then execute a plan (that is, program or programs in that plan). Otherwise, that person must be specifically authorized to EXECUTE the plan with the GRANT EXECUTE authorization mentioned previously.

For security reasons, a specific programmer is generally given authorization to BIND and EXECUTE specific plans; the operator is given authorization to EXECUTE specific plans.

# 3 REVOKING AUTHORIZATION

The REVOKE statement revokes a previous authorization to perform a function. The general format is similar to the GRANT:

```
REVOKE privileges|ALL
  ON table-name|view-name
  FROM authorization-id|PUBLIC.
```

# 4 DB2 AND CICS

Although all the discussion and examples in this book have been on the use of DB2 in batch applications, much of what we have learned is in fact applicable to CICS applications. We now discuss their similarities and differences.

## 4.1 How CICS and Batch Programs are Similar

CICS and batch programs are similar in these respects:

1. SQL statements work in the same manner (except for the COMMIT and ROLLBACK statements).
2. The coding style is basically the same, except where CICS and batch application programs are inherently different (that is, even without DB2). For instance, CICS programs execute within tasks, not program steps.

## 4.2 How CICS and Batch Programs are Different

CICS and batch programs are different in these respects:

1. In CICS programs, we use the CICS SYNCPOINT command instead of the SQL COMMIT statement, the CICS SYNCPOINT ROLLBACK command instead of the SQL ROLLBACK statement.
2. In CICS applications, such requests for commit or rollback are issued in different situations compared to those for batch applications. This is explained in Section 4.2.1.
3. In typical batch applications, there is usually only one plan per program. In CICS applications, many programs are often combined in one plan. This is explained in Section 4.2.3.

**4.2.1 Problem of autocommit on task termination.**    In typical batch applications, we usually issue the SQL COMMIT statement many times in a single run. Otherwise, the locks will remain (resulting in a lower level of concurrency) until program termination.

On the other hand, in CICS applications, there are usually multiple tasks that implement a single data update. If there are errors in the current update and we want to retry it on the next task, we have to issue the CICS SYNCPOINT ROLLBACK command if there were "good" updates in that task; otherwise, DB2 automatically commits the update, which it does at task termination.

**4.2.2 Problem with row to be updated changed by others.**    There is a problem that occurs when using CICS in an update application. When an operator wants to update certain data (say, a VSAM record), those data are first read from the file, then displayed on the terminal, after which the task terminates. This is the pseudoconversational mode of processing.

A data integrity problem is that while the first operator may still be keying changes to the data, another task (run at a different terminal) may already be updating it. This is possible since for CICS, VSAM exclusive control is released when the task is terminated. In DB2, the locks are also released at task termination.

One common solution for this problem (which is easily adopted for CICS applications using DB2) is for each task to store the record key in a temporary storage record and have each task investigate this record to see whether a data record that we intend to update is present there. If so, the update to that data record is momentarily set aside.

### 4.2.3. Single-program plan and problem with XCLT and LINK.   In release 1.3, DB2 does not allow a change of plan within a task. If we use one plan per program (as we generally do in batch), then the CICS XCTL and LINK commands will not work anymore since they execute another program within the task.

The only current solution (until this problem is resolved) is to combine all programs that execute in a single task into a single plan. The problem is that if one program becomes invalid (say, because of a modification), its corresponding DBRM becomes invalid, and the whole plan in turn becomes invalid.

## 5 REFERENTIAL INTEGRITY

Referential integrity deals with the problem of data in one table being consistent with related data in another table. For instance, in Figures 15.4A and 15.4B in Chapter 15, the course numbers in both tables are identical. If we drop a course in the Course table but retain the Offering table as is, there is a problem with referential integrity, since the affected offerings will no longer have a corresponding course.

### 5.1 Referential Integrity with Subordinate and Association Tables

Most discussions on referential integrity deal with rows in subordinate tables and association tables. Many users suggest that DB2 automatically synchronizes their existence with the corresponding rows in the "source" tables. For instance, if a course is deleted, all offerings (sections) for it should be automatically deleted. If a purchase order is deleted, all ordered items belonging to it should be automatically deleted.

This book will not deal further with this question, since the discussion is quite trivial. Instead, we will deal with questions when two tables (say, both kernel) are related, not fully but to some degree.

### 5.2 Referential Integrity with Primary/Foreign Tables

We discuss referential integrity in association with Figure 21.4. We deal with the integrity questions between foreign keys and primary keys, foreign tables and primary tables.

Data examples of Figure 21.4A are shown in Figure 21.5.
Data examples of Figure 21.4B are shown in Figure 21.6.

### 5.3 Data Inconsistency on DELETE

Data inconsistency may occur when a delete is made on a Primary table.

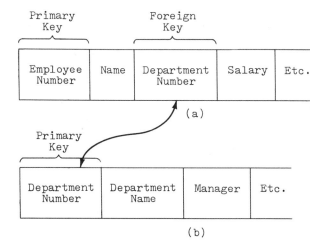

**Figure 21.4a**  The employee table: a foreign table.

**Figure 21.4b**  The department table: a primary table.

| Primary<br>Key | | Foreign<br>Key | |
| --- | --- | --- | --- |
| Employee<br>Number | Name | Department<br>Number | Salary |
| 00005 | BAKER, C. | 003 | 0030000 |
| 00008 | RANDOLPH, R. | 005 | 0029000 |
| 00010 | RICHARDS, M. | 002 | 0031000 |
| 00015 | DAVIS, L. | 006 | 0030000 |
| 00150 | ELLIOT, T. | 005 | 0031000 |
| 00170 | RABINOVITZ, M. | 003 | 0031000 |
| 00190 | LEE, R. | 005 | 0030000 |

**Figure 21.5**  The employee table. a foreign table.

| Primary<br>Key | |
| --- | --- |
| Department Number | Department Name |
| 002 | Accounts Payable |
| 003 | Data Processing |
| 005 | Administration |
| 006 | Finance |

**Figure 21.6**  The department table. a primary table.

**5.3.1 Deleting a row in a foreign table.**    This can be done anytime. Deleting a row (say, employee number 00010) in the Employee table (Fig. 21.5) has no adverse effect on the Department table (Fig. 21.6).

**5.3.2 Deleting a row in a primary table.**    This has an effect on the Foreign table. Deleting a row in the Department table (say, department number '003') means those employees in the Employee table (in this case, employee numbers '00005' and '00170') now belong to deleted departments.

The user has four options.

*5.3.2.1 Option #1: cascading delete.* Here, we allow the delete anytime. In addition, all affected rows in the Foreign table are also deleted. Thus, when a department row is deleted all employee rows belonging to the deleted department are also deleted.

This option is useful if there is a total dependency relationship between one table to the other. For instance, all offerings in the subordinate Offering table are also deleted if the corresponding course in the Course table is deleted. All rows in the Item-ordered table are deleted when the corresponding purchase order is deleted.

However, this option is inappropriate if there is no total dependency between the tables. *For instance, if we drop employee rows, we lose information on those rows that has nothing to do with the department.*

The subquery of one table, using the WHERE [EXIST|NOT EXISTS] operand may be used when deleting (as well as inserting and updating) rows in the other related table.

*5.3.2.2 Option #2: restricted delete.* Allow a delete of the Primary table only if there are no corresponding rows in the Foreign table. Only those departments without any employees assigned to them may be deleted. *This is the most logical way to proceed, the choice for most applications.*

*5.3.2.3 Option #3: neutralizing delete.* Allow the delete anytime. For those affected rows in the Foreign table, the values are changed to LOW-VALUES, blanks, or NULLs. Thus, delete the department row but then change all employee rows belonging to that department (change their department numbers to LOW-VALUES, blanks, or NULLs).

*5.3.2.4 Option #4: no constraint.* Delete anytime and don't bother about the Foreign table. This always results in inconsistency, and is allowed only if the user does not care.

## 5.4 Data Inconsistency on INSERT

Data inconsistency may occur when an insert is made on a Foreign table.

### 5.4.1 Inserting a row in a foreign table. There are several options.

*5.4.1.1 Conditional insert.* Check the Primary table to make sure the value of that foreign key exists in the Primary table. We check if the department number in the new employee record exists in the Department table. If so, the insert is made; otherwise, there is an error.

*5.4.1.2 Insert with Default.* We basically do the same thing as in the conditional insert. However, if the value does not exist (the department number in the new employee record), allow the insertion anyway but use default value, say SPACES, for the department number. Possibly, the Primary table also has spaces as the key of one row that says the department name is "UNKNOWN".

**5.4.2 Inserting a row in a primary table.**    This can be done anytime. A new department is inserted in the Department table without any effect on the Employee table.

## 5.5 Data Inconsistency on UPDATE

Data inconsistency may occur when an update is made on either a foreign or primary table.

**5.5.1 Updating a row in a foreign table.**    The problem is the same as for the insert operation.

*5.5.1.1 Conditional update.*    Check the Primary table to make sure the new value of the foreign key exists in the Primary table. We check if the new department number for the old employee record exists in the Department table. If so, the update is made; otherwise, there is an error.

*5.5.1.2 Update with default.*    We basically do the same thing as in the conditional insert. However, if the new value does not exist (the new department number in the old employee record), allow the update anyway but use default value, say SPACES, for the department number. Possibly, the Primary table also has spaces as the key of one row that says the department name is "UNKNOWN".

**5.5.2 Updating a row in a primary table.**    This is done in the same manner as for the delete operation and therefore this has an effect on the Foreign table. Updating a row in the Department table affects those rows in the Employee table belonging to the department.

The user has four options.

*5.5.2.1 Option #1: Cascading update.*    Here, we allow the update anytime. In addition, all affected rows in the Foreign table are also updated. Thus, if we change the Department table such that department number '003' is changed to '500', then all rows in the Employee table with department number '003' are correspondingly changed to '500'.

*5.5.2.2 Option #2: Restricted update.*    Allow an update of the Primary table only if there are no corresponding rows in the foreign table. Only those departments without any employee assigned to them may be updated.

*5.5.2.3 Option #3: Neutralizing update.*    Allow the update anytime. Then for those affected rows in the foreign table, the values in their foreign key are changed to LOW-VALUES, blanks, or NULLs.

*5.5.2.4 Option #4: No constraint.*    Update anytime and don't bother about the Foreign table. This may result in inconsistency, and is allowed only if the user does not care.

# 22

# *Important DB2 Utilities/Program Products*

## 1 INTRODUCTION

We give a general discussion on important utilities/program products that enhance the use of DB2. In general, these utilities are not directly used by the application programmer, but only by the system and database administrators or system operator.

## 2 THE DATA EXTRACT FACILITY

Data Extract is a separate program product that allows the user to extract data from non-DB2 sources, reformat such data if so desired, and write them into a temporary data set; they are then loaded into a table via the DB2 LOAD utility. It therefore saves rekeying such data if they already exist somewhere else.

Figure 22.1 shows how this is done.

The following apply:

1. The source may be VSAM files, DL/I databases, or physical sequential files.
2. The Data Extract (DXT) program extracts data selected from the source(s) and reformats them for use by DB2.
3. The DB2 LOAD utility in turn loads them into a table.

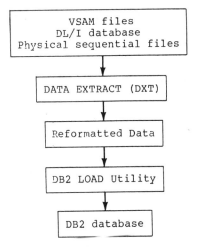

**Figure 22.1**   The data extract facility.

## 2.1 Using DXT

DXT works in four steps.

1. Describe and define the source data.
2. Code and Extract request.
3. Run and Extract.
4. Load the data.

The four steps may be conveniently done interactively. DB2 provides a series of user-friendly panels.

## 3 TUNING THE DATABASE

Many efficiency techniques were mentioned in Chapter 19. The DBA may also promote efficiency by keeping the table spaces, indexes, and subsystem tuned. Such tuning requires statistics generated by DB2 utilities as well as the important REORG (reorganization) utility.

Important utilities to use are RUNSTAT and REORG as previously mentioned, and EXPLAIN (to be discussed), among others.

### 3.1 The RUNSTAT Utility

This utility generates to the DB2 catalog information about a table space and/or index. Such information is used by the DB2 Optimizer (during the BIND process for application programs) to select the most efficient way to access data. Section 3.1.2 provides details on the specific information generated. In general, they are:

1. Information on how a table space utilizes space and how rows are clustered within it.
2. Information on the efficiency of an index.

### 3.1.1 Running RUNSTAT.

RUNSTAT is easily run via the utility option of the DB2 Interactive (DB2I) facility. In Figure 4.2 on page 25, this is option 8. This will take you through a series of user-friendly panels.

### 3.1.2 Information updated by RUNSTAT.

RUNSTAT generates information into DB2 catalog tables that correspond to DB2 objects.

1. *Tables*. There is one row per table or view in the SYSIBM.SYSTABLES catalog entry. Information generated is:
   a. Number of rows in the table.
   b. Number of pages in the table containing rows.
   c. Percentage of total pages containing rows.
2. *Columns*. There is one row per column in a table or view in the SYSIBM. SYSCOLUMNS catalog entry. Information generated is:
   a. Number of distinct values in the column.
   b. Second highest value in the column.
   c. Second lowest value in the column.
3. *Table spaces*. (Another entry following Item 4). There is one row per table space in the SYSIBM.SYSTABLESPACE catalog entry. Information generated is:
   a. Number of active pages in the table space.
4. *Table spaces*. (Another entry previously given in Item 3). There is one row per nonpartitioned table space or per partition in a partitioned table space in the SYSIBM.SYSTABLEPART catalog entry. Information generated is:
   a. Number of rows in the table space or partition.
   b. Number of rows moved from their original position to a nearby position because of an increase in the length of the row.
   c. Number of rows moved from their original position to a faraway position because of an increase in the length of the row.
   d. Percentage of space occupied by rows of data from active tables.
   e. Percentage of space occupied by rows of data from dropped tables.
5. *Indexes*. (Another entry following in Item 6). There is one row per index in the SYSIBM.SYSINDEXES catalog entry. Information generated is:
   a. Whether the table is clustered by the index.
   b. Number of distinct values of the first eight bytes of the first key column.
   c. Number of distinct values of the key.
   d. Number of active leaf pages in the index.
   e. Number of levels in the index tree.

**6.** *Indexes.* (Another entry previously given in Item 5). There is one row per non-partitioned index or per partition in a partitioned index in the SYSIBM. SYSINDEXPART catalog entry. Information generated is:

   a. Number of data rows referenced by the index or the partition of a partitioned index.

   b. When following the order defined by the index, how many times the next data row in the sequence was not in the same page but was near the current row.

   c. When following the order defined by the index, how many times the next data row in the sequence was not in the same page but was far from the current row.

   d. 100 times the average number of pages between successive leaf pages during a sequential access of the index.

## 3.2 The STOSPACE Utility

This utility generates data in the DB2 catalog on how much space is allocated to storage groups, table spaces, and indexes.

   **3.2.1 Running STOSPACE.**    STOSPACE is easily run via the utility option of the DB2 Interactive (DB2I) facility. In Figure 4.2 on page 25, this is option 8. This will take you through a series of user-friendly panels.

   **3.2.2 Information updated by STOSPACE.**    STOSPACE generates information into DB2 catalog tables that correspond to DB2 objects.

   **1.** *Tables.* There is one row per table or view in the SYSIBM.SYSTABLES catalog entry. The information generated is the amount of storage space allocated.

   **2.** *Indexes.* There is one row per index in the SYSIBM.SYSINDEXES catalog entry. The information generated is the amount of storage space allocated.

   **3.** *Storage group.* There is one row per storage group in the SYSIBM. SYSSTOGROUP catalog entry. The information generated is the amount of storage space allocated.

## 4 THE EXPLAIN STATEMENT

The EXPLAIN statement provides the programmer with information on how DB2 will execute a particular SQL statement, including such information as whether an existing index will be used, whether a sort will be made, in which order tables will be joined, and so on. The programmer may thus code several versions of the SQL statement and check which one will generate the most efficient code.

   DB2 does not actually execute the statement that we want explained. It simply provides information on how the statement will be executed.

## 4.1 Format of the EXPLAIN Statement

The statement format (SPUFI) is:

```
EXPLAIN PLAN SET QUERYNO = n FOR
        SQL statement;
```

The following apply:

1. n in QUERYNO is explained in Section 4.3.
2. The SQL statement, which is subordinated to the EXPLAIN statement, is the one we want explained. Any SELECT, INSERT, UPDATE, and DELETE statement may be used. Another EXPLAIN statement is not allowed.

Note that EXPLAIN simply generates statistical information. The programmer will have to use another SELECT statement to extract this information, either in SPUFI or in an application program.

## 4.2 Creating the PLAN_TABLE

The plan_table is used to store the information generated by EXPLAIN. Each user must use his or her own table.

Figure 22.2 is an example of how to create the table.

```
CREATE TABLE PLAN_TABLE
(QUERYNO             INTEGER          NOT NULL,
 QBLOCKNO            SMALLINT         NOT NULL,
 APPLNAME            CHAR(8)          NOT NULL,
 PROGNAME            CHAR(8)          NOT NULL,
 PLANNO              SMALLINT         NOT NULL,
 METHOD              SMALLINT         NOT NULL,
 CREATOR             CHAR(8)          NOT NULL,
 TNAME               CHAR(18)         NOT NULL,
 TABNO               SMALLINT         NOT NULL,
 ACCESSTYPE          CHAR(2)          NOT NULL,
 MATCHCOLS           SMALLINT         NOT NULL,
 ACCESSCREATOR       CHAR(8)          NOT NULL,
 ACCESSNAME          CHAR(18)         NOT NULL,
 INDEXONLY           CHAR(1)          NOT NULL,
 SORTN_UNIQ          CHAR(1)          NOT NULL,
 SORTN_JOIN          CHAR(1)          NOT NULL,
 SORTN_ORDERBY       CHAR(1)          NOT NULL,
 SORTN_GROUPBY       CHAR(1)          NOT NULL,
 SORTC_UNIQ          CHAR(1)          NOT NULL,
 SORTC_JOIN          CHAR(1)          NOT NULL,
 SORTC_ORDERBY       CHAR(1)          NOT NULL,
 SORTC_GROUPBY       CHAR(1)          NOT NULL,
 TSLOCKMODE          CHAR(3)          NOT NULL,
 TIMESTAMP           CHAR(16)         NOT NULL,
 REMARKS             VARCHAR(24)      NOT NULL)
IN tablespace-name;
```

**Figure 22.2**  Creating PLAN__TABLE.

## 4.3 Meaning of Fields in the PLAN_TABLE

The meaning of the columns are as follows:

1. *QUERYNO*. This identifies the query number, which is the one generated by the EXPLAIN statement; if a number is not specified, DB2 will assign a number. The following statement will generate the value of 1 for the QUERYNO field.

```
EXPLAIN PLAN SET QUERYNO = 01 FOR
          SQL statement;
```

2. *QBLOCKNO*. In case there are multiple SQL levels in a single query (for instance, subqueries), QBLOCKNO will indicate which level this row (or rows, since a single QBLOCKNO generates one row per specific PLANNO) belongs to. The main query (the highest-level query) is query block number 1, the first subquery as query block number 2, and so on. For example:

```
EXPLAIN PLAN SET QUERYNO = 01 FOR
          SELECT col1, col2, ....
          FROM ....
          WHERE ....
            (SELECT col3, col4, ....
            FROM ....
            WHERE ....);
```

The main query (SELECT col1, col2, ...) is query block number 1 and the subquery (SELECT col3, col4, ...) is query block number 2.

3. *APPLNAME*. The application plan name if EXPLAIN is used for an application. When used in SPUFI, this is blank.

4. *PROGNAME*. The program name.

5. *PLANNO*. The current step of the plan in which QBLOCKNO is processed. A single SQL statement may be implemented by DB2 in several steps, as for instance a Join. Each step generates one row in the Explain table.

6. *METHOD*. The method used. The values are:
   a. 0 if no join is used.
   b. 1 if a nested loop join is used. This Join is more efficient than METHOD 2 below since it uses existing indexe(s) on the column(s) used in the Join.
   c. 2 if merge scan join is used. This is a less efficient Join since there is a table space scan and possibly a sort operation.
   d. 3 if an extra sort operation is used because of GROUP BY, ORDER BY, UNION or SELECT DISTINCT.

7. *CREATOR*. Creator of a new table accessed in this QBLOCKNO. For the preceding Method 3, this is blank.

8. *TNAME*. The table name accessed in this QBLOCKNO. For Method 3, this is blank.

9. *TABNO*. The number assigned by DB2 to the table. For Method 3, this is 0.

10. *ACCESSTYPE*. The type of access used. The values are:
    a. I if an index was used. This index is identified in ACCESSCREATOR and ACCESSNAME.
    b. R if a table space scan was used.
    c. Blank if accessed by cursor (UPDATE or DELETE using WHERE CURRENT OF . . . ).

11. *MATCHCOLS*. Further information related to ACCESSTYPE.
    a. If ACCESSTYPE is I:
       1. If 0, DB2 did a complete index scan, reading all data rows in spite of also using the index. This is less efficient than 2 below.
       2. Else, the number of index keys DB2 used for a direct read on the data. This is more efficient than 1 above.
    b. Otherwise, 0.

12. *ACCESSCREATOR*. If ACCESSTYPE is I, the index or table space creator; otherwise, blank.

13. *ACCESSNAME*. This depends on ACCESSTYPE. If ACCESSTYPE is I, this is the name of the index; otherwise, blank.

14. *INDEXONLY*. If the value is Y, the request was satisfied with index entries only, without any need to access the data. This is the most efficient access method.

15. Sort fields for real tables. This shows any sort of the original input table(s). Y means a sort was done.
    a. *SORTN_UNIQUE*. For SELECT DISTINCT, UNION, whether a sort was done to eliminate duplicate rows.
    b. *SORTN_JOIN*. For merge scan join (see Method 2), whether a sort was done.
    c. *SORTN_ORDERBY*. For the ORDER BY clause, whether a sort was done.
    d. *SORTN_GROUPBY*. For the GROUP BY clause, whether a sort was done.

16. Sort fields for composite tables. This shows any sort of any composite table(s), as for instance, the output of a join operation. Y means a sort was done.
    a. *SORTC_UNIQUE*. For SELECT DISTINCT, UNION, whether a sort was done to eliminate duplicate rows.
    b. *SORTC_JOIN*. For merge scan join (see Method 2), whether a sort was done.
    c. *SORTC_ORDERBY*. For the ORDER BY clause, whether a sort was done.
    d. *SORTC_GROUPBY*. For the GROUP BY clause, whether a sort was done.

17. *TSLOCKMODE*. The locking mode if table space locking.
    a. IS means INTENT SHARE.
    b. S means SHARE.

    c. IX means INTENT EXCLUSIVE.

    d. SIX means SHARE With INTENT EXCLUSIVE.

    e. X means EXCLUSIVE.

**18.** *TIMESTAMP.* Time DB2 stamped for the query. The format is MMDDYY HHMMSSTTT.

**19.** *REMARKS.* Documentation information of up to 254 characters inserted by the user.

## 4.4 Using the EXPLAIN Statement

The EXPLAIN statement may be used for SQL statements in both application programs and SPUFI. An example in SPUFI is Figure 22.3.

```
Edit --- userid.DB2.TEST.SPUFI(QUERY1)
COMMAND INPUT ===>
****** ********** TOP OF DATA **************************
000100     DELETE FROM PLAN_TABLE WHERE QUERYNO = 1;
000200     EXPLAIN PLAN SET QUERYNO = 1 FOR
000300       SELECT EMPNO, EMPSALARY
000400         FROM XLIM.EMPTABLE
000500         WHERE EMPDEPT = '003';
000600     SELECT QUERYNO, METHOD, ACCESSTYPE, INDEXONLY
000700       FROM PLAN_TABLE
000800       WHERE QUERYNO = 1;




   PRESS:   END to execute
```

**Figure 22.3**   An EXPLAIN statement in SPUFI.

The following apply:

**1.** Line 000100 is used to delete any previous row generated by a previous "QUERYNO = 1" operand. This avoids confusion when displaying the generated information, since only one row for QUERYNO = 1 will always exist (see line 000800).

**2.** Lines 000200 to 000500 show the complete EXPLAIN statement.

**3.** Lines 000300 to 000500 show the statement we want explained.

**4.** Lines 000600 to 000800 display selected columns from the row of information generated by the EXPLAIN statement. The display is the same style as any SPUFI display.

**5.** Note that since these are SQL statements in SPUFI, each independent statement ends with a semicolon (lines 000100, 000500, and 000800).

## 5 DATA RECOVERY

Data recovery involves the use of the DB2 COPY TABLESPACE utility that generates preupdate ("before") image copies of data, the MERGECOPY utility to combine several partial image copies into one, the DB2 postupdate ("after") image log records generated on updates, and the DB2 RECOVERY TABLESPACE utility.

### 5.1 Data Recovery and the DB2 Locking Feature

We mentioned before that DB2's locking feature helps promote data integrity. A corollary of this is its function in data recovery. When DB2 commits changes for a user, it will not only release locked table space or pages but will also create log records so that the pages committed are eventually physically written out, even if a hardware or software error occurs before the physical write is done.

Such log records of "after" images of updated rows are used by DB2 to guarantee that once the commit is made data integrity is preserved.

### 5.2 The Image Copies of Table Space

As a safety measure, periodic copies of the table space are made. The frequency depends on how volatile the table space is.

**5.2.1 The full image copy.**   The user may use the COPY TABLESPACE utility anytime to make a full image copy of the table space or partition of a table space. Generally, if more than 10 percent of pages have been updated since the last copy of the table space or partition of a table space (full image or incremental), then a full image copy should be made.

**5.2.2 The incremental image copy.**   On succeeding periods (after a full image copy), if there is at most only 1 percent of total pages that has an updated row, then the user may opt for a copy of those pages only, thus making an incremental copy. The same COPY TABLESPACE utility determines which pages have been updated since the last COPY TABLESPACE run and copies those pages only.

**5.2.3 The MERGECOPY utility.**   Several incremental image copies may be used as input to the MERGECOPY utility to produce a single incremental image copy. This is useful when recreating a table space and there are too many incremental image copies to handle.

**5.2.4 The RECOVER TABLESPACE utility.**   To recreate a corrupted table space, the user runs the RECOVER TABLESPACE utility. This takes the last full image copy, any incremental image copies after that, and the DB2 log of uncopied "after" image copies of updated rows to produce the reconstructed table space.

**5.2.5 The DB2 log.**    In addition to any MVS or other subsystem (CICS/VS, and so on) logs, DB2 itself produces log records. These are logs on database changes, errors, and regular checkpoints.

Log information on data changes and checkpoints are used for data recovery, while error logs are useful to check software and hardware problems.

*5.2.5.1 The active log.*    When running, DB2 produces active logs on a preallocated VSAM ESDS data set. These data sets are dynamically allocated at DB2 initialization and will remain in the system until DB2 termination.

DB2 intially writes log records in log buffers, each one a VSAM control interval. When that buffer is full, it is then written to an active log data set.

*5.2.5.2 The archive log.*    The archive log, which may be on disk or tape, is written out only when an active log is full. This log is not dynamically allocated at DB2 initialization, but only allocated when needed.

*5.2.5.3 Type of log records.*    There are three types of log records:

1. *Changes to the database.* These are "before" and "after" images to updated rows and are used for data recovery.

2. *Checkpoint records.* These are snapshots of the DB2 subsystem taken at predetermined intervals. They are taken after a user-specified number of log records. They are also automatically written when switching from one active log to another or at the end of a successful restart or at DB2 termination.

3. *At end of successful restart or normal termination.* This is also automatically written out.

# 6 QMF

The Query Management Facility (QMF) is a separate program product that can process DB2 data. If your installation has this product, it would be accessible via the DB2 Interactive (DB2I) facility. It would thus be one of the options in Figure 4.2.

QMF is generally used by nontechnical personnel, mostly as a facility to produce reports fast and on an as-needed basis. Being a fourth generation, user-friendly type application generator, it is also inherently less efficient to use, compared to using application programs.

For nontechnical personnel, QMF allows the user (in addition to using SQL statements) the facility to access data using the query-by-example feature, where the user signifies what he or she wants simply by keying "examples" in a series of user-friendly displays.

QMF is not explained in this book.

# *Index*

## A

ALL, 157
ANY, 157
Authorization:
   granting, 196–98
   revoking, 198
AVG, 36–37

## B

BETWEEN, 43
BIND, 77–79
   panel for, 85–86
   plans, 78–79
   rebind, 79

significance of, 78
validation of authorization, 173
(*see also* Program preparation)
Buffer pools, 171, 179, 186
Built-in Functions (*see* Selecting data)

## C

CICS application programs, 198–200
Cobol programs, 60–75
   basic program skeleton, 73–75
   committing changes (*see*
            Committing changes)
   data names in SQL, 67–68
   indicator variables, 68–70
   Procedure Division, 70

Cobol programs (cont.)
 SQL statement delimiters, 61
 testing of (*see* DB2 Interactive
  Facility)
 Working-storage Section, 61–70
  SQL Communication area (*see*
   SQLCA)
  table/view declaration (*see*
   DCLGEN)
Column, 6
 naming conventions, 19
 selecting in SQL (*see* Selecting
  data)
COMMIT, 72 (*see also* Committing
  changes)
Committing changes:
 CICS programs, 73
 Cobol programs, 60, 70–73, 173
  cursor processing, 112–17
  DB2 action on commit, 72–73
  unit of recovery, 70–71
  when to commit, 72
 SPUFI function, 29–30, 59
Concurrency, 172
COUNT, 37
COUNT DISTINCT (*see* DISTINCT)
Cursor processing:
 committing changes (*see*
  Committing changes)
 deleting rows, 117–22
 selecting multiple rows, 96–103
 updating rows, 104–17
  multiple open/close of cursor,
   112–17
  single open/close of cursor,
   107–12
Cursor stability, 173, 174


D

Database:
 definition, 1
 hierarchical model, 1–2

network model, 2–3
relational model, 4–10
 advantages of, 7
 creating, 176–77
 definition, 4–7
 history, 4
 join, 8–10
 projection, 8
 selection, 7–8
Database administrator (DBA), 13,
  175
DB2:
 access to resources, 11–12
 catalog, 21
 definition, 11
 integrity procedures:
  locking, 21, 190–96
  recovery of data, 21, 212–13
 objects:
  creation of, 13
  database, 12, 176–77
  index, 13, 185–88
  permission to use, 14
  storage group, 12–13
  table, 13–14, 181–84
  table space, 13, 171–80
  view, 13, 184–85
 operating environment, 11–12
 security procedures, 20
DB2 Interactive Facility (DB2I), 12
 prepare/test application programs,
   79–88
  BIND panel, 85
  COMPILE/LINK/RUN panel, 87
  executing program preparation
   steps, 87–88
  invoking TSO, 80
  PRECOMPILE panel, 84–85
  program preparation panel, 80–82
  saving generated JCL, 79, 88
 SPUFI function, 22–30
DCLGEN, 65–67
Deadlock condition, 106–7
DECLARE cursor statement (*see*
  Cursor processing)

Delete rows:
  application program:
    current row only, 119–22
    multiple rows, 126–29
  SPUFI and general discussion, 58
  subquery, 158
Design:
  logical:
    final, 140–48
    preliminary, 133–39
  physical, 149–53
DISTINCT, 33, 37

**E**

Efficiency techniques:
  coding SQL statements, 162–67
  DB2 resource management, 168–74
Entities, 134–38
  primary key, 138–39
  relationship among, 136–37
EXIST, 157
EXPLAIN, 207–12

**F**

Foreign table, 200–203
FREEPAGE, 53, 179, 186
FROM, 23

**G**

GROUP BY, 23, 46–47, 49

**H**

HAVING, 23, 47–48

**I**

IMS/DC, 12
IN, 43, 155

Index:
  clustered, 5, 186
  creating, 185–88
  efficiency factors, 169–70
  how it looks in DB2, 53–54
  pages of, 153
  relationship to data (diagram), 152
  unique, 5, 186
  updated on row insertion, 53–54
  use in Join, 45
  when useful, 168–70
Insert rows:
  application programs:
    multiple rows, 132
    one row, 129–32
  SPUFI and general discussion,
      51–57
    efficiency via free space, 52–53
    indexes updated, 53–54
    placement of row, 52–53

**J**

Join, 44–45
  subquery comparison, 159
  use of index in, 45

**L**

LIKE, 43
LOAD (*see* Utilities)
LOCK TABLE, 173, 191, 195–96
Locking, 21, 173–74, 190–96
  owner of, 191
  page (locks), 192–95
  purposes of, 190–91
  recovery of data, 212
  table space (locks), 193–94
  (*See also* LOCKSIZE and LOCK
      TABLE)
LOCKSIZE, 106, 172–73, 178, 191
Logging, 212–13

## M

MAX, 36
MERGECOPY (*see* Utilities)
MIN, 35–36

## N

Normalization, 140–48
NOT, 42
NULL, 44, 182–83

## O

ORDER BY clause of SELECT, 23,
    49–50

## P

Page size (*see* Design, physical)
PCTFREE, 53, 171, 179, 186
Plans (*see* BIND)
Primary key, 138–39
Primary table, 200–203
Program preparation 76–88
    BIND process (*see* BIND process)
    database request module (DBRM),
        76
    steps in, 76–78

## Q

QMF, 12, 213

## R

Recovery of data, 212–13
Referential integrity, 200–203
REORG (*see* Utilities)

Repeatable read, 173–74
ROLLBACK, 73, 173
Row:
    physical sequence by key, 5
    representation of an entity, 6
RUNSTAT (*see* Utilities)

## S

SELECT statement, 22–23 (*see also*
        Selecting data)
Selecting data:
    application programs, 89–103
        multiple rows, 96–103
        one row, 90–95
    SPUFI and general discussion:
        columns, 23, 31–38
            all columns, 31–32
            built-in functions, 34–38
            computed columns, 34
            distinct values of columns, 33
            specific columns, 33
        rows (*see* WHERE)
        tables/views, 39–40
Sort, 172
SPUFI, 12, 22–30
    changing defaults in, 26–27
    committing changes in, 29–30
    common SQL verbs used in, 22
    clauses of, 22–23
    entering SQL statements in, 27–28
    running SQL statements in, 28
    use of SQL statements in, 22–30
SQL (Structure Query Language):
    advantages of, 17–18
    most common statements, 17
    using with application program, 19
    using without application program,
        18
SQL return code (SQLCODE), 29
    Cobol programs, 61
        select rows, 89
        update/delete/insert rows, 106–7

SQL return code (SQLCODE) (cont.)
  SPUFI function:
    delete rows, 58
    insert rows, 51
    select rows, 29
    update rows, 57
SQLCA (SQL Communication area):
  definition, 61
  explanation of fields, 64–65
  including in Cobol programs, 62
  precompiler-generated version, 62
  use of, 62–65
SQLCODE (*see* SQL return code)
Storage group, 175–76
STOSPACE (*see* Utilities)
SUBPAGES, 173, 186
Subquery, 154–59
  correlated 158–59
SUM, 34–35
Synonyms, 188
System administrator, 13, 175

**T**

Table:
  altering, 189
  creating, 181–84
  dropping, 188
  example of invalid, 6
  how many per table space, 180
  idealized, 141
  naming conventions, 19
  primary key, 5, 138–39
    no UPDATE permission, 5
  two-dimension nature, 5
  View as virtual table, 15
Table space, 177–80
  altering, 189
  creating:
    partitioned, 171, 179–80
    simple, 177–79
  dropping, 188

simple versus partitioned, 177

**U**

Union, 160–61
Unit of recovery (*see* Committing changes)
Update rows:
  application program
    current row only, 107–12
    multiple rows, 123–26
  SPUFI and general discussion, 57–58
  subquery, 158
Utilities, 204–13
  COPY, 212
  DXT, 204–5
  LOAD, 180
  MERGECOPY, 172, 212
  RECOVER, 212–13
  REORG, 170–71
  RUNSTAT, 170, 205–7
  STOSPACE, 170, 207

**V**

View:
  creating, 16, 184–85
  definition, 15
  dropping, 188
  examples, 15–16
  naming conventions, 19
  reasons for, 15
  update restrictions, 16
Virtual storage, 172, 180

**W**

WHENEVER exceptional condition, 63

WHERE, 23, 41–45
    operators in:
        arithmetic, 43
        BETWEEN ... AND, 43
        comparison, 42–43
        comparison on conditions, 44
        IN, 43
        LIKE, 43
        NOT, 42
        NULL, 44